British Defence Policy in a Changing World

First published in 1977, *British Defence Policy in a Changing World* provides an analysis of the changes which have taken place in Britain's security policies since the Second World War. Domestic political, economic, and social factors are discussed as well as the range of international circumstances which have influenced policy. The approach is essentially a thematic one, isolating several key issues and examining them in detail. The authors use their skills to study a comprehensive range of affairs relating to Britain's security policy since 1945.

The book may be divided into four main sections. The first looks at the relationship between foreign policy and defence policy in general and more specifically at the three circles of British policy: East of Suez, the 'special relationship', and Europe. The second section looks at the place of nuclear weapons in defence policy. The third section is concerned with defence economics, national priorities, and the recurring dilemmas of decision-making, while the final section concentrates on issues of civil military relations and discuss public attitudes towards defence in terms of their political implications. This is a must read for scholars and researchers of international politics, British politics, defence and strategic studies.

British Defence Policy in a Changing World

Edited by John Baylis

Routledge
Taylor & Francis Group

First published in 1977
by Croom Helm

This edition first published in 2024 by Routledge
4 Park Square, Milton Park, Abingdon, Oxon, OX14 4RN

and by Routledge
605 Third Avenue, New York, NY 10017

Routledge is an imprint of the Taylor & Francis Group, an informa business

Publisher's Note
The publisher has gone to great lengths to ensure the quality of this reprint but points
out that some imperfections in the original copies may be apparent.

Disclaimer
The publisher has made every effort to trace copyright holders and welcomes
correspondence from those they have been unable to contact.

A Library of Congress record exists under ISBN: 0856643742

ISBN: 978-1-032-45196-1 (hbk)
ISBN: 978-1-003-37586-9 (ebk)
ISBN: 978-1-032-45198-5 (pbk)

Book DOI 10.4324/9781003375869

BRITISH DEFENCE POLICY IN A CHANGING WORLD

Edited by JOHN BAYLIS

CROOM HELM LONDON

©1977 Croom Helm

Croom Helm Ltd, 2-10 St John's Road, London SW11

British Library Cataloguing in Publication Data

British defence policy in a changing world.
   1. Great Britain — Military policy 2. Great
   Britain — History, Military — 20th century
   I. Baylis, John
   355.03'35'41   UA647

   ISBN 0-85664-374-2

Printed in Great Britain by Biddles Ltd, Guildford, Surrey

CONTENTS

ACKNOWLEDGEMENTS

The Editor would like to express his thanks to Doreen Hamer and Marian Weston who helped with the typing of the manuscript and to Jane Davis for her valuable assistance with the index. David Greenwood also wishes to express his thanks to Margaret McRobb.

LIST OF CONTRIBUTORS

C.J. Bartlett has taught in the Universities of Edinburgh and the West Indies, and currently is Reader in International History in the University of Dundee.

Phillip Darby is a Senior Lecturer in International Relations at the University of Melbourne.

John Baylis is a Lecturer in International Politics at the University of Wales, Aberystwyth, and is an Academic Advisor at the National Defence College, Latimer.

Stephen Kirby is a Lecturer in International Relations at the University of Hull and is currently the holder of a NATO Research Fellowship.

A.J.R. Groom is a Lecturer in International Relations at University College, London.

John C. Garnett is a Senior Lecturer in International Politics at the University College of Wales, Aberystwyth, and is an Academic Advisor at the National Defence College, Latimer.

David Greenwood is Reader in Higher Defence Studies at Aberdeen University and Director of the recently-established Centre for Defence Studies there.

Michael Dillon is a Lecturer in Politics at the University of Lancaster and Co-Director of the Rockefeller Programme on Arms Sales and Public Accountability in Western Europe.

John Sabine is a Lecturer in the Department of Political Theory and Government at the University College of Wales, Swansea.

David B. Capitanchik is a Senior Lecturer in Politics at the University of Aberdeen and an Associate of the University's Centre for Defence Studies.

INTRODUCTION

The Meaning and Nature of Defence Policy

This book is about British defence policy in the period since the Second
World War. The term 'defence policy' is widely used by both the lay-
man and the specialist in strategic studies but its meaning is rarely
defined with any precision. Despite its apparent simplicity, the term
hides a multitude of activities, some of which are emphasised in
some uses of the term and others in other uses. Some use the term to
refer to purely military policy or operational capabilities, others to refer
to strategy or strategic policy, and still others to the whole spectrum of
national security policy. It may therefore be useful at the outset to try
to clarify the term and provide a clear delineation of the parameters of
the area of political activity covered by it.[1]

The initial difficulty arises over what is meant by 'policy'. Most
writers identify a link between policy and decision. Some writers, like
Heclo, in fact, see policy as a series of decisions.[2] This is a useful
starting point in the sense that it suggests an ongoing process, or what
Sartori describes as 'continuous decisions'.[3] It is this connotation of the
word, perhaps, which makes precise definition difficult, if not in fact
misleading. The dynamic and fluid nature of the process makes it difficult to encapsulate the meaning of the term in a simple convenient sentence. The problem of definition is not made any easier either by the
fact that besides suggesting a bundle of decisions over a period of time,
the term also seems to have other implications as well. William Wallace
emphasises the importance of an overall programme or common orientations. He argues that the term 'policy' denotes 'a stable set of attitudes, an implicit or explicit plan or some general guiding principles or
attitudes determining or influencing decisions'.[4] A slightly different
interpretation is given by David Vital, who highlights the link between
the decisions and the eventual goals which they are designed to achieve.
Policy, he says, involves the

> formulation of desired outcomes which are intended (or expected)
> to be consequent upon decisions adopted (or made) by those who
> have the authority (or ability) to commit the machinery of state and
> a significant fraction of the resources to that end.[5]

This stress on goal-oriented decisions is again taken a stage further by some writers who argue that it is the actions which are all-important in any understanding of the term. John Garnett, for example, suggests that policy 'can best be thought of not as a series of finite decisions, but as a flow of purposive action over a period of time'.[6] Whether it is always purposive is perhaps debatable but again this statement highlights an important connotation of the term. It incorporates what a government has done as well as what it is trying to do. Like the other individual meanings discussed, however, it doesn't provide us with a comprehensive view of the term. Indeed, 'policy' would seem to imply all of the aspects mentioned rather than any one on its own. The term denotes a flow of decisions; a set of orientations or principles; an overall plan or framework; *and* a series of actions designed to achieve the objectives of the programme as a whole. All appear to be equally important notions implicit in the term.

Besides the different meanings emphasised by various writers, the term 'policy' is also used in different ways. Distinctions, for example, can be usefully made between 'declaratory policy', that is policy which has been announced but not as yet put into operation; 'planned policy', which involves the course of action which the government really intends to implement; and 'actual policy' which involves the actions which are resultant from the decisions made by the government, as they evolve in reality. Sometimes these are the same; that is to say, the policy which the government declares it is going to follow is the same as that which it actually intends to follow and does in fact follow when the decisions are implemented. Very often, however, they do not coincide, either intentionally because of government policy, or because of the limitations, restrictions and changing circumstances outside governmental control. Very often the term used in a 'declaratory' sense refers to policy statements which have as their objective certain political or psychological effects. At the same time the government may have a 'planned policy' different from that which has been announced, which refers to the general guidelines which it believes should and will in reality govern its actions in various contingencies. It is not, however, always possible for a government to implement policies in the precise way in which it intends. Due to the changing nature and variables of both domestic and international society, the government is often forced to modify its policies in the light of the exigencies of the moment, making it impossible for the authorities to fulfil their original objectives. Such changing circumstances often give policy the appearance of inconsistency and incoherence, making it far from 'the settled course of action adopted and followed' implicit in some dictionary definitions.[7]

These inherent inconsistencies have been ably expressed by Roger Hilsman, a former American State Department official, who argues that:

> Very often policy is the sum of a congeries of separate or only vaguely related actions. On other occasions, it is an uneasy, even internally inconsistent compromise among competing goals or an incompatible mixture of alternative means for achieving a single goal ... rather than through grand decisions or grand alternatives, policy changes seem to come through a series of slight modifications of existing policies emerging slowly and haltingly by small and usually tentative steps, a process of trial and error in which policy zigs and zags, reverses itself and then moves forward in a series of incremental steps.[8]

Like policy, 'defence' is another difficult word to interpret, at least in the context of the term defence policy. Largely for political and propaganda purposes, War Offices have been retitled Ministries of Defence in most countries, and the use of the term military policy has generally been dropped in favour of defence policy, partly at least because of its more favourable connotations in peacetime. In reality, of course, defence policies have often involved far from purely defensive actions. States frequently use their armed forces in an offensive and aggressive manner against other states as part of what they call their defence policy. Defence policy thus defined in general terms involves the provision, deployment and use[9] of military resources to facilitate not only the protection but also the pursuit of the perceived national interests of the state. This can involve provision and direction of the necessary resources designed to secure the protection of the homeland and population both from the enemies within and foreign invasion, and it may also involve measures intended to provide protection of overseas territories and population, as well as the safeguarding of what are seen as the political and economic interests of the state in the world as a whole. Defence policy in this sense is concerned in large part with the selection of the objectives which must be achieved by the armed forces to ensure that the foreign policy, and in some circumstances the domestic policy, of the state has the necessary support. It is concerned also with the selection of priorities, the allocation of resources and the elaboration of the permissible parameters of government action related to the security of what are perceived to be the important interests of the country. Defence policy therefore is more than just the state's military operational capability. It involves the political direction of a nation's defence resources as a whole with a view to ensuring national security, protecting vital interests and furthering the international aims of the state.

Bearing these characteristics in mind, it is useful to try to differentiate between 'defence policy' and 'strategy'. With the obsolescence of the older, narrower, purely military definitions of the term presented by military writers such as Clausewitz and von Moltke, strategy is now usually conceived as 'the art of distributing and applying military means to achieve the ends of policy.'[10] There would seem therefore to be very little difference between 'defence policy' defined in terms of the political direction of a nation's defence potential to achieve state aims and 'strategy', defined by one author as the use of military force by a state for ends clearly defined by political authorities.[11] Robert Osgood has gone as far as to suggest that

> military strategy must now be understood as nothing less than the over-all plan for utilizing the capacity for armed coercion — in conjunction with economic, diplomatic and psychological instruments of power — to support foreign policy most effectively by overt, covert and tacit means.[12]

The connection is made even more explicit by Henry Kissinger when he argues that 'it is the task of strategic doctrine to translate power into policy.'[13]

Despite the over-lap in the meanings of the terms 'defence policy' and 'strategy', they are nevertheless obviously not synonymous. Defence policy involves strategic decisions, concerning the use of force, and it is based on strategic concepts; but it also involves more. It involves domestic decisions related to the provision of human and material resources which make up the units of force. Defence policy in this sense consists of both strategic and organisational decisions.[14] Strategic decisions being those pertaining to the nature of the military forces at the disposal of the state together with their deployment; and organisational decisions being those relating to the administration, structure and finance of those military forces. All major defence policy decisions have both strategic and organisational aspects. As Samuel P. Huntington points out, a decision to defend a certain territory with ground forces, for instance, involves a strategic action with the use of force. It also implies certain actions to ensure that the forces and weapons necessary for the mission are in existence. These actions in turn may imply decisions on budgeting (increasing ground force expenditure either by

raising the total military budget or reallocating resources from other
forces), on personnel (conscription or higher pay may be necessary to
get the additional men required), on material (changes in procurement
and base construction policies), and possibly on organisation (enhancing
the position of the ground forces in the over-all defence organisation).[15]

Defence as a Boundary Problem

Apart from the difficulties of defining the term, the study of defence
policy, like foreign policy, involves what William Wallace calls
'boundary problems'.[16] In the first instance, it takes place on the boundary of both military and political activity. For many years political
scientists wrote extensively about political ideas, governmental processes and institutions, paying little attention to the use of the military
as an instrument of government policy. Similarly those concerned with
the analysis of strategy often did so, in predominantly military terms
without reference to political limitations, in a belief 'that strategic prescriptions can be made without reference to constitutional habits and
political idiosyncracies of the patient'.[17] The student of defence policy,
however, is very much concerned with exploring the essential features
of the border region between political and military activity and studying
the relationship between these two phenomena.

Besides the political and military facets, defence policy is also a
boundary problem in another important respect, in that it exists in two
worlds; the domestic and the international. To those concerned with
policy-making, defence policy concerns that area of politics, which, like
foreign policy, bridges the all-important boundary between domestic
and international politics.[18] As an instrument of foreign policy,
defence policy is concerned with the protection and promotion of the
state's interests in the international environment in which it exists. In
the last resort states pursuing their perceived national interests (in a
world in which there is no over-all international authority capable of
keeping law and order and ensuring the peaceful solution of
differences) have the opportunity, if they so desire, of resorting to
force, of utilising their military resources to settle their disputes with
one another. In this sense, defence policy exists very much in the world
of international politics. Governments make defence policy, however,
in the context of domestic as well as international pressures. It is
affected as much by pressures from its domestic environment as it is by
influence from the international environment. Defence policy is made
in a domestic context, and as such it is usually influenced by interest
groups, political parties and social classes with their conflicting interests

and goals, just like other areas of government policy. Indeed, most of
the distinctive characteristics of a state's political processes in general
are to be found in the processes by which it makes defence policy.
Those who are concerned with the analysis of defence policy therefore
must be concerned with the institutional structure by which governments make and implement their defence policies, as well as with the
whole domestic political process as it affects policy-making.

Developments in the Study of the Subject

Until relatively recently the field of British defence policy in the period
since 1945 was a largely neglected area of study, particularly amongst
British academics. The literature which did exist, especially in the
1960s, was written mainly by retired military and scientific specialists
who brought their professional experience and technical knowledge to
the study of a subject which they saw as being very much their preserve.[19] Writers like Basil Liddell-Hart, Sir John Slessor, Rear-Admiral
Sir Anthony Buzzard and later Air Vice-Marshal Kingston-McCloughry
tended to dominate the field with works which often went far beyond
the study of purely British military problems and embraced the wider
strategic problems facing the Western powers as the Cold War gathered
momentum. Not surprisingly, perhaps, much of their work tended to
be of a prescriptive and often polemical nature, urging the acceptance
of this or that strategy upon Western policy-makers struggling to cope
with the problems of the nuclear age. Similarly, important contributions to questions of operational capability as well as to the strategic
debate on massive retaliation and graduated deterrence were made by
various scientists involved in military affairs in the mid-fifties. Leading
figures in the scientific community, like Professor P.M.S. Blackett and,
later, Sir Solly Zuckerman, saw themselves as being just as well-placed
to write and theorise about the major issues of war and peace in the
new post-war environment as military specialists. Some scientists, like
Blackett, were concerned to warn of the profound moral as well as military implications of the new technology in the nuclear age while others,
like Zuckerman, were interested in the more practical aspects of the
science of war.

Influential as these writings may have been in setting the foundations for the great debate on nuclear weapons in the West and subsequently for the development of strategic studies in the late fifties and
early sixties, there was little attempt in most of the works to provide a
detailed study of specifically British defence policy. The contemporary
lessons of the Second World War, individual service operational im-

provements and strategic theory were discussed in detail in the defence journals and books of the period, but the nature and practice of defence policy as a whole was largely neglected. Much the same was true of other writings on defence issues in Britain at this time as well. Outside the ranks of those directly involved in the military field, interest in defence matters seems to have been generally low. The contributions which were made were directed, like those of the military and scientific writers, mainly at the contemporary strategic debates and tended to be confined to a small group of interested civilians, which included men like Sir Stephen King-Hall, politicians like John Strachey and Denis Healey, and a small number of academics, of whom Alistair Buchan and Michael Howard were amongst the most prominent.

With the blossoming of academic interest in military affairs in the United States in the late fifties and early sixties, however, the systematic study of British defence policy began to be undertaken. It was therefore perhaps not surprising that the field, initially at least, became very much the preserve of American scholars. Indeed, the first major work which attempted to break away from the largely prescriptive studies of the fifties and to concentrate instead on a more detailed survey of the nature and evolution of specifically British policy was written by an American writer. In 1964 William P. Snyder produced a book on *The Politics of British Defence Policy,* in which he adopted an essentially analytical approach to explain different aspects of Britain's military policy and to trace its development from 1945 to 1962. Snyder's emphasis on the domestic determinants and dimensions of British policy were particularly illuminating and, although dated, the book still remains indispensable reading for serious students of the subject.

During the late fifties and early sixties, interest in defence matters began to grow in British universities,and various professional institutions, like the Institute for Strategic Studies, Chatham House and the Royal United Services Institution,[20] attempted with some success to explain defence issues to a much wider audience. The growing interest in various defence questions in the sixties was reflected in the works of a small number of British writers. Amongst the most notable of these studies were Anthony Verrier's *An Army for the 60's*, Peter Gretton's *Maritime Strategy* and Neville Brown's *Arms without Empire.* Apart from these books, however, the major works on British defence policy in general still tended to flow from the pens of overseas and mainly American academics. Following the publication of two short works by H. de Weerd and Emanuel J. de Kadt,[21] the next significant contribution to the literature was made by Richard Rosecrance of the University of California. In 1968 he published a study entitled *The Defense of the Realm* which, together with Snyder's book, helped to highlight British defence policy as a separate area of study in its own right. Focusing his attention on such issues as nuclear weapons, European and overseas defence and the 'special relationship', Rosecrance emphasised the continuous and painful post-war struggle to adjust defence to Britain's reduced position in the international system. Despite his somewhat optimistic conclusions, the picture presented was, in most respects, one of declining influence, especially from 1955 onwards. Most of the major works written subsequently have tended to follow this general picture of continuous retreat which Rosecrance described.

Since the publication of these two important studies by Snyder and Rosecrance, the literature on British defence policy has been considerably enriched by a number of major contributions; contributions which increasingly reflected the growing interest of British academics in the subject. In 1969 Professor L.W. Martin, one of the leading figures in the strategic studies field in Britain, produced an Adelphi Paper entitled 'British Defence Policy: The Long Recessional', in which he concentrated his attention in particular on the East of Suez debate. Following this study, the 1970s have seen the publication of a series of important works on defence policy in general, as well as on specific areas of that policy. In 1972 C.J. Bartlett from Dundee University produced a thorough and comprehensive follow-up to Richard Rosecrance's study, entitled *The Long Retreat,* in which he traced the history of Britain's over-all defence effort up to 1970. The same year another American writer, Andrew Pierre, published a work on *Nuclear Politics* which concentrated specifically on the development of, and the debates concerning, Britain's nuclear deterrent from 1939 to 1970. This was followed in 1973 by the publication of Phillip Darby's doctoral thesis, which, like Pierre's book, concentrated on one aspect of policy: in this case British defence policy east of Suez from 1947 to 1968. Like Pierre's book, the main value of Darby's work was that the author was careful to set his study in the wider context of defence policy in general, relating the east of Suez role to other important areas of policy.

The literature on the subject was taken a stage further in 1974 with the publication of Margaret Gowing's two-volume work entitled *Independence and Deterrence.* Following up her earlier work, particularly that covering the history of Britain's atomic energy programme between 1939 and 1945, Professor Gowing became the first British academic to gain access to the post-war government documents. In so doing, she was able to write an authoritative 'official' history of the development of nuclear weapons in Britain between 1947 and 1952. As such, her work is likely to provide the starting point for research in this field for some time to come. On a similar theme, but covering a longer period and without the benefit of access to government documents, A.J.R. Groom produced a book in the same year tracing *British Thinking about Nuclear Weapons.* This study, which formed the basis of John Groom's doctoral thesis, concentrated on the different attitudes of 'political parties, the military intellectuals as well as the Unions and Churches towards developments in the nuclear field', rather than specifically on government policy.

Such contributions as these by historians and political scientists have been matched in recent years by important studies by economists working in the defence field. One British economist in particular has made this field very much his own. David Greenwood, who recently established a Centre for Defence Studies at Aberdeen University, has produced a number of influential studies, including *Budgeting for Defence,* published by the Royal United Services Institution in 1972, and numerous special surveys under the acronym ASIDES*. These studies have helped to fill an important vacuum which has existed for some time in the literature. Another British writer, Dr Gavin Kennedy, has recently contributed another useful, but more general, work on *The Economics of Defence,* published in 1975.

Economic analysis and the financial constraints on defence planners also form a significant part of a study edited by Professor L.W. Martin, published under the title *The Management of Defence* in 1976. This work consists of a number of papers by civil servants, military officers and academics presented in a seminar at the National Defence College, Latimer. The study is designed, in part at least, to cover another relatively neglected area of the subject: defence decision-making. The survey in some ways complements and updates Michael Howard's RUSI pamphlet on *The Central Organization for Defence* published in 1970, F.A. Johnson's *Defence by Committee* published in 1960, and Dr David Owen's rather disappointing study of *The Politics of Defence,* published in 1972.

Writing in 1972, Martin Edmonds and A.J.R. Groom commented that 'British defence policy since 1945 is largely a virgin field in which there are no standard works.'[22] No doubt a similar statement made today would cause contemporary undergraduate and postgraduate students studying the subject some quiet amusement. In general, the

*Aberdeen Studies in Defence Economics.

literature has now reached sizeable proportions in both qualitative and quantitative terms. If this is the case, then the question arises, why should we burden our students further? What, if anything, does the present work have to offer? The claims we make for this study are modest. Most of the books written so far tend to fit mainly into two categories. They are either general chronological accounts covering British defence policy as a whole, like those of Rosecrance and Bartlett, or they are detailed, more specific studies, like those of Darby and Pierre. This study is somewhat different, in that it adopts an essentially thematic approach within an historical framework. All of the authors take as the backdrop to their study British defence policy in the post-war period. Each of them, however, takes a different theme and attempts to study it in depth while at the same time, as far as possible, relating it to the wider context of defence policy as a whole. The essays are designed to stand on their own. Taken together, however, it is hoped that the themes chosen represent a reasonably comprehensive picture of the major features of British defence policy since 1945.

One of the main purposes of the study also was to bring together historians, political scientists and economists to use their particular skills to throw light on a subject which interests them all, by looking at the material available from different angles and perspectives.[23] The disciplines presented are obviously not the only ones which could have been usefully utilised. Sociologists and natural scientists in particular undoubtedly have an important contribution to make to our understanding of different aspects of defence policy. Besides the problems often created by speaking different sorts of language, however, such scholars as these who are interested in defence tend to be a rather rarer breed in Britain than in the United States. Their studies, nevertheless, are to be welcomed and indeed encouraged.

In Chapter 1, C.J. Bartlett provides a general over-view of 'The Military Instrument in British Foreign Policy'. In his survey he begins by setting the post-war process of adjustment between foreign and defence policy into the wider historical context of the disparity which has been growing since the nineteenth century between Britain's world-wide interests and commitments on the one hand and the resources available on the other. Then, concentrating his attention on the period since the Second World War, he discusses the significance of Britain's changing military power in the Third World, in NATO and in relations with the United States. In so doing, he attempts to highlight the efficacy as well as the limitations of the use of military forces as an instrument of policy and comes to the conclusion that despite the mistakes

(and mistakes there have been), 'the fact remains that by some combination of good luck and good judgement the services were remarkably
successful in meeting the needs of British foreign policy' (p. 48). He is
somewhat more critical, however, of the political direction of military resources. Not only was the reassessment of foreign and defence policies
from the later 1960s undertaken, he argues, rather belatedly, but it is
'far from clear that adequate new guidelines have been devised by the
mid-1970s' (p. 49).

The next three chapters deal in turn with each of the important
areas of policy which Dr Bartlett identifies: east of Suez, European
security and 'the special relationship'. In Chapter 2, Phillip Darby uses
the framework of the radical critique of Western military involvement
in the Third World to undertake, in his words, 'a restatement and
assessment of the purposes of the British deployment of power east of
Suez after Indian independence, taking into account changing assumptions and interpretations of the relations between the West and the
Third World' (p. 52). Phillip Darby reviews the 'radical approach' in
general and then considers three main questions with particular reference to British policy towards the east of Suez states. These questions
are: To what extent did policy-makers have clear ends in mind? How
far were interests furthered or seen to be furthered? What was the
nature and function of political ideology? On the basis of this discussion
about ends, interests and ideology, Dr Darby's analysis yields rather
mixed conclusions about Britain's east of Suez policy. He doesn't doubt
the sincerity of moral purpose of British policy-makers (p. 63) but in
terms of their perceptions, he argues that the 'benefits were less substantial and enduring than had earlier been supposed' (p. 64). Despite the undoubted success of the services in many of their operations in the region,
he concludes that Britain's overall contribution to the stability of the
newly emerging states was 'modest and not without costs' (p. 64).

In the third chapter the spotlight is focused on Anglo-American
relations in the defence field. John Baylis attempts to analyse the
nature and motivation behind the 'special relationship' in defence and
to assess the advantages and disadvantages to Britain. The first part of
the paper suggests that although tradition, culture and sentiment obviously played (and are still playing) an important role in determining
the close collaboration, calculations of interest have generally been of
relatively greater importance. The argument is that, as mutual interests
were seen to diverge, the spectrum of collaboration declined. In the
second part of the chapter, it is argued that despite certain harmful
effects resulting from the 'special relationship', on balance, if the post-

war period as a whole is considered, Britain has undoubtedly been '"a net beneficiary" from the partnership' (p. 88).

Chapter 4 deals with the third of Churchill's three circles – Europe. Stephen Kirby traces the evolution of Britain's foreign and defence policies towards Europe and highlights the problems of co-ordinating the two in this particularly important area of British interest. In his analysis he shows that although the continuous military presence in Europe 'has been the most consistent feature of Britain's post-war defence policy' (p. 95), successive governments, until recently, have lacked enthusiasm for the role. In fact, he argues, of all Britain's commitments, the commitment to Europe has been least in harmony with Britain's foreign policy aspirations. In his survey he charts the hesitant and often painful adjustment to the realities of power. The process of reassessment which has taken place, he concludes, has led, however, to the eventual recognition that 'of all her defence interests, only that in "European security was, and will remain, irreducible" ' (p. 95).

The next two chapters deal with nuclear weapons and strategic thinking in Britain. A.J.R. Groom, in Chapter 5, discusses the evolution of British nuclear policy. Just as European security described in the last chapter has loomed progressively larger in the calculations of defence planners in recent years, so the priority given to nuclear deterrence has gradually declined. In his survey Dr Groom identifies four principal factors which have moulded successive governments' policies towards the deterrent: the perception of threat (German and later Soviet); great power status; the Anglo-American relationship; and cost. As far as the future is concerned, John Groom argues that 'bureaucratic momentum may keep the deterrent in being, but only while the cost is modest' (p. 153). If so, he identifies three alternatives as being the most likely ones: buying unwanted Polaris missiles and perhaps submarines from the United States; purchasing Trident I for existing submarines; purchasing, or producing independently, cruise missiles.

In Chapter 6 John Garnett widens the discussion by analysing the nature of strategic thought in Britain more generally. He begins by looking at thinking about the role of military force in peacetime and highlights in particular the lack of creative thinking amongst serving officers. Most of the interesting contributions in the fifties, he argues, came from retired officers like Sir John Slessor and Sir Anthony Buzzard. It was their writings and lectures on massive retaliation and graduated deterrence which helped to widen 'the market for strategic ideas in Britain' in the middle and late fifties. This expansion in the market was also encouraged by the growing community of strategic thinkers in the United States. John Garnett argues, however, that the American approach to strategic thinking has been somewhat different to that of the British. He sees the American approach as generally more conceptual and theoretical compared with the more pragmatic approach of the British. The distinction he draws is between pure and applied strategic thought. One area of strategic thinking which particularly interests the author is the relationship between the wider category of strategic thought and official policy together with the delay which often occurs between ideas and policy. He illustrates his arguments by looking at strategic delivery systems, Indian independence, the erosion of empire, the bases strategy and various concepts of mobility. Despite the British contribution to insurgency theory, the author concludes by looking at the diminution of strategic thinking in Britain in the sixties and seventies and tries to provide some explanations why this has been so. It has been largely due, he suggests, to Britain's decline as a great power and the economic problems which have progressively prevented Britain from taking a leading part in the technological development of strategic weapon systems.

One of the central themes running through most of the chapters in the book is the critical impact of economic considerations on defence policy and strategic thinking since 1945. It is this very important domestic dimension which David Greenwood deals with in Chapter 7. In this chapter, the writer is particularly concerned to take issue with two commonly held assumptions about the relationship between economic criteria and British defence policy. He criticises firstly, the widely accepted notion that the state of the economy has directly *forced* changes in British defence effort, and secondly, the view that British defence policy has been characterised by a continuous process of diminution since 1945. On the first point he emphasises the importance of political choice. Faced with particular economic circumstances governments, he points out, choose between alternatives on the basis of their values and priorities. On the second point he is concerned to take issue with the widely accepted view that British defence policy has been characterised predominantly by decline and contraction. He shows that although in some respects contraction has taken place (in terms of the percentage of GDP spent on defence, service manpower and units of equipment), viewed from a different perspective an alternative picture emerges. He argues that if inflation is taken into account, defence spending in real terms has been remarkably stable over the post-war period. He also maintains that 'it just is not true that the United Kingdom now disposes evidently less military might than five, ten or twenty years ago' (p. 189). Comparisons are very difficult, but it would be wrong to suggest, he argues, that the military forces of today are significantly inferior to those of the 1950s. What has happened is that a process of reshaping has taken place within defence itself so that resources have been spent in different ways on different things. After the confused priorities of the period 1955 to 1964 David Greenwood shows that greater emphasis has increasingly been given to European theatre forces rather than to the deterrent or extra-European forces and, as such, new and clearer priorities have now been established for the future.

The question of priorities is, of course, at the heart of the whole problem of defence decision-making. In Chapter 8, Mike Dillon provides an over-view of the organisational and procedural changes which have taken place in defence decision-making in the post-war period. In his survey he puts particular emphasis on the persistence of dilemmas and the role of rationalism in resolving them at the level of rhetoric (p. 208). Dr Dillon points out that defence provides a fertile environment for the adoption of the rationalist and managerialist approach to decision-making. As far as the UK is concerned, he argues, 'the changed strategic environment . . . , its persistent economic decline, the retreat from empire and the development of collectivist politics were some of the principal reasons why rationalism became a dominant theme in the post-war decades' (p. 210). He sees the whole process of centralisation which has taken place in defence organisation in Britain as representing the desire by defence planners to move towards the 'rationalist ideal' in an attempt to solve 'recurring and persistent difficulties and dilemmas' (p. 212). To illustrate this general trend, Dr Dillon firstly examines in depth an area which has been central to defence decision-making: 'the managerial processes and organisational structures associated with technological development and weapon system procurement' (p. 213). He then goes on finally to discuss the even more difficult contemporary dilemmas which arise from standardisation and rationalisation of equipment within the NATO context. He concludes that 'political and administrative initiative is required more than before to thrash out the essential policy understandings to specify and accept common courses of action and to ensure their implementation' (p. 225).

Another domestic area of defence policy which is of contemporary interest is that of civil-military relations. With the contraction of defence commitments, the emphasis on a more UK-based army and a voluntary system of recruitment, questions of civil-military relations have taken on a renewed significance. Terrorism in Northern Ireland and bombings on the mainland have also made the subject a more sensitive one as the army operates on the doorstep in a domestic context. Although generally accepted, the army on the streets of Britain and contingency planning with the police create a degree of suspicion in a society which still remembers Cromwell. In such circumstances areas of military and civilian responsibility have a tendency to become blurred and friction can easily arise. It is in this situation that important questions of political control arise and take on an even greater significance than usual. Although he doesn't confine himself to the present, it is this important area of civil-military relations which John Sabine deals with in Chapter 9. In his survey he argues that 'Britain provides the most long-standing example of a state which has maintained civil control of its armed forces' (p. 230). He points out that although Britain's armed forces have most of the attributes which give the military everywhere the unique opportunities to impose their will on civilian governments, they nevertheless lack that vital ingredient which Finer calls 'the disposition' to intervene in civil affairs. John Sabine discusses four types of circumstances which might engender such a disposition. These include: equivocal orders; the redefinition of the sphere of military autonomy; the association of the military with sectional interests; and a sense of alienation on the part of the military *vis-à-vis* the nation as a whole. He sees the contemporary situation in particular as posing a number of strains on civil-military relations in Britain. While he dismisses the complacency of those who reject the possibility of direct military intervention in British politics in the future, however, he concludes that the tradition of civilian supremacy is one which is likely to continue. The awareness by service leaders of the small size and limited resources of the forces they command as well as all the problems of political responsibility is likely, he argues, to reinforce their acceptance of the long tradition of political control.

Apart from these important questions of political supremacy, civil-military relations also deal with 'Public Opinion and Popular Attitudes towards Defence'. In Chapter 10, David Capitanchik considers the commonly accepted view that the public has remained strangely disinterested in defence during the post-war period despite the profound changes which have taken place. He is concerned in particular to answer two important questions. First, why it is that the public have acquiesced in the reductions of the armed forces, the withdrawal from empire and the decline in Britain's status? Second, how, in the absence of direct security threats but with widespread concern over domestic

problems, have British governments found it possible to spend a relatively high proportion of GNP on defence without wider public debate
or controversy? In his discussion of these two questions David
Capitanchik ranges over a wide field. He deals not only with public
opinion polls on defence but also with defence as a parliamentary issue,
defence as an electoral issue, interest groups and specialist publics and
defence, and the coverage of defence by the mass media. On the basis
of the evidence available he comes to the conclusion that in general
'questions of defence policy and provision have been of such low
saliency in political debate in Britain since 1945, that they have evoked
relatively little expression of public opinion' (p. 279) It doesn't follow
that public attitudes have no influence on policy-making. Capitanchik
points out that in fact they have had an influence by impinging
'subtly, obliquely, indirectly within the central process of "setting
national priorities"' (p. 255). But the influence has been smaller than
might have been expected and this, he believes, is due to the fact that
'in the main defence has been a business which society at large has
chosen to leave to its government' (p. 279).

The fact that this has been so helps to explain some of the characteristic features of British defence policy over the post-war period. It
helps to explain in particular the failure of governments to ask crucial
questions about the purposes of defence policy. Successive governments since the war have tended to look to the 'macro-economic'
effects of defence expenditure. They have usually turned to defence
when reductions in public expenditure have been needed. Defence in
this sense has been a reasonably 'soft touch', especially in terms of the
domestic political repercussions of cuts in spending. Whenever this has
occurred, and it has occurred more and more often from the mid-
sixties onwards, there has been a fairly predictable service reaction –
'this is the last cut we can bear and still maintain a credible defence',
'We've reached rock-bottom,' and so on. Significantly, however, what
has never occurred within the political system has been any sort of
fundamental debate about the purposes of the defence posture as a
whole.

This reluctance to broaden the debate about the nation's defence
posture has placed the defence effort in a curiously paradoxical position. In terms of expenditure, defence has been a significant item. As
David Greenwood points out, only in 1962 was it exceeded by spending
on social services and 1969 by education. It still remains third in the list
of national priorities. Even in the latter part of the 1970s also Britain
still spends a higher proportion of GNP on defence than most of the

other members of NATO. Given that governments are constantly under
pressure to spend resources on education, hospitals, houses and roads, a
reasoned observer would perhaps think that defence was regarded by
successive governments as of vital importance. However, when one
surveys the long history of cuts after each successive defence review,
one is left with the impression that governments attach such a low
priority to defence that it is the first thing they think of when expenditure reductions are called for. The question seems not to be 'how
much is enough' but rather 'how little is enough'?

The inability to consider more fundamental questions stems partly
from the lack of public discussion about defence but also because it
seems far easier for politicians to think in incremental terms than to
question established values. Indeed incrementalism or 'muddling
through' seems to have been as much a feature of the defence decision-
making field as of other fields of government policy. It is far easier to
think about replacing obsolete aircraft, tanks or destroyers with newer
models than to worry about why you had those weapons systems in the
first place. It is usually more convenient to make alterations at the
margins than to consider the whole. As we move towards the end of
the 1970s many commentators believe that the problem of the incre-
mentalist approach to defence decision-making in Britain is becoming
increasingly serious. In the Second Report from the Parliamentary
Expenditure Committee in March 1977, dealing with the *Cumulative
Effect of Cuts in Defence Expenditure,* the implications of such an
approach to defence were clearly spelled out.[24] Since the 1974 Defence
Review, which initiated cuts of £4.7 billion spread over the ten years
from 1975-6 to 1983-4, four further cuts in planned expenditure were
announced up to March 1977, totalling £1,224 million (at 1976
prices).[25] In July 1975 Defence Ministry officials announced that the
limit had virtually been reached and that any further reductions would
have serious effects on the equipment programme. Between July 1975
and December 1976 three further cuts were nevertheless made. If the
'limit' really had been reached in 1975 then presumably Britain's
defences are now below what Ministry officials consider necessary.
What exactly is meant by the 'limit' and on what criteria it is determined is not altogether clear. Indeed some would argue no doubt that
there is no limit to defence cuts, apart from zero expenditure. There is,
however, a sliding scale of effectiveness of Britain's armed forces in
relation to the tasks which they may be called upon to perform. The
incremental erosion of Britain's defences therefore and the approach
which treats defence like any other area of public expenditure is one

which causes many contemporary observers of the defence scene considerable anxiety.

Aberystwyth   John Baylis
April 1977

Notes

1.   Some of what follows is taken from an article by the editor entitled 'Defence Policy Analysis: the study of change in post-war British Defence Policy', in *International Relations,* Nov. 1973.
2.   H. Heclo, 'Review Article: Policy Analysis', *British Journal of Political Science,* Vol. 2, Jan. 1972, p. 84.
3.   G. Sartori, 'Will Democracy kill Democracy? Decision-making by majorities and by Committees', *Government and Opposition,* Vol. 10, 1975.
4.   W. Wallace, *Foreign Policy and the Political Process* (London, Macmillan, 1971), p. 11.
5.   D. Vital, *The Making of British Foreign Policy* (London, Allen and Unwin, 1968), p. 11.
6.   John C. Garnett, 'Some Constraints on Defence Policy-makers', in L.W. Martin (ed.), *The Management of Defence* (London, Macmillan, 1976), p. 30.
7.   *The Concise Oxford Dictionary* (London, Oxford University Press, 1964).
8.   R. Hilsman, *To Move a Nation* (New York, Doubleday, 1967), p. 5.
9.   'Use' refers to the threatened use, the physical use (directly in operational terms) or the diplomatic use (arms sales, etc.).
10. B.H. Liddell-Hart, *Strategy: The Indirect Approach* (London, Faber and Faber, 1967), pp. 335-6.
11. John C. Garnett (ed.), *Theories of Peace and Security* (London, Macmillan, 1970), p. 14.
12. R.E. Osgood, *NATO: The Entangling Alliance* (Chicago, Chicago University Press,) 1962, p. 5.
13. H. Kissinger, *Nuclear Weapons and Foreign Policy* (New York, Harper and Row, 1957), p. 7.
14. See S.P. Huntington, *The Common Defence* (New York, Columbia University Press, 1961).
15. Ibid., p. 4.
16. Wallace, op. cit.,p. 7.
17. Huntington, op. cit., p.x.
18. Defence policy also tends to take place at the boundary of various academic subjects, political science, international politics, history, economics and sociology.
19. For a fairly comprehensive analysis of the works written on British defence policy, particularly most of those mentioned in this introduction, see Martin Edmonds and A.J.R. Groom, 'British Defence Policy since 1945', in R. Higham, *The Sources of British Military History* (London, Routledge, 1972). See also the short bibliography on page 283.
20. The RUSI, in particular through its lectures and its journal, provided an important forum for debates about operational capability, strategic theory and defence policy throughout the post-war period.

21.   H. de Weerd, *British Defence Policy and NATO* (Santa Monica, 1964), and E.J. de Kadt, *British Defence Policy in the Nuclear Age* (London, Frank Cass, 1964). Two very good theses were also written by Americans during this period. One was De Witt Armstrong's 'The Changing Strategy of British Bases' (Ph.D. thesis, Princeton, 1960), and the other was W.J. Crowe's study of 'The Policy Roots of the Modern British Royal Navy 1946-63' (Ph.D. thesis, Princeton, 1965).

22.   Edmonds and Groom, op. cit.,p. 568.

23.   Another purpose was to bring together mainly British academics working in this field.

24.   'Cumulative Effect of cuts in Defence Expenditure', Second Report of the Expenditure Committee, Session 1976-7 (H.C. 254).

25.   Ibid., p. xi.

1 THE MILITARY INSTRUMENT IN BRITISH FOREIGN POLICY

C.J. Bartlett

Andrew Jackson once remarked that a general cannot guarantee success; he can only conduct himself so as to deserve it. The same might be said of many fields of human activity. After 1945, there was a widespread feeling in Britain that foreign and defence policies in the 1930s had not only been unsuccessful but that they had not deserved success. The aftermath of the Second World War found the leadership of both Conservative and Labour parties anxious to learn the lessons of the past. There should be less disparity between the foreign interests of the nation and its capacity to defend them; the nation's military preparations should not be allowed to lag so far behind possible rivals; and the dangers of appeasement should not be forgotten. A Labour Prime Minister's defence of National Service to the House of Commons on 12 November 1946 underlined just how far British thinking had been transformed by events since 1938:

> The development of modern warfare has made this country more vulnerable. We are now part of the Continent . . . While in the past we always had a breathing space . . . [now] we must have trained reserves who can take their part right away without waiting for six months' training.

Yet one of the most fundamental lessons of the 1930s was that there were no easy solutions. The disparity between Britain's resources on the one hand and her world-wide interests and commitments on the other had been growing since the end of the nineteenth century. The Anglo-Japanese alliance, the *entente*, appeasement itself (at least in part), and the half-hearted search for an agreement with the Soviet Union in 1939 had all been among the expedients employed to try to bridge this gap. In the defeat of the Axis in 1941-5, the Americans and the Russians had played much the largest parts. British strategists therefore by 1945 could not fail to recognise how far the traditional bases of British power were being eroded. Britain's security had long rested on her island position, her economic strength, the existence of a satisfactory balance of power in Europe, the weakness of Afro-Asian peoples, and the British possession of India. The latter was not an unmixed blessing, but the service chiefs viewed with dismay the approaching independence of the sub-continent without some satisfactory defence arrangement with the successor state or states.[1]

It is true that for some time after the war uncertainties rather than immediate threats were most in evidence. There was no immediate abandonment of all hope of continued co-operation — at least in an attenuated form — with the Soviet Union: certainly there was no general expectation of an early military conflict.[2] But the long-term prospects were unpromising given Britain's relative economic decline — even when the damage and distortion inflicted upon the economy by the war had been made good. The advance of military technology, and especially the development of nuclear weapons, had increased British vulnerability. Russia, though grievously injured by the war, was now powerfully placed in Eastern Europe, and seemed more likely to realise its huge economic and military potential than at any time in its past history. The economic, social and political dislocation wrought in Central and Western Europe by the war meant that this region, or much of it, might also prove vulnerable to Russian influence, either from sheer weakness or revolutionary movements, quite apart from any deliberate Soviet or Communist activities. Britain herself could neither protect Europe from such threats, nor provide the economic assistance needed to renew the political and strategic strength of the Continent. Only the United States possessed the means for such an undertaking, and in 1945-6 it was by no means clear how far or for how long that country was prepared to involve itself in the affairs of Europe. Comparable uncertainties surrounded British interests in some other parts of the world.

At the end of the war, therefore, although a rough tabulation of Britain's global interests might be attempted, it was clear that Britain unaided had no prospect of defending all of them. Furthermore, given the existence of nuclear weapons, and the as yet unappreciated political potential of the Afro-Asian peoples as a whole — and not merely those of India — the nation's past experience of the place of military instruments in her foreign policy was not necessarily a good guide to the future. Indeed, states such as Germany and Japan were to discover roads to prosperity in which the military instrument played a much smaller part. But speculation as to how Britain might have fared after 1945 with different, less traditional, and less ambitious foreign and defence policies must be excluded. The aim of this chapter must be to explain briefly some of the choices that were made and to evaluate the role of the military instrument in that context.

In the first place it cannot be emphasised too much how far British policy was determined by the relationship with the United States. For good or ill, Britain clung to a largely traditional interpretation of her foreign interests, and to a great degree the American response made that interpretation seem both realistic and attractive for many years to come. The American loan of 1946, despite its controversial terms, ensured from the outset that there were no significant or early cuts in British pretensions to act as a world power. True, several years had to elapse before Britain was sufficiently assured of American support to commit herself to firm policies in Europe or the Middle East.[3] In the meantime the British showed their readiness to proceed independently with the development of nuclear weapons. There were, it is true, early doubts as to whether any defence of Britain would be feasible in the dawning nuclear era,[4] but no major war was expected in the immediate future, and much defence planning appears to have gone ahead on the basis of general considerations rather than with any specific enemy in mind. The decision to develop an atomic bomb at the beginning of 1947 was made without special reference to the Soviet Union.[5] The belief of both Conservative and Labour leaders that Britain should remain a great power, in so far as her economic strength permitted, explains this decision.[6]

Britain's former imperial possessions lost during the war were promptly reoccupied. But there were important doubts too. Later suggestions that the loss of the army of India should have prompted a drastic reconsideration of British policy in the Middle East neglect the fact that a tentative start was made to such a review. In practice it was overtaken by events. There was no simple case of inertia. The Chancellor of the Exchequer, Hugh Dalton, recorded in his memoirs that there was a meeting of some of the Cabinet at Chequers in the middle of February 1946. The Prime Minister introduced an interesting line of thought.

Attlee is fresh-minded on Defence. It was no good, he thought, pretending any more that we could keep open the Mediterranean route in time of war. That meant we could pull troops out of Egypt and the rest of the Middle East, as well as Greece. Nor could we hope, he thought, to defend Turkey, Iraq or Persia against a steady pressure of the Russian land masses. And if India 'goes her own way' before long, as she must, there will be still less sense in thinking of lines of

Imperial communications through the Suez Canal. We should be prepared to work round the Cape to Australia and New Zealand. If, however, the U.S.A. were to become seriously interested in Middle Eastern oil, the whole thing would look different.[7]

The idea was discussed with sufficient seriousness by the Cabinet for Montgomery to claim in his memoirs that the Chiefs of Staff jointly threatened resignation early in 1947 unless the Middle East were held.[8] Similarly, with respect to Europe, there was much anxious discussion as to how far Britain dare commit herself to a Continental strategy without a strong European ally or until or unless the United States should make plain its long-term European plans. Thus Churchill, in 1945, favoured an air-sea strategy for Britain so long as there was the danger of another Dunkirk.[9] Both the Attlee Cabinet and the services were divided on the question.

The American Ambassador in London was told on 11 June 1947[10] that Britain was decreasing her defence commitments, but in the event of war she hoped to be able to retain certain key points until the United States intervened. Communist influence in France and Italy was much feared, and the British were uncertain what line they would be able to hold in the Middle East. Indeed, in the long run they looked to friendly co-operation with the peoples of the region as the best defence against Communism. Unfortunately, the British lacked the economic power readily to attract such co-operation at that time, just as there was little that Britain could do by herself to revive the economies of Western Europe. The occupation zone in Germany and aid to Greece and Turkey (and then only until 1947) were strain enough.

As American fear of and hostility towards Communism strengthened, and as American consciousness of the weakness of Europe and of Britain grew, so there was a renewed desire to work closely with Britain. But at the same time, there had also to be the promise in American minds that Britain and Europe were worth supporting, and that they were willing to help themselves. Without such a promise there were fears in Washington that the American public might become more isolationist — hence the growing anxiety in the State Department, in particular from 1947, for clear evidence of firm and positive British policies in Europe and the Middle East.[11]

Despite the claims of many American revisionist historians, American foreign policy was not conducted with single-minded self-confidence at this time. Thus the National Security Council concluded in the winter of 1947-8:

It would be unrealistic for the United States to undertake to carry
out such a policy [i.e. one of opposition to a Soviet advance in the
Near and Middle East] unless the British maintain their strong strategic, political and economic position in the Middle East and Eastern
Mediterranean.[12]

This attitude was being steadily extended to many of Britain's imperial
positions throughout the world, so that what had once appeared as
obsolete relics of a decaying imperial past were increasingly seen as
valuable assets in the struggle to contain Communism. The United
States, though showing rather more awareness than the British of
nationalist potential throughout the world at this time (in Cyprus, for
instance), was nevertheless anxious that no position should be given up
if it were likely to fall into hostile hands.[13]

By the end of 1947 the British Foreign Secretary, Ernest Bevin, and
the American Secretary of State, George Marshall, had agreed that
parallel Anglo-American policies should be possible in much of the
Middle East.[14] Attlee himself, as we have seen, had commented early in
1946 that if the Americans showed an interest in the Middle East this
would make a British stand there against the Soviet Union less unrealistic.[15] As relations deteriorated with the Russians, and given doubts
as to the defensibility of Europe in the immediate future, the British
service chiefs were very anxious to hold as much of the Middle East as
possible. In particular, they wanted air bases from which to bomb
southern Soviet cities, and to retain control of the Mediterranean. As
we shall see, many circumstances conspired to undermine this strategy
in the next decade, but before the effective development of NATO in
the 1950s this British preoccupation with the Middle East is
understandable.

Bevin, elated by American interest in the Near and Middle East, next
strove to draw from Washington similar or stronger assurances concerning the security of Western Europe — or preferably the whole
North Atlantic region. But again Washington was anxious to see what
Britain (and her possible Western European allies) had to offer. Bevin
was told: 'You are in effect asking us to pour concrete before we see
the blueprints.'[16] The British therefore took the lead in the formation
of the Brussels treaty with France and the Benelux states in March
1948, though Bevin still had difficulty in securing sufficiently firm
commitments from the rest of the Cabinet to a Continental strategy.[17]
He had done enough, however, to pave the way for the North Atlantic
Treaty Organization of 1949. Earlier, in the spring of 1948, the British

had again been in demand when the Americans, fearful of at least a partial Communist take-over in Italy, considered military counter-moves, including the possible occupation of Sicily and Sardinia. Here Britain's diverse military capabilities and bases in the Mediterranean were seen as of great value, and tentative promises were duly secured.[18] The Berlin blockade of 1948-9 brought the RAF into play as a vital contributor to the famous air-lift which leap-frogged the Russian closing of the land links. In the summer and autumn of 1948 Britain emerged as basically an unsinkable aircraft carrier from which American air power could strike, if necessary, at the Soviet Union. At this time, although war was still thought to be improbable, the West looked to American nuclear power as its main defence (and deterrent). No extensive build-up of conventional forces began in Western Europe until after the outbreak of the Korean War in June 1950.

The American desire for a military ally with both European and extra-European capabilities thus greatly enhanced British influence at a time when Britain's economic weakness might, in other circumstances, have left her weak and exposed. As we shall see later, although her economy was in a healthier state at the time of Suez in 1956, it was still too vulnerable to sustain the foreign policy objectives of the government. In the later 1940s, there were several variations on the idea that Britain might ultimately recover some of her former influence either through the Commonwealth and/or in conjunction with revived Western European states to form some sort of 'third force' in the world. This was not yet remotely feasible, but it helps to explain the British determination to hold Malaya, a great dollar-earner, and the nation's general sensitivity concerning the economic and political future of the Commonwealth. The American Ambassador in London in August 1948 described Britain's subordination to the United States as 'a bitter pill for a country accustomed to full control over her national destiny'.[19] Yet, as Bevin was finding, useful though more coal exports and other forms of economic power might have been, even in 1947-8 the varied capabilities of his country's armed forces and her unique array of strategic bases throughout the world, including the island position of Britain herself, gave him some, if not easily measurable, influence over American policy. The forces did not so much protect Britain as help to secure protection from the United States. Bevin's opposition to many proposed cuts in the armed forces at this time might not have served the economy well, but those armed forces helped to give Britain the premier place for the time being among Western European nations, as well as the first place among America's allies.

Britain's defence spending exceeded that of the rest of the Brussels
pact: it was natural that the first commander within that organisation
should have been British, and that British officers should have held so
many key posts when NATO was formed and developed from 1949.
The remarkably close relations that existed between Bevin and both
Marshall and Dean Acheson, and Acheson and the British Ambassador
in Washington were based on more than personal ties. When war broke
out in Korea in 1950, appreciative though the American administration
was of British efforts in the struggle against Communism in many parts
of the world, the belated arrival of a British brigade was vital to calm
ill-informed critics of Britain in America. By the beginning of 1951
British naval strength in Korean waters had reached two carriers, four
cruisers and seven destroyers. Britain also embarked upon a massive
rearmament programme, mainly to help strengthen NATO. British
Ministers desired to influence the Americans against escalation of the
conflict in Korea or the commitment of a disproportionate amount of
their strength in the Far East at the expense of Europe. It is doubtful
whether British policy could do much more than strengthen those
elements in the United States already predisposed to this position.
Nevertheless, in recognition of Britain's special efforts, the United
States provided additional financial aid in 1952, noting that her arms
production exceeded that of her European NATO partners combined,
and that Britain alone possessed the resources entitling her to treatment
as an independent military power.[20]

Britain's debts to her military power for her influence within NATO
and with the United States did not necessarily mean that military
power could be used to equal effect in all problems in foreign affairs.
It is true that the British still found themselves engaged between 1945
and 1975 in relatively straightforward displays of force to demonstrate
their strength of purpose, and their ability to outweigh the
opposition.[21] These were of varying form and intensity, occurring over
such questions as the fishery disputes with Iceland, the future of
Gibraltar against Spain, British Honduras against Guatemala, or the
Falkland Islands against Argentina. These incidents often necessitated
delicate and skilful handling by the Foreign Office and by British
officers on the spot, but they do not call for special treatment here.
Within Britain's colonial territories there were also many policing and
counter-terrorist operations, notably in Malaya, Kenya, Cyprus and
Aden. With the dramatic rise in national consciousness in the Third

World, it was no longer possible for a power such as Britain to employ
her armed forces to the same effect as in the great age of imperialism.
By and large, the British had hitherto been able to prevail, usually with
relatively small forces, against Asiatic and African peoples because the
mass of the population — and often the rank and file of the enemy
armies — lacked a sufficient sense of commitment against the British.
There were often divisions among the rulers and local élites themselves
which could be readily exploited. British power had rested on more
than the machine-gun and other technical — or even organisational —
advantages, and this is seen when, in the twentieth century, in so far as
qualitative advantages were retained, they were progressively undermined by the new sense of political commitment among more and
more of the people of Africa and Asia. Terrorist bombs and small arms
were often all that was required to constitute an effective military
threat by determined opponents.

The above considerations must be borne in mind in order to understand the efficacy of Britain's armed forces in the major clashes of
interest with the peoples of the Third World, especially in the Middle
East. There were many reasons by 1950 why the British wished to
maintain a strong strategic presence in the Middle East, and in particular
to retain the use of the extensive and elaborate base at Suez. There had
been efforts to reach a satisfactory settlement with Egypt on this
matter since 1946, and these had failed, partly because of Egyptian
aspirations to the Sudan, which Bevin wished to hold to neutralise any
enemy presence in Egypt. Cyrenaica was another alternative to the
Suez base.[22] By 1950 the British were determined to retain Suez, even
against Egyptian ill will. In practice they found themselves with a large
number of troops tied up in the defence of a vulnerable base against
Egyptian terrorist attacks, and increasingly the drawbacks of trying to
hold this base in hostile territory came to outweigh its advantages.
British policy was reviewed from 1952, and a compromise was reached
with Egypt in 1954, whereby the British agreed to evacuate their Suez
base in return for the right to reactivate it in certain circumstances over
the next seven years. British interest in bases in this area, however, led
them into further crises in Cyprus in the 1950s, and Aden in the
following decade, only to be defeated on each occasion by local terrorism and by the absence of sufficient local support. Aden, indeed, only
became a first-class base as British power was crumbling.

Apart from the question of bases, there were four other very significant Middle Eastern crises between 1951 and 1961 when the place of
force in the defence of British interests had to be considered. When the

Anglo-Iranian oil company's assets were nationalised in 1951, more was
at stake in British eyes than compensation for those assets. There was
the broader question of Britain's standing in the Middle East; too
conciliatory a policy might be treated as weakness by others, and lead
to further encroachments. Hence the British insistence both on compensation for the assets which had been nationalised and on damages
for what was held to be an illegal act. An impasse ensued. British
forces had obviously to be on hand to protect British lives, but beyond
that the Foreign Secretary, Herbert Morrison, considered the possibility of seizing the Abadan refinery itself in July, and holding it indefinitely. 'Quite a little Pam,' commented a Cabinet colleague.[23] Sufficient forces, however, were not available, and Attlee was convinced
that an act of force would prove morally and politically disastrous to
British standing in Asia. The need to keep in step with a hesitant
United States was accepted by this government, and by its Conservative
successor under Churchill. A compromise was finally secured with Iran
through the effect of economic pressure, and by Anglo-American ex-
ploitation of political divisions within that country.

   The wisdom of this course, however reluctantly it was pursued by
many British Ministers, was amply demonstrated by later events. In the
mid-1950s the British Government was still convinced that the nation's
interests in the region could best be defended by largely traditional
methods, and this accounts for British participation in the Baghdad
Pact of 1955, an attempt to reconcile retention of British bases in Iraq
with Iraqi self-respect. In practice the pact helped to worsen British
relations with Egypt and to embroil Britain even more deeply in the
rivalries dividing the Arab world. The pact forms part of the tangled
story leading up to the Suez adventure.[24] For the purpose of this essay
our interest in Suez is limited to the question as to whether the British
might have found a military solution to this crisis, especially if they
had been able to act promptly after the nationalisation of the canal, or
if the military operations could have been conducted quickly enough to
forestall the intervention of the United States and United Nations in
October-November 1956.

   It must first be noted that Britain lacked the forces to strike quickly
in August, immediately after the act of nationalisation, that forces
were laboriously assembled in the ensuing six weeks, and that the
planning for the operation was over-cautious, being based on over-
estimates of Egyptian strength. The British were reluctant to take risks
with their own forces, a fact which caused some friction with their
French partners. Nevertheless, from September, the timing of the oper-

ation was determined by political considerations, even to the extent that the operation itself was spread over more than two or three days because of the government's refusal to despatch sea-borne forces from Malta ahead of the ultimatum to Egypt. There were no military reasons why the canal should not have been seized earlier and more quickly. As it was, despite the many constraints under which they were operating, the Anglo-French forces could have speedily completed the seizure of the canal had the British Government not bowed to outside pressures. Unfortunately for the British Government, the canal was only the nominal battlefield, and even complete victory there might have meant little.

It is idle to speculate on all the possibilities had the British Government decided to persist. If there was some rallying of public opinion behind the government in Britain, the nation was still badly, and almost evenly, divided. More risks might have been run with the nation's gold and dollar reserves and the American bluff called. An earlier and speedier operation here might have eased the government's exposed position a little. Yet hostility to the government's action would have remained high both at home and abroad in all circumstances, and severe damage to the economy was always likely. Had the Cabinet felt able to brave all these dangers, the fact remained that possession of the canal did not necessarily end Egyptian resistance, entail the overthrow of President Nasser, or deter Arab hostility elsewhere in the Middle East. The British had but recently evacuated the Suez base in the face of Egyptian guerrilla tactics. Possession of the canal would probably have exposed Britain and France to a costly and, in the end, profitless defensive operation. As for the emergence of a more co-operative Egyptian Government, the British had been in search of that elusive entity since the time of Disraeli and Gladstone, with little success. Even success there would not necessarily have swayed anti-British Arab opinion elsewhere. In so far as British policy might have been guided by a sense of reality, the Suez operation can only be seen as an act of desperation inspired by the hope that it might somehow improve Britain's bargaining position. The evidence so far published perhaps gives some support to this approach, but in general British policy appears more ambitious, emotional and nebulous. Of the British armed forces it may be said that they did reasonably well what they were so unreasonably asked to attempt.

This did not mean that the British services had no part to play in the nation's foreign policy in the Middle East. In particular there were occasions when they were able to lend useful support to friendly governments, provided the latter had some reasonable prospects of survival. These were not always easy to evaluate, could depend to some extent upon chance, and could involve British support of régimes which were unprogressive or undemocratic by British standards. One salutary effect of Suez at least appeared to be greater British sensitivity to local political situations in the Middle East. Policy became more discriminating. Thus when a military *coup* overthrew a friendly government in Iraq in July 1958, generating fears that a similar fate awaited King Hussein of Jordan, the British responded cautiously to the King's appeal for help.[25] The concurrent troubles in the Lebanon meant, however, that the United States was already to some extent interested in the stability of the region — quite apart from the general professions of interest to be found in the Eisenhower Doctrine of 1957. The small force which the British were able to send to Jordan was highly vulnerable, so that American support was vital. The final outcome was more satisfactory than the politicians had really dared to hope. There were Russian and Arab protests, but the British and Americans had intervened with limited objectives, and once the viability of governments in both countries was assured, the tension gradually lifted, and the forces were withdrawn.

Several times between 1952 and 1959 the British were able to give aid to the Sultan of Muscat in sundry frontier and internal troubles. Some fighting was involved, and in 1957 ground troops were needed to reinforce the air strikes. But if local powers of resistance were growing, and if outside opinion showed some concern, these were still basically old-fashioned policing operations within the well-known context of tribal, feudal or family rivalries.[26] The British only ran into serious trouble in the Arabian peninsula in the 1960s when disturbances in Aden and the neighbouring protectorate came to include deeper nationalist and revolutionary movements. A more important incident occurred in 1961 when the newly independent state of Kuwait appealed for British aid against a reported threat to its independence from the neighbouring state of Iraq.[27] Controversy has persisted over the seriousness, or even the reality, of this threat. The British, however, had to be guided by the following considerations. The Iraqi Government of the time had a reputation for unpredictability. If the Iraqis intended to attack, the vulnerability of Kuwait to a quick occupation was such that the British had to arrive well in advance of the attackers to provide an effective defence. Not to have responded to the Kuwaiti appeal would have damaged British credibility in the Middle East. Furthermore, Kuwait was, at that time, in view of its huge sterling balances and its large oil exports to Britain, of critical importance to the British economy. Indeed, so vital were the ties between Britain and Kuwait in these years that there was even some vague and irresponsible discussion of this as a region where Britain might possibly wish to use nuclear weapons outside the context of the Anglo-American alliance.[28] In 1961, however, only conventional forces were needed, and these were assembled without too much difficulty. True, there were doubts as to their full fighting efficiency in the circumstances in which they found themselves, but as a display of strength the operation met the needs of the British Government. Of vital importance, moreover, was the opposition of other Middle Eastern states to Iraq's pretensions, and the solidity of opinion in Kuwait itself. Unlike Suez, the political situation complemented the military move.

British success here, and in the suppression of mutinies in Kenya, Uganda and Tanganyika at the request of their governments early in 1964, encouraged many British politicians – of both parties – diplomats and senior officers to exaggerate the ability of Britain to perform services of this kind in the future.[29] Lord Montgomery, in retirement, spoke of the army finding increasing occupation outside Europe (where nuclear deadlock prevailed) in conjunction with the air force and navy. The chiefs of staff produced an important paper in 1962 on joint service operations outside Europe.[30] Various threats to British interests and those of her friends and allies east of Suez were envisaged from Nasser, other extreme Arab nationalists, revolutionaries of all kinds, Sukarno of Indonesia, and the variegated activities of the Soviet Union and Communist China. When the Berlin crisis early in the 1960s gradually appeared to confirm the existence of a military-political stalemate in Europe, and with Communist and subversive activities of many kinds being stepped up in Asia and Africa, it was natural that much more attention should be paid to the East. There was much interest, even in the Labour Party, partly through the enthusiasm of many of its members for a genuine multiracial Commonwealth. It also formed part of Labour's reaction to the Common Market. The brief war between India and China in 1962 aroused much concern, with Harold Wilson in 1964 expressing interest in a possible British contribution to a Western nuclear umbrella for India. This came to nothing, but it was an interesting example of the sort of ideas that were circulating at this time. Some in the Labour Party showed interest in the idea of British forces playing a role in the East as the agent of the United Nations.

The Conservatives, until their loss of office in 1964, had very ambitious plans for the provision of efficient, highly mobile forces. Their successors, while entertaining serious reservations as to the cost (extensive re-equipment of the services for their Eastern roles could not be long delayed), were quick to appreciate the place of British forces outside Europe in the maintenance of the 'special relationship' with the United States. As early as a Cabinet meeting of 11 December 1964, according to Richard Crossman,[31] the Defence Minister, Denis Healey, following a visit to Washington, reported the deep American interest in Britain's retention of her footholds in Hong Kong, Malaya and the Persian Gulf, 'to enable us to do things for the alliance which they can't do. They think our forces are much more useful to the alliance outside Europe than in Germany.' The Crossman diaries further suggest that until the Prime Minister, Harold Wilson, began to look to the EEC, he was convinced that British survival was dependent upon the 'special relationship', and that both this and British influence in Washington were heavily dependent upon the British military presence in the East.[32] Other reasons included the extent of British economic interests (Middle Eastern oil being only the most important and obvious), and Britain's many Commonwealth and other commitments. Stability was not to be expected in a region where so many states were but newly independent, and where so many political and nationalist forces competed for power.

In general, down to the early 1960s the British had just managed, though often only with help from the United States (and to a lesser extent from other friends), to provide the military forces required to support their foreign policy. To some degree this had been done with equipment inherited from the Second World War or from the Korean emergency. It had been done by bearing a heavier defence burden than their main industrial rivals. Conscription, which was ending in the early 1960s, had supplied manpower, and though volunteer forces with better equipment were more efficient, they were very costly. By the early 1960s, too, Britain's possible opponents were much stronger, as nationalism gathered force in the Third World, and even if potential foes were unable to build sophisticated weapons themselves, there was no lack of supplies from the Soviet Union. Britain, with difficulty, had sustained the triple burden since 1945 of developing a nuclear deterrent, making a significant contribution to NATO, and at the same time supporting considerable forces outside Europe. Although the 1962 Nassau agreement with the United States ensured that Britain retained a nuclear force at a bargain price, the modernisation of her conventional forces for both European and extra-European roles could only be carried through at great cost. Recognition of these harsh truths coincided with the growing appreciation that all was not well with the British economy itself — that compared with Japan and Western Europe British economic growth was sluggish, and that efforts to accelerate it brought serious balance of payments problems. Not surprisingly the mid-1960s were years when the Foreign Office lived in dread of commitments outrunning military resources.[33] Paul Gore-Booth, as Permanent Under-Secretary (1965-9), has recorded that the main theme in policy-making was 'as ever, finance', and the tension between foreign, defence and financial policy considerations caused 'moments of great bitterness which endured until 1968'.[34] The margin had often been perilously narrow in the past, but in the 1960s the strains within government over policy choices were further acerbated by more serious balance of payments problems than any since 1952, and by domestic pressures to divert more resources to economic growth and social reform. The question was also being more insistently debated as to whether British economic interests east of Suez really needed military backing.

Apart from these conflicting forces, the mid-1960s were the years of final disillusionment for the British concerning the future of the Commonwealth. The Labour Government from 1964 soon found that its hopes of increased Commonwealth trade and of closer ties of other kinds were all illusory. The Commonwealth ideal was damaged by British immigration policies, and by the crises over Rhodesia. Advocates of military intervention against the white settlers' act of unilateral independence failed to appreciate the political furore this would have caused in Britain herself. Nor was military intervention vital for the purposes of British foreign policy, given the decay of the Commonwealth. In time the Wilson government concluded that another bid for entry to the European Economic Community was necessary, and though this failed in 1967, the movement in the priorities in British foreign policy was unmistakable. Even so, there was still a great reluctance to make a clear, quick break from military commitments east of Suez, however much the government might try to lessen the cost of its Eastern policies. The desire to influence and avoid the displeasure of Washington remained strong; there were still fears that sudden British withdrawals could cause instability, or damage trade and investment.[35] There was, furthermore, in the mid-1960s a major crisis between Indonesia and the new British-supported federation of Malaysia, an episode which both seemed to underline the need for some sort of British presence, but which also in time generated alarm at the cost and open-ended nature of such commitments.[36]

It is possible that the way in which the Malaysian federation was established — to meet British as well as local interests — may have been counter-productive in the sense that it made more likely a military clash with Indonesia in the tense and emotional atmosphere that prevailed in that region in the early 1960s. If so, the British had to pay a heavy price in terms of the commitment of large military forces to stabilise the situation. These forces had to perform two roles. Light land and air forces were needed to patrol the 1,000-mile borders of Sabah and Sarawak and fight off Indonesian infiltration. Sophisticated air and sea forces were also necessary to deter any Indonesian temptation to escalate the conflict by making use of the advanced Soviet weapons at their disposal. Both these tasks were admirably performed by British and Commonwealth forces, a wise restraint being imposed on operations with the object of winning the 'hearts and minds' battle among the local population. The military aim was to 'out-guerrilla' the guerrilla. Patience, endurance and imagination were the vital qualities, but there were times when it seemed the Commonwealth forces were committed to an expensive, if very limited, conflict with no obvious end in sight. It was thus fortunate that internal divisions in Indonesia came to their aid in 1965-6 — a new régime making a settlement possible. British personnel in the area had been increased by no less than 50 per cent between 1963 and 1966. The operations also made servicemen very conscious of deficiencies in much of their equipment.[37]

'Confrontation' was thus one of several causes encouraging the Wilson government to review the need for a large British presence east of Suez. By the summer of 1967 the government had decided to give up their bases in Malaysia and Singapore, probably before 1975.[38] They were, however, strengthening the British presence in the Persian Gulf. Healey argued that British forces should remain there so long as they acted as a tranquilliser. The government was still thinking of deploying forces in the East when occasion demanded and if circumstances permitted. Yet the Six Day Arab-Israeli War of June 1967 demonstrated the irrelevance of British forces either in the context of the defence of specific British interests — such as an assured flow of oil — or the exercise of British influence in the crisis. Matters were brought to a head by the economic crisis in November 1967, which necessitated devaluation and a drastic pruning of government expenditure. The abandonment of a British military presence east of Suez by 1971 provided the government with defence economies which were important in themselves, but which were also necessary to win back-bench Labour support for cuts in the government's domestic programmes.[39] A Conservative Government from 1971, despite some professions to the contrary, basically accepted this retreat.

This switch to an essentially European defence policy was clearly vital, given the state of the British economy. It also fitted in with the general orientation of British policy away from the Commonwealth and towards the EEC. The continuing growth of Russia's military strength and rising doubts as to the firmness of the American commitment to NATO from the late 1960s similarly made this new concentration very timely. Even east of Suez itself, the new policy worked out better than might have been expected, given a reasonable measure of stability in both the Persian Gulf and in Malaysia. Britain's economic interests were not adversely affected. Yet had matters been otherwise, it is difficult to see how Britain could have acted to much effect in the East without damage to her economy and to her contribution to the defence of Europe. Circumstances and chance rather than calculation had determined the evolution and outcome of British policy, and the nation could count itself fortunate that the last decade of its extra-European strategic involvements had ended so satisfactorily.

Meanwhile, various justifications had been offered in the 1950s and early 1960s for the maintenance of a British nuclear force, with special emphasis being placed upon its 'independence' by the Conservative Party.[40] In practice it was almost impossible to conceive of circumstances in which it might be used 'independently' of the United States, and talk of its possible use to act as a 'trigger' to the American deterrent also lacked plausibility. As with the security of the British Isles themselves, this could only be considered in the context of relations with the United States and NATO. But the fact that Britain had developed an H-bomb by 1957, and had the beginnings of a nuclear delivery force, encouraged the United States to break down the remaining barriers to nuclear co-operation with the British. Independent nuclear development had thus ultimately gained for Britain much of the nuclear relationship with the United States to which she had aspired in 1945-6. From the late 1950s the maintenance of Britain's nuclear forces was both more effective and much cheaper. The climax was reached with the Polaris agreement at Nassau at the end of 1962. The argument that this agreement was bought at the expense of worse relations with de Gaulle — with the consequent veto on British entry to the EEC in 1963 and therefore the exclusion of Britain from Europe for another ten years — is unlikely to be sustained when all the relevant archival material becomes accessible to historians. De Gaulle had too many reasons at that time to feel that British membership would be an embarrassment to France — reasons which could not have been overborne by an Anglo-French nuclear partnership.[41] The price of such a partnership would in any case have been daunting, both in terms of extra material costs to Britain and the overall damage which it would have inflicted on the Anglo-American relationship.

Britain's influence on the United States in the early 1960s, by reason of her nuclear capabilities and her other contributions to Western defence, is not easily evaluated. Under President Kennedy, many in the American Administration would have preferred a phasing-out of British nuclear forces in return for larger conventional contributions, including that to NATO to make feasible the strategy of 'flexible response'. There was some disappointment during the Berlin crisis of 1961 both over Britain's political stance and her failure to increase her conventional forces in Europe.[42] But Britain could not significantly increase her contribution to NATO without either weakening her forces east of Suez (which the Americans did not want) or having recourse to at least selective service (to provide additional manpower) and much higher defence expenditure. The fact that Britain could secure Polaris in 1962 on such favourable terms is an impressive demonstration of her bargaining power, while in the Laotian and the Cuban missile crises, and the negotiations leading up to the partial test-ban treaty of 1963, Kennedy certainly listened to, if he did not always act on, British advice.[43] Perhaps in the missile crisis Kennedy was doing no more than to seize the opportunity in his exchanges with Macmillan and the British Ambassador to see the crisis from a non-American perspective. In the background to the test-ban treaty British persistence and ingenuity may well have heartened and assisted the moderates in both Washington and Moscow. Britain's standing as a power was still of some significance, but thereafter the decline was rapid. Her efforts to find solutions to the war in Vietnam later in the decade were ineffectual, and damaged what influence she had in Washington. But in any case, quite apart from the decline of Britain's weight in the Western alliance as a whole, Anglo-American interests were tending to diverge in the later 1960s, and this was to be especially apparent with the start of the Nixon-Kissinger era in 1969.

In the early 1970s, despite the liquidation of most military commitments outside Europe, Britain's weak economic base left her hard-put even to maintain those forces which gave her influence in NATO. The 1975 Defence Review prompted the House of Commons Expenditure

Committee to comment early in 1976 that any further significant reductions might seriously damage Allied confidence in Britain as a competent military member of NATO. She still retained an advanced arms industry, with an impressive scientific base. The possession of all-volunteer forces gave her some qualitative advantages over her European allies. But the seriousness of Britain's economic problems, and the need to restore national morale and confidence made it unlikely that armed forces would be provided in the immediate future on the scale that British national interests and aspirations appeared to indicate. This would be true of policy under either Labour or Conservative governments.

A defence White Paper in 1966 described the armed forces as the servant of foreign policy. Neither, however, could be divorced from the economic condition of the country, even if a great deal might be achieved by ingenious improvisation over limited periods. But for much of the time from 1945 the British were not conscious of the fact that their foreign policy was over-ambitious. Indeed, with some notable exceptions, British foreign policy seemed remarkably successful, all things considered, and there was much truth in Churchill's contention that Britain was the influential common point in three interlocking circles — the United States, Europe and the Commonwealth. Britain was able to lean heavily on the United States, and even to exert some influence given the American need for an ally of her calibre. If there was a delay in the economic recovery of West Germany, Japan and France, their military resurgence was still slower. Apart from Britain's current economic and military resources, she could draw upon her reserves of accumulated prestige. It was natural both to Britain and others that she should be in the forefront. Only in the 1960s was the change in Britain's circumstances increasingly, yet still reluctantly, perceived. Similarly, it was not until then that the ability of Britain was questioned to maintain simultaneously a significant nuclear deterrent, an army, an air force and a navy — each of the services with a very wide range of capabilities.

Down to the mid-1960s, therefore, criticisms of the armed forces tended to start from the assumption that they ought to be equal to Britain's basically unquestioned strategic requirements as a world power, and where this was not the case it was either the fault of government or the services themselves. Certainly mistakes were made. Decision-making both in government and the services can be criticised on many grounds. The aircraft procurement programmes are a notorious example. Nevertheless the fact remains that by some combination of good luck and good judgement the services were remarkably successful in meeting the needs of British foreign policy in this period. This, of course, helped to perpetuate the basic complacency. Criticism tended to centre upon the difficulties experienced by the services in providing forces at short notice for a wide variety of roles. Yet it was not reasonable, within the expenditure devoted to the services, to expect them to meet with equal facility a terrorist emergency in Cyprus, a large-scale three-service operation against Egypt, or a logistically difficult if relatively small movement into Jordan. A large proportion of the defence estimates had to be earmarked for the nuclear deterrent and the British contribution to NATO, and it was impossible to maintain an adequate range of forces for the variegated type of crises that might develop in the many territories outside Europe where Britain had commitments. All too often, therefore, the services had to try to fit square pegs into round holes. This they did with no mean success from Korea to Kuwait, and East Africa to the East Indies. Indeed, in the process, Britain earned the first place in the Russian Ministry of Defence's survey of 'imperial aggression' since the Second World War, published in June 1976.

One hesitates to use yet again so hackneyed a phrase as an age of transition. Yet such an age it was as Britain moved from the status of a world power to second-class status in Europe. If the final outcome was very different from the assumptions of successive British governments, a fair measure of success was achieved in ensuring that the British withdrawal should be reasonably orderly and that a fair measure of stability should ensue. Relative failures in Palestine, Cyprus and Aden may be contrasted with some measure of short-term success elsewhere. The final outcome in Kenya, Malaya and Borneo was more satisfactory than many can have dared to hope, and if for the services the task was essentially the tedious, back-breaking one of holding the ring until political sanity, or at least a political compromise emerged, their work was no less valuable in consequence. Military success, indeed, was dependent upon intelligent political objectives, but in turn it was vital that the services used only such degree of force as would not endanger those political objectives. This they succeeded in doing in Kenya, Malaya and Borneo, after some trial and error, and sometimes with a sense of frustration. But these were operations which conformed to and vindicated the *dicta* of Clausewitz.

Britain's armed forces also played a critical part in the Cold War down to the 1960s. If Britain's economic health suffered as a result of her ambitious post-war foreign policies, with their expensive defence requirements, they helped to bring about the growing American commitment to Europe of the late 1940s. It might be argued that the American national interest, or American perceptions of that interest, would have brought the same result. But from the available evidence one can point to significant uncertainties among American policy-makers in 1946-8. In consequence it would be premature to discount Britain's role. Both at this juncture, and well into the 1960s, Britain's armed forces were one of her most valuable assets in her endeavours to influence American policy. Thus, although Britain's armed forces could no longer provide for her defence against a major opponent, they could still exercise much influence in the context of an international alliance.

It is vital, however, that post-war successes of the kind summarised above should be seen in their proper context. Power equations in international rivalries are highly complex — no mere quantitative analysis is enough, while the qualitative contributions are often difficult to measure. The contrast between Britain in 1947-8 and 1956 is stark. In practice Britain might have found herself on other occasions in as exposed a position as at the time of Suez. The recasting of her foreign and defence policies from the later 1960s was belated, nor is it by any means clear that adequate new guidelines have been devised by the mid-1970s. Indeed, they can be no more than tentative until the British economy is soundly based.

Notes

1. Sir Arthur Bryant, *Triumph in the West: 1943-6* (London, Collins, 1959), pp. 532-3.
2. A.J. Pierre, *Nuclear Politics* (London, Oxford University Press, 1972), p. 71; Margaret Gowing, *Independence and Deterrence: Britain and Atomic Energy, 1945-52* (London, Macmillan, 1974), i, pp. 186-7.
3. C.J. Bartlett, *The Long Retreat: a short history of British defence policy, 1945-70* (London, Macmillan, 1971), pp. 15-22.
4. *The Economist*, 8 Feb. 1947 and 27 Mar. 1948.
5. Gowing, op. cit., i, pp. 179-87, 209-10.
6. Ibid., chapters 3-4, 6-7.
7. Hugh Dalton, *Memoirs, 1945-60: High Tide and After* (London, Frederick Muller, 1962), pp. 101, 105; P. Darby, *British Defence Policy East of Suez, 1947-68* (London, Oxford University Press, 1973), p. 15.
8. Viscount Montgomery of Alamein, *Memoirs* (London, Collins, 1958), p. 436.
9. Sir Llewellyn Woodward, *British Foreign Policy in the Second World War* (London, HMSO, 1962), pp. 272, 464.
10. *Foreign Relations of the United States: Diplomatic Papers* (hereafter

FRUS), 1947, i, pp. 751-8.
11. Ibid., 1947, i, pp. 716-18, 750-1; v, pp. 485-626; 1948, iii, pp. 765-9.
12. Ibid., 1948, iii, pp. 765-9. For some American doubts concerning Britain as an ally, and hence the importance of a strong British foreign policy, see W. Millis (ed.), *The Forrestal Diaries* (London, Cassell, 1952), pp. 288, 296, 301.
13. *FRUS*, 1948, iii, pp. 1091-108.
14. Ibid., 1947, v, pp. 625.
15. Dalton, op. cit., p. 101.
16. *FRUS*, 1948, iii, p. 13.
17. Montgomery, op. cit., pp. 498-501.
18. *FRUS*, 1948, iii, pp. 767-9, 844.
19. Ibid., 1948, iii, pp. 1113 ff.
20. Bartlett, op. cit., pp. 64-5.
21. This type of operation is admirably analysed by James Cable, *Gunboat Diplomacy: political applications of limited force* (London, Chatto and Windus, 1971).
22. *FRUS*, 1947, i, pp. 751-8; v, pp. 499 ff. On the British hope to hold a line from the Taurus mountains to Aqaba, see E. Monroe, 'Mr. Bevin's "Arab Policy"' in A. Hourani (ed.), *St. Antony's Papers*, no. 11 (London, Chatto and Windus, 1961), especially p. 19.
23. B. Donoughue and G.W. Jones, *Herbert Morrison: portrait of a politician* (London, Weidenfeld and Nicolson, 1973), p. 498.
24. On Suez see especially A.J. Barker, *Suez: the seven day war* (London, Faber and Faber, 1964), Hugh Thomas, *The Suez Affair* (London, Weidenfeld and Nicolson, 1967), and for general diplomatic background, F.S. Northedge, *Descent from Power: British foreign policy, 1945-73* (London, Allen and Unwin, 1974), pp. 124-41.
25. Harold Macmillan, *Riding the Storm, 1956-9* (London, Macmillan, 1971), pp. 505-23.
26. Darby, op. cit., pp. 131-3. This was nevertheless an interesting operation in that the government was anxious not to provoke too much foreign criticism; the British forces were used as sparingly as possible. But Macmillan also felt the operation revived British prestige in some parts of the Middle East, and helped to prepare the way for the interventions in Jordan and Kuwait (see *Riding the Storm*, pp. 271-7).
27. Darby, op. cit., especially p. 221.
28. Pierre, op. cit., p. 173.
29. Darby, op. cit., pp. 155 ff.
30. Ibid., p. 276; Bartlett, op. cit., p. 168.
31. Richard Crossman, *The Diaries of a Cabinet Minister* (London, Hamish Hamilton, 1975) i, p. 95.
32. Ibid., i, pp. 117, 156, 456, 540.
33. Paul Gore-Booth, *With Great Truth and Respect* (London, Constable, 1974), pp. 330 ff.
34. Ibid., p. 330.
35. Darby, op. cit., especially pp. 284, 288.
36. J.A.C. Mackie, *Konfrontasi: the Indonesia-Malaysia Dispute, 1963-66* (London, Oxford University Press, 1974), *passim*.
37. Sir Walter Walker, 'How Borneo was Won', *Survival* (March 1969), pp. 79-87.
38. Darby, op. cit., pp. 304 ff.
39. Harold Wilson, *The Labour Government, 1964-70* (London, Weidenfeld and Nicolson and Michael Joseph, 1971), pp. 479-86.

40.   Pierre, op. cit., pp. 170 ff.; A.J.R. Groom, *British Thinking About Nuclear Weapons* (London, Frances Pinter, 1974), especially chapters 13, 17, 27-8.
41.   E.A. Kolodziej, *French International Policy under de Gaulle and Pompidou* (Ithaca, Cornell University Press, 1974), pp. 309-15.
42.   David Nunnerley, *President Kennedy and Britain* (London, The Bodley Head, 1972), p. 68.
43.   Harold Macmillan, *At the End of the Day: 1961-3* (London, Macmillan, 1973), chapter 7.

2 EAST OF SUEZ REASSESSED

Phillip Darby

From the vantage point of the mid-seventies much of the political thinking behind Britain's world role appears lacking in depth. Generalised conceptions about maintaining stability in Asia and Africa and ensuring the viability of the successor states of empire over a transitional period sit uneasily alongside changing perspectives of the true nature of the relationship between the metropoles and the periphery. Yet the literature on Britain's world role remains largely undisturbed. The currents of radical thought in other areas of Western involvement in the Third World have passed by British defence policy, leaving little more than ripples. In part this may be attributed to the fact that the decisions which spelt the end of Britain's overseas military role were taken piecemeal over a period of time, and more on the basis of limited resources and alternative methods than in the light of any intellectual rejection of the role itself. There was never any great debate about the ends of policy; rather the arguments related to how much disengagement and at what rate. In this respect Britain's military withdrawal from Asia and Africa took a substantially different course from that of France, the United States, Portugal and other Western states.

Whether the radical critique of Western military involvement in the Third World has much applicability to the British case or whether the British case casts doubt on some aspects of the radical critique remain unexplored. The object of this chapter is to attempt a restatement and assessment of the purposes of the British deployment of power east of Suez after Indian independence, taking into account changing assumptions and interpretations of the relations between the West and the Third World.

There is always a danger of seeing one period through the lenses of another and we would do well to recall Sir Lewis Namier's warning about the tendency to 'imagine the past and remember the future'.[1] Ideas are conditioned by their times and what seems self-evident to one generation requires explanation to the next. Just as policy-makers often interpret the world on the basis of maps of their formative years, so it is seductively easy for scholars to transpose the concerns of today to an earlier era. It would be mistaken, however, to limit enquiry to the thinking of the time. If policy-makers failed to ask fundamental questions or if they were content to settle for over-simplified answers to others, it is necessary to ask why. Explaining the gaps in thinking may be as important as analysing the content of thinking. The vantages of hindsight and distance enable us to probe more searchingly and to see the issues of the moment in broader context.

Changing Perspectives

Over the past decade several schools of thought have made plain the extent to which traditional accounts and interpretations of Western overseas policies in the fifties and much of the sixties proceeded within narrow confines. Dependency theory, the revisionist historiography of the Cold War and the scholarship associated with peace research hold out alternative hypotheses which, whatever their respective strengths and weaknesses, raise new issues and recast old ones.[2] The course of the war in Vietnam blew open the debate, with the result that a new generation of students approaches Western policies with a greater scepticism about official explanations and a presumption that military involvement held back the processes of social change in the Third World.

It is immediately apparent that the bulk of radical literature is either cast in general terms or specifically related to American foreign policy. In the former case, critics have been concerned to explore the wellsprings of Western — meaning capitalist — action, which is assumed to be much of a piece. In the latter, attention has been directed to the United States as the pre-eminent imperialist power. Either way, there are difficulties in relating particular arguments to the special historical, economic and cultural circumstances of the United Kingdom. Equally, it is clear that the radical critique cannot be lifted from its context and directly applied to Britain's role east of Suez. None the less, radical perspectives can serve as signposts to inform, raising questions which make for a wider debate and more extensive reference to the involvement of other Western states. Despite the differences in approach and judgement among the critics, it is possible to identify certain general themes which give rise to a world view far removed from that customarily associated with Western policy-makers in the two decades following the Second World War. Four lines of thinking convey the gist of the critics' approach and serve as a sounding-board for our subsequent analysis of British purposes east of Suez.

The first relates to the primacy of economic interest. Though by no means a novel view, it is now presented with greater sophistication and receives a wider currency. The rhetoric of peace, stability and anti-Communism or the logic of power balances and security calculations

are seen either as a cloak to conceal an underlying economic purpose or
at least as running in parallel with a wider economic interest. At times
it is simply asserted that statesmen knew their best interests and acted
accordingly in the particular case. Increasingly this has given way to
more generalised explanations in terms of a socio-economic structure
which inevitably propels overseas involvement. One does not need to
find some neat correlation between economic interests and specific
intervention; nor is it necessary to establish that policy-makers know-
ingly acted in pursuit of economic interests. Another approach associated with dependency theory is more circumstantial still. The economic
basis of overseas policy is assumed or implied by the characterisation of
an unequal relationship between the developed and the underdeveloped,
in which the wealth of the former is seen as structurally related to the
poverty of the latter.

Second, and related to the first, is the view that the leadership of the
new states lacks legitimacy and often effectiveness as well. In part this
assertion follows from the new models of the economic relationship
between the developed and the underdeveloped. In place of the earlier
and cruder economic theories of imperialism which postulated two sets
of actors — one which dominates and the other which is dominated —
there is a complex interplay between related élites. Dominance is per-
petuated through the activities of collaborating élites in the Third
World whose private interests run counter to those of the masses and
are furthered through a bargaining process with external groups. Thus
the existing régimes, or most of them at any rate, far from promoting
the prospects for economic growth and political stability of the new
states, in fact impede them. Further support for this interpretation is
drawn from the succession of military *coups* in Asia and Africa, the
apparent failure of the development plans of the fifties and sixties, and
the increasing reliance on coercion and repression.

The third line of argument rejects the appropriateness of the ends
which supposedly shaped the course of Western and especially British
overseas policy in the post-war era. It is not by accident that order,
stability and the minimisation of violence were taken as guides to
action in that they are deeply embedded in the history of European
thinking about international politics and represent an externalisation of
internal values grounded in the legitimacy of the rulers or the existence
of orderly processes of securing economic and political change. With
some force, it is contended, this situation has few parallels in the Third
World. Given an international order and national systems which hold
few prospects of non-violent change, the attempt to freeze the distribu-

tion of power between the new states and the metropoles, between new states themselves, and between Afro-Asian élites and masses meant creating the very conditions for instability in the longer term. In the context of economic modernisation and political change in Africa and Asia, what was required was a good deal more emphasis on rights and justice and a good deal less on peace and order.

Finally, and more generally, it is asked on what moral basis did Western statesmen take upon themselves the task of influencing the course of the new states. The ethnocentrism and boundless self-confidence of the West in the days of empire now flowed along different channels but the psychology remained the same. The attempt to recast the Third World in the mould of the old was no better than, and in most cases related to, the determination to secure economic advantage. How could this be seen as anything other than a continuation of imperialism? As such it stands automatically condemned.

A closer analysis of Marxist conceptions, dependency theory and revisionist historiography would make clear the extent to which these views proceeded on different bases and involved different hypotheses. Our purpose here is not to pursue the course of radical debate but to explore its implications in the British case. These relate to ends, interests and ideology. To what extent did policy-makers have clear ends in mind? How far were interests furthered or seen to be furthered? What was the nature and function of political ideology?

Means and Ends

An analysis of the ends of British policy furnishes only a partial ex-planation of why the defence system east of Suez endured after Indian independence. Although there were always individuals with a clear and far-sighted conception of Britain's role and there were regular attempts to appraise and present policy in the light of changing interests, assess-ments and circumstances, the continuance of the system itself seemed beyond the reach of logical enquiry or action at the centre. There is little in the British record which offers support to those, either of the left or the right, who see policy as a product of careful calculation. In-deed, the evidence available cannot help but raise doubts as to the use-fulness of many generalised accounts of the policy-making process and alert scholars to the risks of rationalisation after the event.

Unlike the student of foreign affairs, most decision-makers worked with a limited span of time in mind. Both the Cabinet and the Foreign Office were invariably preoccupied with the issues of the moment, often to the neglect of longer-term interests and assessments. According to one Conservative Minister, the Defence Committee was little more than 'a clearing-house for short-range decisions' — a view with which the Chiefs of Staff expressed wholehearted agreement.[3] Until the mid-sixties the Foreign Office appears to have had an inbuilt prejudice against forward planning and a distaste for grappling with purposes and objectives.[4] The result was that British policy flowed naturally along established channels guided more by the experience of an imperial past than by any conception of a post-imperial future.

The course of events overseas reinforced existing patterns of thinking and led to adjustments in the structure of British military power which ensured its continued viability. Pragmatism proved self-perpetuating. The insurgencies in Malaya and Kenya, and the war in Korea, were seen as campaigns to be fought and won, not developments prompting reflection on why and where to in the longer term. Much later the Iraqi threat to Kuwait, the Sino-Indian conflict and Indonesia's confrontation with Malaysia became grist to the east of Suez mill. They were taken to demonstrate the diplomatic dividends of continued involvement, though they might equally have been seen to illustrate the military costs. It was as if the momentum of events made the running, but it was a course few wished to change. Similarly, a succession of military difficulties — the emergence of the air barrier in the Middle East, the loss of bases and staging posts, doctrinal disputes and budgetary cuts — were viewed as challenges to be faced rather than pointers to an untenable future. Thus the structure and doctrines of Britain's overseas defence policy were refurbished to meet the demands of a different era.

The difficulties of determining an overseas role in keeping with British interests, and then adjusting defence to suit, were compounded by the division of responsibility between several departments of state, the individual services, and officials at home and abroad. During the two decades following the Second World War the picture which emerges is of a rough and ready coalition at the top, while below the various branches of government made policy in accordance with their own precepts or historical purposes. The Admiralty and the Colonial Office in particular give the impression of acting almost as governments in their own right. On occasions this led to inconsistent or even contradictory policies being pursued by the different departments. Officials could maintain that the left hand did not know what the right was doing — and, one might add, in some cases preferred not to know either. After the advent of the Wilson government in October 1964 major changes were taken to rationalise and streamline the bureaucratic

structure but by then economic exigencies had sealed the fate of the
east of Suez role.

The fragmentation of responsibility for overseas defence invested the
Defence Committee with exceptional importance. It was here that
national interests and purposes had to be drawn from conflicting assessments and recommendations, often loaded with the particular interest
of the department concerned. Yet they were not. Although the records
remain closed, it seems clear that the Defence Committee proved an
ineffectual body for resolving the larger questions which crossed departmental boundaries and involved assessments over the longer term.
In part, explanation must be sought in institutional terms — in the inad-
equacy of the Cabinet and committee system when faced with fundamental issues which impinged upon a range of vested interests. Fundamental issues are seldom practical politics and the natural inclination is
to hedge or compromise. In practice, the issues were not always presented in a clear-cut manner because they were too divisive, too disruptive or too open to accident. In such cases Ministers and departments
preferred ambiguity and uncertainty to a decision which might run
against them.

The weave of British policy-making thus runs counter to the notion
that the politics of the overseas role had some fixity of purpose, some
bolder design. New ends could be found and fashioned, the White
Papers could rationalise and link together the various pieces, but the
men who shaped the structure of British power were not unduly
troubled about what it was for or even less where it was heading. One is
reminded of Viscount Curzon's comment to Hamilton: 'The Government of India is a mighty and miraculous machine for doing
nothing.'[5] Surveying the tangled web of interests, assumptions and doctrines from which policy emerged, there is reason also to be cynical of
any conception of underlying rationality which finds its way to the
surface through patterns of socialisation and bureaucratic habits. The
touchstone of Britain's role was in the past — in the achievements and
shortcomings of empire. Its changing ends were heavily influenced by
available means. 'We were there because we were there,' observed one
very senior official.[6] He might equally have added, 'and our tasks were
determined by our tools.'

All this is not to deny the relevance of official thinking about the
purposes of Britain's role but rather to narrow its significance. The
point is simply that political justifications and doctrines of responsibility did not represent the bases of the overseas deployment of power.
They did, however, help shore it up. To some extent assumptions about

the relationship between a military presence, diplomatic leverage and the protection of economic interests affected the direction of strategic doctrine. Without question, a strong sense of moral duty to the successor states and a preferred pattern of world order influenced the course of policy as it developed on the ground. We thus turn to the considerations which motivated official thinking, what they meant and where they led.

Hard Interests

The importance of hard interests in the formulation of policy cannot be divorced from the values of those involved in decision-making. Quite apart from the practical difficulties of judging the question of motive and deciding to whom to impute it, the notion of interests is meaningless unless amplified by the weighting attached to it in a particular context at a particular period of time. Accepting the interrelationship, it is none the less appropriate to consider the more general preferences of policy-makers separately.

In the play of international politics we are accustomed to thinking of interests primarily in national terms. Military security and material advantage are by and large assumed to fit within national frames.[7] Yet in the British case this was by no means always true. On the one hand, different arms of government promoted their own distinctive conceptions. On the other, the interests at stake were as often as not supranational, or at least Western rather than specifically British.

That the east of Suez role survived for some two decades after its original rationale had gone must in some measure be attributed to the promotion of service interests which were seen to be anchored overseas. At different times each of the three services used overseas defence as a means of securing the largest possible share of the defence vote and the weapons and forces they favoured. To this end they became advocates of the world role as well as beneficiaries. In 1957, for example, confronted by the threat to the aircraft carrier mounted by the then Minister of Defence, Duncan Sandys, the Admiralty launched its plan for the development of sea-borne task forces with the carrier as hub. This led the navy to shift its emphasis from general to limited war and from Europe to east of Suez. In addition to these changes in strategic doctrine, the navy embarked on an inspired campaign both in Whitehall and overseas to stress the continuing importance of British interests in the area.[8] Some three years later the RAF turned to the east of Suez role and presented an alternative to carrier air power. Faced with the passing of the nuclear deterrent to the navy and lessened prospects for

new procurements of aircraft, the Air Staff proposed a new fleet of aircraft and a chain of island bases.[9] It would be a gross misreading of the
historical record and do serious injustice to the men concerned to see
service politics simply in terms of the desire for larger forces and expensive equipment. Their thinking was heavily influenced by a sense or
habit of imperial responsibility and an almost instinctive identification
of a powerful navy or air force with the national interest. The fact
remains, however, that sectional interests distorted national judgement.
Much the same can be said of the Colonial Office and the Commonwealth Relations Office, each of which, though in different ways, had
vested interests in the traditional order. As John Kenneth Galbraith has
observed with respect to the American case, 'an overseas bureaucracy,
once in existence, develops a life and purpose of its own.'[10]

The significance of direct economic interests overseas to the formulation of British policies varied according to the particular area concerned, but over all, seems less consequential than might have been expected. In the background lay the well-worn but widely accepted
notion that a military presence safeguarded overseas investment and the
flow of trade. Until the mid-sixties, however, little attempt was made to
draw up a ledger or to dissect the east of Suez role to determine which
parts were profitable and which were not.[11] During the Healey re-
appraisals beginning in 1965 the subject received more serious attention,
but agreed conclusions could never be reached. The arbitrariness of
costing a military presence and the difficulty of quantifying the economic stakes were obvious hurdles, but the main obstacle lay in the
relationship between the two. Here the techniques of cost effectiveness
had no relevance and judgement necessarily depended upon individual
assessments of the nature of international politics and the utility of
military power. In general and taking into account other factors which
weighed in official thinking, economic interests were important in the
Middle East, much less so in the Far East, and scarcely at all in Africa.
In Southern Arabia and the Persian Gulf Britain's involvement had always been narrowly conceived – first communications, later strategy,
finally oil. In the Far East, British imperialism had taken root and its
moral and political aspects were seen as compelling in themselves.

There is some evidence that economic considerations receded in importance as the years went by. For one thing, it became more widely
recognised that nationalisation and expropriation did not necessarily
result in a halt in production. For another, the need to protect the flow
of trade was seen as less compelling with the passing of the Cold War.
There was also considerably more scepticism in Whitehall in the sixties

about the relevance of military power to the protection of specific
economic interests. A case could be argued, however, that the declining
significance of direct economic interests was counterbalanced by the
emergence of strong American pressure on Britain to maintain its overseas role and by a new and more subtle expression of economic interest
in the doctrines of stability and keeping the peace.

Sustained American interest in the east of Suez role can be dated
from late 1961, when the Kennedy administration first revealed the
importance it attached to a continuing British presence. In the view of
the administration the United States could not be expected to under-
write the stability of Asia and Africa on its own. At the same time
Robert McNamara was anxious to resist US service calls for an American
presence in the Indian Ocean. It seems likely that American representa-
tions and the British desire to maintain a 'special relationship' with the
United States strengthened the resolve of both Conservative and Labour
governments to remain east of Suez. It is possible that in the final
round of defence reviews some Ministers saw economic implications in
co-operating with American designs for Asia. On the evidence available,
however, economic considerations did not weigh heavily and certainly
could not be seen in terms of an implicit *quid pro quo*.

In the sixties when Britain's role came to be presented as a contribution to the peace and stability of Africa and Asia, official statements
carried the message that military involvement could not be seen as
arising from any selfish concern. The interests which Britain sought to
secure were general rather than specific, international more than
national. The task was one which came almost by default. In 1966 Mr
Wilson asked, 'If we abdicate responsibility who will exercise that role?'
At first such generalised conceptions drew considerable political support, but later the debate turned mainly on resources: either way there
was little incentive for policy-makers to carry their thinking further or
to explore the question of interests in detail. Clearly such a world view
had its economic dimension, though it was hardly one which could be
separated from and analysed apart from the rest. The fact remains that
military intervention was more selective than the rhetoric might
suggest. Many of the calls for military assistance by new states went un-
answered. When support was extended, policy-makers appear to have
been more influenced by ties of history and moral obligation than by
economic interest. Nor should it be assumed that as a matter of course
military intervention assured the protection of economic interests. The
patron did not always control the client. Contemporary historical
analysis shows that often the client was able to manipulate the patron.[12]

It is of interest that in a recent book Corelli Barnett argues that at the
outbreak of the Second World War the empire was a net liability
rather than an asset. It represented 'an immense structure of entanglement' which the English had failed to deal with 'in terms of English
power'.[13] One can accept Barnett's assessment of the costs of Empire,
and for that matter the significance of the education system and the Non-
conformist sects to the changing moral temper of the United Kingdom.
It is quite another thing to assume that the Empire was pliant and manageable and that had British will been stronger it might have been
turned or turned more fully to Britain's advantage.

Viewed historically, the concept of national interest has always been
of limited explanatory capacity in understanding the global policies of
great powers. In general, big nations have acted big and this has
variously been interpreted by some assumption that interests expand
proportionately with capabilities or investing power with a logic of its
own.[14] Similarly, a corollary might run, interests cast long shadows and
continue to influence the policies of powers in decline. Contemporary
international trends, including the growing interdependence of states
and the greater likelihood that certain domestic developments will have
external implications, enable the argument to be updated and elaborated somewhat differently. Robert Tucker, for example, has put forward the concept of security 'in its greater than physical dimension' as
at the root of America's post-war expansion.[15]

Whatever force is attributed to philosophical conceptions of this
kind, it does not derive simply from an analysis of interests as such. We
are offered a portmanteau approach which fails to determine how far
expansion is a means or an end; a compendium of security and economic interests, values and ideas about power. The debate is elevated to a
rarified plane. At this level of abstraction the lines of argument say
more about the writer than the statesman; like beauty, historical interpretation is in the eye of the beholder.

A Preferred Order
The language of British overseas policy was less effusive, but in similar
vein to the American. The Atlantic charge was taken to be the defence
of international order, the promotion of regional stability, the maintenance of the peace. The realities, however, were different. Beneath the
rhetoric, anti-Communism was the drawstring of United States policy.
Despite the phraseology, the principles that informed Britain's action
east of Suez arose from her imperial past.

The fact of Empire provides the substance and the continuity of

British thinking about the east of Suez role from the end of the Second World War to the dismantling of the system in the late sixties and early seventies. The fears of the Cold War in the fifties and the concern for international order in the sixties were like clouds which cast shadows but left the landscape essentially unchanged. Seen in broader context, Harold Wilson's memorable phrase that 'our frontiers are on the Himalayas' was nearer the mark than the views of many of his detractors. Though hardly good politics, it was sound history in that it highlighted the centrality of the legacies of empire, both at home and overseas, to the evolution of British policy. In short, Britain's commitment was to the viability of the successor states of empire. The formal devolution of power could not bring an immediate end to the material, ideological and moral ties between Britain and her former colonies. Over a transitional period neither internal minority groups nor external forces should be allowed to disrupt the state system by resort to violence.

This understanding of the purposes of overseas defence was not divorced from British interests but neither did it run in parallel. Indeed, paradoxically, it can be argued that the clearer the political conception the less it reflected hard British interests. Thus, in the sixties, when the sense of purpose was strongest and to some extent Britain's role was broadened as a result, its economic rationale was at its weakest. If from 1962 to 1965 the doctrine of keeping the peace became almost an article of faith, the role itself was fast becoming an exercise in altruism. By and large, Noam Chomsky may be right that articles of faith have a function;[16] as a rule of thumb, Coral Bell may be correct that altruism is not a very powerful motive in international politics.[17] The fact remains that neither judgement seems applicable to the politics of the east of Suez role in the 1960s.

One might go further and suggest that the British case is less exceptional than might appear at first sight. There is one school of thought to the effect that ideologies are most likely to emerge in situations of change where policy-makers are forced to express and amplify what had earlier been subconscious or secondary. It has also been observed that ideologies can be counter-productive inasmuch as they distort judgement by catching elements or perceptions of the past and holding them rigid and immobile.[18] Both points are well illustrated by the development of a Portuguese imperial ideology in the latter part of the sixties under the stress of the wars in Mozambique, Angola and Guinea-Bissau. The vision of a multiracial Portuguese-speaking commonwealth only took shape after mercantilism had been brought to an end and the economic advantages of European association were becoming apparent.

The commitment to the successor states cannot be understood apart
from the sense of moral obligation which pervaded the thinking and
influenced the judgement of generations of British decision-makers. It
has become commonplace to decry the significance of the moral factor
in the formulation of national policies. And with some reason. Both the
rhetoric and many of the studies of American foreign policy have been
loaded with moralism, yet the disclosures associated with the war in
Vietnam have undercut their credibility. The benchmark has become
the March 1965 memorandum from John McNaughton, Assistant Secretary of Defense, to Robert McNamara, setting out American war aims
as 70 per cent to avoid a humiliating US defeat, 20 per cent to keep
South Vietnamese territory from Chinese hands, and 10 per cent to
permit the people of South Vietnam to enjoy a better, freer way of
life.[19] There is, however, no reason why American disclosures should
influence judgement about British motives. Few, if any, who have
worked or talked with British policy-makers would doubt the sincerity
of moral purpose.

Whether the implications of that moral purpose were fully
appreciated is more open to doubt. There are some who would concede
no right of intervention on the principle of absolute sovereignty and
others who would condemn any action in support of the new states,
including economic aid, as imperialism. Such arguments cannot adequately be dealt with here. More general considerations aside, British
policy-makers in the period did not start with a clean slate; the formal
grant of independence redefined but did not extinguish the rights and
obligations which linked the parties. Discussion must turn instead on
the claim that the moral perspectives were skewed; that stability was
overweighted and too often seen in terms of perpetuating the *status
quo*; that violence was too readily assumed to be simply disruptive and
lacking in popular support; that thinking was framed primarily in terms
of states and there was too easy an identification of interests between
national leaderships and the people they supposedly represented. While
to varying degrees these points are well taken, it can also be argued they
are in part misdirected. They are linking what can be seen as two different moral worlds. British thinking about the successor states was more
in terms of their international viability than their domestic future. It
was a matter of imperial devolution in the context of international relations, not economic and social change in the context of nation-
building.

Whatever view is taken of the basis of evaluation, there can be no
assessment across the board. Just as the circumstances of Britain's in-

volvement were different in the Middle East and the Far East, so the critics' case is stronger in the Persian Gulf than in Malaya (sia). On the face of it, intervention in East Africa in January 1964 was of a different moral order from that in South Arabia from 1964 to 1967. The record cannot be assessed in detail until we know more of the occasions when assistance was declined and until the archives reveal the extent and nature of diplomatic prodding and the pressures which were brought to bear.

One point remains which must qualify the influence of the moral factor. Given the understanding that Britain's responsibility was to secure the safe passage of the new states through a transitional period, the matter of timing was of primary importance. Yet it was not well judged. For too long former colonies and protected states were able to act in the comfortable assurance that British support would continue indefinitely. There was thus little incentive to put their houses in order or to begin the process of making alternative, probably indigenous, security arrangements. Then, in the second half of the sixties, the apparatus of military support was dismantled too quickly. When economic pressures crowded in, the Labour Government defaulted on its commitment to stay the process of withdrawal and to maintain a special military capability for overseas intervention. In the final analysis the record of shifting deadlines and broken pledges must be explained in terms of political expediency more than economic exigency.

Reflecting on Britain's east of Suez role in the terms in which policy-makers saw it, we are left with the thought that the benefits were less substantial and enduring than had earlier been supposed. The achievement of the services in developing an effective system for the extension of military support to the successor states is undoubted. Many of the operations were executed with great skill. But as a contribution to the peace and order of the new states Britain's role was modest and not without costs. The passage of time scales things to size. Recent historical research has shown that Empire itself did not impinge deeply on the life of the colonies. Similarly, Britain's post-war policies only marginally shaped the course of the successor states.

Notes

1.   L.B. Namier, *Conflicts* (London, Macmillan, 1942), p. 70.
2.   Among the more important and representative works are: R. Owen and
      B. Sutcliffe, *Studies in the Theory of Imperialism* (London, Longman,
      1972); R.I. Rhodes (ed.), *Imperialism and Underdevelopment* (New York,

Monthly Review Press, 1970); K.J. Fann and D.C. Hodges (eds.), *Readings in United States Imperialism* (Boston, Sargent, 1971); W.A. Williams, *The Roots of the Modern American Empire* (New York, Random House, 1969); G. Kolko, *The Roots of American Foreign Policy* (Boston, Beacon Press, 1969); I. Howe (ed.), *A Dissenter's Guide to Foreign Policy* (New York, Praeger, 1968); H. Magdoff, *The Age of Imperialism: The Economics of U.S. Foreign Policy* (New York, Monthly Review Press, 1969); J. Galtung, 'A Structural Theory of Imperialism', *Journal of Peace Research*, 2 (1971), pp. 81-117; T. Hayter, *Aid as Imperialism* (Harmondsworth, Penguin, 1971).

3. P. Darby, *British Defence Policy East of Suez 1947-1968* (London, Oxford University Press for RIIA, 1973), p. 138.

4. See Sir W. Hayter, *The Diplomacy of the Great Powers* (London, Hamish Hamilton, 1960), p. 46.

5. Quoted by Anil Seal in J. Gallagher, G. Johnson and A. Seal, *Locality, Province and Nation: Essays on Indian Politics 1870-1940* (Cambridge, Cambridge University Press, 1973), p. 1.

6. Darby, op. cit., p. 155.

7. There is of course one line of radical argument, mainly relating to the United States, which sees the multinational corporation as the key agent of overseas expansion. Thus the interests served are those of the corporations rather than society as a whole. Recent analyses, however, have stressed the links between the multinational corporation and the national economy, concluding that in the final analysis there is an organic interrelationship between the two — a unity of capitalist interest. See, for example, J.H. Dunning (ed.), *The Multinational Enterprise* (London, Allen and Unwin, 1971).

8. Darby, op. cit., pp. 110-13.

9. Ibid., pp. 261-5.

10. J.K. Galbraith, 'The Plain Lessons of a Bad Decade', *Foreign Policy*, 1 (1970-1), pp. 31-45 at p. 39.

11. In 1959 and 1960 the Future Policy Committee considered the question, but its report was pigeon-holed and had little influence.

12. A line of approach pioneered in R. Robinson and J. Gallagher, *Africa and the Victorians* (London, Macmillan, 1967).

13. C. Barnett, *The Collapse of British Power* (London, Methuen, 1972), p. 232.

14. P. Darby, 'The West, Military Intervention and the Third World', *Brassey's Annual 1971* (London, Clowes), pp. 65-79 at p. 74.

15. R. Tucker, *The Radical Left and American Foreign Policy* (Baltimore, Johns Hopkins Press, 1971), especially pp. 105-6, 109-10.

16. N. Chomsky, *The Backroom Boys* (London, Fontana, 1973), pp. 69 and 70.

17. C. Bell, *The Debatable Alliance* (London, Oxford University Press for RIIA, 1964), p. 98.

18. Even Noam Chomsky is prepared to concede 'that ideology can have a life of its own, contributing to the design and implementation of policy in a way that may, on occasion, even conflict with the interests from which it arose.' *American Power and the New Mandarins* (London, Chatto and Windus, 1969), p. 237.

19. *The Pentagon Papers* (New York, Bantam Books, 1971), p. 432.

3 THE ANGLO-AMERICAN RELATIONSHIP IN DEFENCE

John Baylis

British defence policy since 1945 has been strongly influenced, indeed perhaps even dominated, by the close and continuous relationship between Britain and the United States. In many respects it is in the defence field that the intimate relationship between the two countries has assumed its most visible and tangible form. It is often argued, with some justification, that the partnership in security matters has not only generally mirrored the changing pattern and fortunes of Anglo-American relations but has also been the most important element in the wider alliance.[1] For many scholars, defence collaboration has been regarded as the central core of what is usually described as the 'special relationship'.[2]

Although the term 'special relationship' has rarely been defined with any precision, most writers use the term to suggest a partnership which has been unusually close and intimate;[3] a relationship characterised by a mutual responsiveness in a whole range of political, economic and military matters such that each state has regarded the other as its primary ally. This has been symbolised in the defence field in particular by the depth and comprehensiveness of co-operation in such things as strategic planning and weapons research; by the informality of contacts between the services and defence departments of the two countries; as well as by the preferential treatment of one ally by the other, especially in the field of atomic energy.

The general consensus over the form the 'special relationship' has taken, however, tends to obfuscate a basic divergence of opinion amongst scholars on Anglo-American relations about the reasons or motivation behind the close alliance between the two states. For some the close bonds binding Britain and America together have been the product above all of a wide variety of common interests. According to this argument, both sides have seen relations with the other as being more important than with third states because of the mutuality of interests between them. Both countries have had more interests in common than with any of their other allies and consequently, not unnaturally, have worked closely with each other. Other writers, however, have suggested that the alliance has more to do with sentiment than

66

with interest. According to this view, the relationship is 'exceptional'
or 'special' in the sense that sentimental attachments, cultural affinities
and historical traditions are seen as more important determinants of
policy than cold political calculation.[4] To this school of thought, it is
the play of these intangible values which elevates the alliance to a qual-
itatively different plane in comparison with most other international
relationships. 'Special' in this sense denotes a relationship which is not
only close and intimate but one which is, in a way, 'different in kind'
from those with other states; a relationship conditioned by different
criteria from those of 'normal' inter-state relations. Which of these two
interpretations is closest to reality is a moot point and remains the subject of lively debate. The argument presented in what follows, however,
tends, on balance, to support the former rather than the latter view.

Undoubtedly the origins of the 'special relationship' in the security
field are to be found deep in the roots of history. From the beginning
of the nineteenth century the maintenance of a two-power naval standard and the dominance of the Atlantic by Britain provided the indispensable shelter for the declaration of the Monroe doctrine of 1823 and
in turn allowed the Civil War of 1861-5 to be fought without the involvement of European powers.[5] Despite this long history, a strong case
can be made that the term itself only has real meaning, however, when
used to refer to the unique partnership between the two countries between 1940 and 1945. H.C. Allen is surely right when he argues that

> the second world war . . . formed an altogether fitting climax in the
> long drama of Anglo-American friendship. It saw, in the words of
> General Marshall, 'the most complete unification of military effort
> ever achieved by two allied nations'. It saw a co-ordination between
> the political authorities of two sovereign states possibly unsur-
> passed in history. It saw a maturing of the cordiality between the
> two peoples more swift and complete than all but the most opti-
> mistic prophets of the Anglo-American comity had hoped.[6]

The term 'special relationship' was apparently first used by Winston
Churchill in his Fulton Speech on 5 March 1946 when, referring to the
wartime alliance, he urged the continuation of 'a special relationship
between the British Commonwealth and Empire and the United
States'.[7] For Churchill, the potential threat from the Soviet Union
necessitated a new policy by the Western states in which 'the core of
every measure of defence must be the Anglo-American unity.'[8] It was
essential, Churchill argued, that the wartime alliance be revived and con-

tinued in the post-war period.

By the summer of 1945 and the defeat of Germany, however, the *raison d'être* of the alliance had quickly disappeared. The clashes of interest which had been largely, but not totally, sublimated during the war became increasingly more pronounced in the latter part of 1945 and early 1946. Suspicion in many American quarters of the new socialist government in Britain, the abrupt cancellation of lend-lease in August 1945 and the bad feelings generated by the loan agreements, as well as the serious differences which emerged over Palestine,all led to a major curtailment of the wartime 'special relationship' in this early post-war period.[9] Economic and political differences were also paralleled by a dwindling away of the close partnership in the defence field. In September 1945 President Truman approved a policy statement calling for the dissolution of several of the Combined Boards which had been the main instruments of Anglo-American co-operation during the war. Even the prestigious Combined Chiefs of Staff Committee, the symbol of Anglo-American integration in the defence field, although continuing to function, did so in a very desultory manner. The flow of information between the services was also greatly reduced and joint Anglo-American military planning ceased to all intents and purposes.

This breakdown in defence co-operation was especially evident in the field of atomic energy. The close collaboration on the Manhattan Project and the wartime agreements at Quebec in August 1943 and Hyde Park in September 1944 led to the expectation in many quarters in Britain that the atomic partnership would continue after the war.[10] Concern that the United States might not honour these agreements took the Prime Minister, Mr Attlee, together with the Canadian Prime Minister, Mr Mackenzie King, to Washington in November 1945. Once again, however, 'full and effective co-operation' was promised by President Truman and enshrined in the Truman-Attlee-King Concordat as well as in the Groves-Anderson Memorandum of 16 November 1945.[11] Continuing executive interest in international control of atomic energy and mounting pressure from nuclear monopolists in the United States, however, soon revealed to the British the hollowness of the President's assurances. Despite promises to the contrary, technical co-operation had virtually ceased by April 1946 and by August, the McMahon Act finally slammed the door on further exchanges of nuclear information between the two countries. As Andrew Pierre realistically points out, 'from the viewpoint of America's national interest, there was no visible incentive for maintaining the special relationship on nuclear matters with Britain or in any way encouraging her separate development of atomic energy.'[12] Britain, on the other hand, clearly saw the need for her own atomic energy programme and in January 1947, as Margaret Gowing has authoritatively shown, the decision was made by a small *ad hoc* group of Ministers to go ahead with the production of Britain's own atomic weapons.[13]

There is little doubt that there was a feeling of disappointment in Britain over her treatment by the American Administration, but evidence has recently come to light which suggests that the issue may not have been as much a source of friction as is often suggested.[14] Lord Sherfield, who as Roger Makins played a leading role in negotiations on atomic energy with the Americans, has recently revealed that both the Quebec and Hyde Park agreements were 'on strict interpretation, valid for the war period only, and they therefore provided a rather weak basis for the claim that collaboration and exchange of information should continue in time of peace'. Lord Sherfield has also indicated that even the Truman-Attlee-King Concordat of November 1945 was 'a somewhat fragile agreement'. From his point of view, therefore, American actions, although regrettable, were not as surprising or indeed as outrageous as some commentators have suggested.[15]

There is further evidence also to show that although in some respects the immediate post-war period was one of disenchantment in Anglo-American relations, there were nevertheless some important lingering ties, especially in the defence field. British officers were still allowed to enter many US research establishments and, significantly, in the field of chemical and biological warfare 'programmes remained so closely in step as to be virtually integrated.'[16] Evidently, in the important field of intelligence, the machinery of collaboration also continued without interruption.[17] Even in the vexed field of atomic energy, agreement was reached in May 1946 on the allocation of uranium supplies, which contributed in an important way to the continuation of both atomic weapons programmes.[18] It is also worth noting that, despite all the friction over the American loan in 1945, Britain was only really able to continue her wide-ranging defence commitments in the immediate post-war period due to American financial support. Thus, as one commentator observes, 'although the Americans and British in the first post-war months kept their distance and were not inordinately fond of one another, they were still closer to each other than to any third power.'[19] Even in this period of relative detachment there was 'a nexus of common interest' or mutual self-interest between the two countries which prevented a complete breakdown of the 'special relationship'.

Certainly members of the new socialist government in Britain didn't
have the same attachment to the United States which Churchill had
developed, but there seems to have been nevertheless a deep conviction
amongst the 'inner circle' that in the changed circumstances of the post-
war world, Britain could not do without American help. Despite left-
wing pressures and clashes of interest on a number of issues, the Foreign
Secretary, Ernest Bevin, realised that no effort should be spared to
renew the alliance with the United States.[20] Britain pushed ahead with
her own atomic energy programme in particular, largely in the hope of
re-establishing her close alliance with the Americans in this field.

Paradoxically, just at the moment when Anglo-American relations
seemed to be at their lowest, in August 1946 when the McMahon Act
was passed, relations between the two countries started to improve.
From late summer 1946 American attitudes towards Britain began to
change as common interests increasingly focused on the twin issues of
the fear of the Soviet Union and the economic reconstruction of
Europe.[21] Co-operation with Britain over the Soviet threat to Iran and
the fusion of the British and American zones in Germany in 1946 laid
the foundations for the far-reaching change in American foreign policy
symbolised by the Truman doctrine and the Marshall Plan in 1947. As
the Cold War intensified, so an informal anti-Communist alliance between the two Anglo-Saxon states was developed. Field-Marshal
Montgomery reveals in his memoirs that on his visit to the United
States in September 1946 he found a number of American military and
political chiefs 'wondering when on earth the British would face realities and frankly broach the question of co-operation in all spheres of
defence'.[22] At Montgomery's 'Sequoia' meeting on 16 September 1946
with the US Chiefs of Staff, agreement was apparently reached on the
commencement of discussions which would cover 'the whole strategic
concept of the West in a third world war, together with the best way of
handling the business of standardisation and combined action.[23]

These discussions were followed up swiftly by the respective air
forces of the two countries announcing in December 1946 an agreement
to continue their wartime collaboration in staff methods, tactics, equipment and research. In January 1947 further agreement was also
reached on an extension of co-operation in officer exchanges for
training purposes. Co-operation was not confined only to the air forces,
either. Of particular importance in this blossoming informal defence
partnership was a directive issued in December 1946 by the Co-ordinating Committee of the US War and Navy departments. According to
this new directive.

all classified military information, including the United States order
of battle, and all information about combined research and development projects to which the United Kingdom had contributed or was
contributing, and United States research and development projects,
could be released to the United Kingdom.[24]

Although atomic energy was omitted from the directive, it did nevertheless cover an extremely wide range of other military information
including 'intelligence, technical and scientific information on weapons
and methods of manufacture and non-technical information about
United States forces'. By the end of 1947, the Combined Chiefs of
Staff Committee, which had been in a state of suspended animation
since the end of the war, was, according to many reports, reaching
its former effectiveness. Indeed, there is a hint from one source that the
amount of co-operation was greater than was perhaps even politically
sanctioned. As one American officer put it, there was a considerable
amount of 'healthy hanky-panky' taking place through a variety of
Anglo-American channels at this time.[25]

Undoubtedly the most far-reaching and significant event in the proliferation of informal contacts between Britain and the United States
occurred as a result of Soviet pressure on Berlin in 1948. The intensifica-
tion of the Cold War led to the arrival at three RAF stations in East
Anglia in July of 60 American B29 Superfortresses.[26] Despite the fact
that Britain was now thrust into the front line of any future war with
the Soviet Union,[27] no formal agreements covering their use were
signed. As the Secretary of State for Air revealed in the House of
Commons on 28 July 1948, the American units were not visiting
Britain under a 'formal treaty' but 'under informal and longstanding
arrangements between the two air forces for visits of goodwill and
training purposes'.[28] The size of the US presence, initially made in
response to the Czech *coup* and the Berlin blockade, was soon
increased to 90 bombers based at seven RAF stations and by 1954 over
45,000 American military personnel were in Great Britain. It was only
in 1951, in fact, that, before leaving office, Prime Minister Attlee signed
an agreement with President Truman on the use of American aircraft
from British bases. Even then the agreement was somewhat vague and
open-ended. As Prime Minister Harold Macmillan revealed to the House
of Commons on 12 December 1957, the 'use of bases in an emergency
was accepted to be a matter for joint decision by the two Governments
in the light of circumstances prevailing at the time'.[29]

Perhaps, not unnaturally, US officials were surprised at the casual way in which their planes were received in Britain. Ambassador Douglas was even instructed by Washington to ask the Foreign Secretary, Ernest Bevin, whether the British Government had fully explored and considered the effect of the arrival of American aircraft in Britain on public opinion.[30] In June 1949 also, the Commander of the American Air Forces in Britain emphasised the unusual nature of the arrangement at a press conference, when he pointed out that 'never before in history has one first-class power gone into another first-class power's country without any agreement. We were just told to come over and "we shall be pleased to have you."'[31]

These informal and unwritten understandings of 1948 and the close ties which they implied between the respective air forces can, however, be contrasted with parallel negotiations which were taking place at this time over the sharing of nuclear information. Atomic energy seems to have been the one area which was not part of the same pattern of improving and increasingly intimate relations between the two states.[32] Concern in the United States over the growing awareness of the existence of a British veto on the American use of the atomic bomb contained in the 1943 Quebec agreement,[33] together with the American need to secure more uranium supplies, led to a renewal of interest in responding to British appeals for greater collaboration in the atomic energy field. Some key American political figures, like Secretary of State Dean Acheson, wanted increased co-operation because they were concerned that the United States had broken the wartime agreements.[34] There were others, however, like Senators Vandenburg and Hickenlooper who wished to remove the 'intolerable' restriction on the use of American power contained in the Quebec agreement.[35] To them, American interests dictated an agreement which restrained Britain's nuclear effort rather than accelerated it, while at the same time facilitating an extension of the US atomic programme. The American official historians on atomic energy developments, Hewlett and Duncan, emphasise that in general it was this calculation of the national interests involved which was paramount in the minds of the American authorities.

> They had apparently agreed that they would strive to abrogate the wartime agreements, to acquire British ore stocks, to get a much greater share of Congo production, to restrict the storage of raw materials in Britain to a minimum and to obtain British and Canadian support for ore negotiations with South Africa. In return the United States would give *some* information.[36]

The result-was a *modus vivendi* negotiated at Blair House in January 1948. According to this agreement, Britain's power of veto over the American use of atomic weapons was removed; the United States received a larger share of uranium ore; and Britain was to receive nuclear information in nine specific areas concerned with health, safety and certain other subjects *not* related to military weapons.[37]

From the British point of view, although the agreement represented a step forward, it was far from satisfactory. Despite important concessions over the British veto and the supply of uranium controlled by Britain, the agreement never lived up to the expectations in London that it would open up a new era of collaboration in atomic energy.

To some observers, the failure of British negotiations in 1948 and 1949 to use the important cards in their hand, especially the control of ore supplies, demonstrates a certain altruism on Britain's behalf which is not explicable by traditional alliance theory.[38] Richard Rosecrance, in particular, argues that Britain might have used its virtual monopoly of vital raw materials to obtain greater information from the United States.[39] The fact that this was not done, he argues, suggests a generosity by Britain not usual in international relations. Similarly the 'extraordinary act of self-abnegation' involved in Britain's offer in 1949 to concentrate its nuclear effort in the United States and to content itself with a stock of bombs from the United States is often viewed in a similar light. The apparent willingness virtually to abandon a national nuclear programme that was near completion suggests to those who hold this view that the legacy of the past and traditional affinities between the two peoples were, at least in these cases, more potent forces in the Anglo-American alliance than calculations of national interest.[40]

On the basis of the evidence available these arguments, however, do not seem particularly convincing. Contrary to what is sometimes suggested, there is little dqubt that British negotiators did in fact consider using their control of uranium to modify American policy but were dissuaded from doing so because they didn't see it in their interests.[41] Senator Vandenburg in the United States had made it very plain indeed that agreement in 1948 was linked with Congressional support for Marshall Aid, so necessary to Britain's economic recovery.[42] Similarly in the face of the perceived threat in 1948, British national interests also seemed to necessitate, to those responsible for these decisions, a strong alliance with the United States. NATO, created in April 1949, represented the culmination of Mr Bevin's endeavours to 'entangle' the Americans in Western European security, following the Czech *coup* and the Berlin blockade. The imminence of the threat, especially after the Soviet atomic explosion in August 1949, which was 'a profound shock to Britain', also provided good reasons for a nuclear alliance with the United States. Whether Britain used the high cards in her hands very adroitly is debatable, but the concessions she was prepared to make were hardly made for altruistic reasons.[43] The United States was the main source of Western defence against the Soviet Union and as such, in the last resort had to have a continuing supply of uranium to expand her nuclear programme.[44] The integration of the British nuclear programme with that of the United States, although it never materialised, likewise offered immediate advantages in the form of a freer flow of information and a stockpile of bombs under British control much sooner than her own independent programme could have produced them.[45] For both states calculations about vital interests seem to have been very much at the heart of the atomic energy issue.

Such calculations were also important in terms of conventional military collaboration as well. Atomic energy may have remained something apart from all the other strands that were weaving a new and stronger 'special relationship' for some time to come, but in other areas of security policy the late 1940s witnessed a renewed intimacy. In both military operations and weapon systems, both states did a great deal to harmonise their policies in the light of the perceived Soviet threat.

During the Berlin airlift and the Korean War close partnership between the two countries enabled the services to enjoy a depth of cooperation comparable in many ways to that achieved during the Second World War. Soviet policies had a 'galvanic effect' and helped restore the Combined Chiefs of Staff as an 'effective, dynamic institution'.[46] Korea in particular did a great deal to cement the alliance. Even at this time, however, as one British Minister has pointed out, 'none of us was taking the alliance for granted.'[47] For this reason Britain was prepared to undertake a massive rearmament programme in 1950 and 1951 to support American operations in Korea.[48] It was felt that the United States had to be shown that the British were prepared to play their part in Western defence if the Americans were to be tied in with the security needs of Western Europe. Despite the damaging effect on the British economy the rearmament programme does seem to have had the desired effect.[49] It demonstrated to the American authorities that Britain was still the most powerful Western European country and as such deserved to be treated as a partner. British arms production exceeded that of her European NATO partners combined at this time and despite the vulnerability of her economy it still occupied a unique place amongst Western European economies.[50] Industrial production was still

30 per cent of non-Communist Europe and was vastly superior to that
of either France or Germany in the early 1950s. As an American survey
written in August 1951 pointed out, Britain alone of the Western European states had the resources which entitled her to be viewed as an independent military power.[51] It was perhaps not surprising, therefore,
that the Anglo-American partnership was the mainspring of Atlantic
defence.[52] Following Korea this was to be formalised in the NATO
command structure with British and American personnel taking most of
the major appointments.[53] At both the bilateral and multilateral levels
it was this collaboration in the defence field which emphasised the
growing harmony of relations between the two states. Indeed, such was
the extent of the co-operation and mutual reliance during this period
that one journalist wrote at the time, 'if the Anglo-American alliance
should be dissolved, every military plan in the Pentagon would have to
be torn up.'[54]

Co-operation was particularly close in the weapons field as well as in
the operational field. Despite the problems over atomic energy an agreement on the exchange of information on guided missiles was ratified in
February 1950. It seems that the early 1950s also saw the signing of a
'plethora of unpublished agreements' on the exchange of military information. One of these arrangements concluded in 1950, known as the
Burns-Templar Agreement, apparently allowed for the interchange of
certain military secrets, about weapon systems 'within the limits of
national policy'.[55] With the Mutual Defence Assistance Act of 1949
and the Mutual Security Act of 1951 the importance of her British ally
was further revealed by the amount of both equipment and defence
support aid given to Britain by the United States. Deliveries of military
equipment covered a wide spectrum and included such items as aircraft,
anti-tank rocket-launchers, medium self-propelled guns as well as elec-
tronic and engineering equipment. Between 1951 and 1956 Britain received altogether over £400 million worth of defence aid and over £300
million of off-shore procurement from the United States, which was of
great assistance in helping to maintain her considerable commitments
around the world.

The early fifties, however, were still characterised by friction as well
as harmony in Anglo-American relations. As the immediacy of the
Soviet threat receded, so clashes of interest became more pronounced,
such that by 1956 the alliance reached its lowest point in the post-war
period. Problems over the recognition of China, as well as over Egypt,
Indochina and the deterioration of personal relations, particularly
those between Anthony Eden and John Foster Dulles, led to a cyclical

relapse in the relationship in certain important areas. Even in Europe, the arena of greatest Anglo-Saxon solidarity, differing interests threatened the cohesion of the partnership. Different attitudes towards European integration came to a head over the cool reception given to the proposed European Defence Community in London in the early fifties. The hiatus stemming from the failure of France to ratify the EDC treaty caused Secretary of State Dulles to threaten his famous 'agonizing reappraisal of American foreign policy' and to warn Britain privately that the United States might go over to a policy of hemispheric defence with an emphasis on the Far East. The threat to the alliance was sufficient to 'evoke from Mr Eden what was perhaps the most adroit diplomatic operation of his career' when he resolved the crisis through the Paris agreements in 1954.[56]

The post-war nadir of Anglo-American relations, however, came in 1956 with the Suez crisis. Shortly before the crisis, disagreements over Palestine as well as over the British base in Egypt and the hesitations by the United States to join the British-sponsored Baghdad Pact should perhaps have warned the decision-makers in both countries of their diverging interests. For Britain, the Middle East was a critical area of her traditional policy. The presence of British forces and the uninterrupted use of the Suez Canal had been axioms of British policy for nearly a century. With the nationalisation of the canal President Nasser was seen as the 'Hitler of the Nile' with a finger on Britain's jugular vein. To the United States, on the other hand, the canal was not an historic lifeline and Egypt was not 'a testing ground of national prestige'. Mr Dulles undoubtedly felt that the main enemy in the region was not Arab nationalism, but Soviet Communism. As H.G. Nicholas clearly demonstrates, 'as far as Anglo-American relations are concerned, the basic trouble was that in connection with the complex of issues which Suez represented, there was no mutuality of interests between Britain and America'.[57] In this vital area both sides were clearly preoccupied by very different considerations.

The initial ambivalence of the American response, the intensity of her subsequent opposition and the rigidity of Prime Minister Eden's perceptions produced a clash which shook the very foundations of the alliance. Not only did American military forces indirectly hamper the invasion of the Canal zone but more importantly financial speculation in Washington brought Britain to the verge of bankruptcy and economic disaster.[58] When the cease-fire was conceded on 6 November, it was clearly the result, more than anything else, of pressure from the United States.

Considering the traumatic experience of Suez, however, the remarkable thing was that within two years, the alliance, although never quite the same again, had resumed much of the intimacy of the late 1940s and early 1950s. The new Prime Minister, Harold Macmillan, made the restoration of the close partnership with the United States the cornerstone of his foreign policy. President Eisenhower similarly worked hard to restore cordial relations. The symbols of this renewed determination to work together were particularly evident once again in the defence field. The Bermuda meeting in March 1957, described later by President Eisenhower as 'by far the most successful international conference that I attended since the close of world war two',[59] gave Britain an IRBM capability in the form of 60 Thor missiles. These missiles, which were deployed in East Anglia, were controlled under a two-key system by both Washington and London. The two allies also collaborated closely, rather ironically, in two Middle East crises in 1958. Threats to the stability of both Lebanon and Jordan in July 1958 were met by British and American operations which were characterised by a high degree of co-ordination in both planning and execution. As Robert Murphy confirmed, 'the British navy provided support in the Mediterranean and made facilities in Cyprus available to us while the United States gave logistic support by flying supplies into Jordan for the British contingent there.'[60]

The most significant and perhaps surprising area of collaboration following the Suez debate, however, was in the field of atomic energy, which had for so long been the exception to the rule in the 'special relationship'. Continued pressure by Britain for a relaxation of the terms of the McMahon Act had produced an important amendment in 1954.[61] The growing importance of tactical nuclear weapons in NATO strategy necessitated a sharing of some limited information on the external characteristics of atomic weapons. If the strategy was to be effective the Allies would have to know about such things as the size, weight, shape, yield and effects of these new weapons. So, following the amendment, in June 1955 an agreement was signed which provided for 'the exchange of information on military aspects of atomic energy including defence planning and training in the use of nuclear weapons.'[62] This breaking of the log-jam, although modest in the amount and nature of information released, was significant for Britain because in June 1956 it enabled the American Government to provide Britain with data on nuclear reactors which later enabled her to take advantage of the Polaris missiles offered at Nassau in December 1962.[63]

The amendment of the Atomic Energy Act in 1958 was of even

greater importance to Britain. It brought to a 'climax Britain's long drive to share nuclear information and to take part in American strategic planning for nuclear war — rights to which she believed she had a claim as a former atomic collaborator, and which she sought as a close ally'.[64] Following Britain's own thermonuclear explosion in 1957 and the Soviet launching of Sputnik in October of the same year, the new amendments were clearly intended to give Britain preferential treatment. According to the legislation, the exchange of information about the design and production of nuclear warheads and the transfer of missile materials was to be permitted but only, significantly, with countries that had already made 'substantial progress in the development of atomic weapons'.[65] At the time Britain was the only nation to qualify under this stipulation. On 3 July 1958, immediately after the amendments, an 'Agreement for Co-operation on the Uses of Atomic Energy for Mutual Defence Purposes' was signed with Britain, which allowed her to make 'important technical advances in design and production of nuclear warheads'.[66] The 1958 legislation also led to the agreement in May 1959, under the terms of which Britain was entitled to buy from the United States 'component parts of nuclear weapons and weapons systems and to make possible the exchange of British plutonium for American enriched uranium'.[67]

The return to the 'special relationship' symbolised by this preferential treatment was paralleled by even closer informal ties between the services in the late 1950s. This was particularly true in the case of the air forces of the two countries. Britain's own thermonuclear test and the deployment of her own delivery system, in the form of the V-bombers, brought an even closer informal partnership between Bomber Command and Strategic Air Command based in the United Kingdom. During this period, according to one senior RAF officer, 'a complete interchange of views on nuclear strategy, nuclear weapons, bombing tactics and equipment' began, which 'continued right up to the demise of Bomber Command in 1968'.[68] At about this time also 'the integration for operational purposes' of British and American nuclear striking forces took place and joint targeting procedures were established through direct links between Bomber Command Headquarters and the Headquarters of Strategic Command at Omaha, Nebraska.[69] Such was the partnership between the two air forces that they apparently even assisted each other in their respective inter-service disputes and budgetary battles in Whitehall and Washington.[70]

This renewed partnership in defence following Suez is again seen by some scholars as emphasising the secondary importance of interests in the Anglo-American alliance. For those holding such views the clash over Suez should have destroyed the partnership.[71] Instead, the alliance survived and indeed went on to prosper, particularly with the proposed Skybolt and Polaris deals. The conclusion reached, once again, is that personal ties as well as historical factors and cultural affinities have been crucial to the alliance, rather than peripheral.

While not denying the importance of personal relationships and the underlying cultural bonds, this view would seem to be somewhat idealistic. Certainly close relations between President Eisenhower and Prime Minister Macmillan, as well as between President Kennedy and Prime Minister Macmillan, had an important impact on the relationship.[72] Undeniably sentimental attachments and cultural bonds influence perceptions about who one's friends are.[73] Common values obviously bind states together. There were, however, other very good reasons why the alliance survived after the 1956 breach which have more to do with common interests than sentiment. Despite the short-term differences over Suez, these were relatively less important to both governments in the long run than the perception of the Soviet threat and the recognition that both countries needed each other. The Soviet thermonuclear explosion, the growing belief in the bomber gap and subsequently after Sputnik in the missile gap, tension over Hungary, as well as Khrushchev's ultimatum over Berlin in 1958, all seemed to threaten Western interests as a whole. To both the United States and Britain each was the other's major ally and it was considered necessary to repair the alliance in order to work together in the face of the perceived common threat.

The partnership may have been increasingly unequal, particularly in the weapons field, but there is little doubt that both sides benefited from it. Britain benefited enormously, for example, from the changes in atomic energy legislation in the United States, but it must be remembered that she had also made substantial progress of her own in this field and was consequently able to play a part in the pooling of information.[74] The American authorities even believed that collaboration with Britain would lead to some financial savings for themselves. Britain was also able to contribute to the American nuclear programme by making certain of her facilities available to the United States. In 1961-2 the British Government allowed the United States to use Christmas Island for high-altitude hydrogen bomb tests in exchange for the use of the American underground site in Nevada. Similarly Britain made important contributions in the more conventional areas of defence as well. Specifically, equipment like the steam catapult, the angled deck and improved landing aids were all pioneered by the British navy in the

1950s and were speedily imitated in the United States.[75]

Despite these contributions in some areas of defence, Britain was nevertheless becoming increasingly reliant on the United States. This was particularly so in the missile field. In 1955, for example, Rolls Royce secured access to details of the liquid-fuelled engine of the Atlas missile developed by the North American Aviation Company, which was used in the British Blue Streak missile. Indeed, licensing arrangements with the United States were said to have lopped five years and £400 million off the original estimates for this weapon.[76] Once Blue Streak had been cancelled in April 1960 Britain became even more dependent on American technology initially with the offer of Skybolt and later with the sale of Polaris missiles. In the Skybolt agreement a clause was included binding Britain to joint consultation with the United States before the missile was used.[77] At Nassau, despite the politically necessary let-out clause, the sale of Polaris missiles almost completed Britain's dependence on the United States in the strategic weapons field.[78] In many respects such dependence, however, served American interests. On the one hand it gave the American Government a measure of control over the 'independent' British deterrent and, on the other hand, it helped maintain Britain as a major ally. It was in this latter respect in particular that Britain made her greatest contribution to the alliance in the late fifties and early sixties. Britain was able to offer in return for US technology her invaluable diplomatic support in a number of contemporary international crises such as those over Quemoy and Matsu, Berlin, the Congo and Laos. Even the Skybolt crisis, caused by the American decision to cancel the project, was resolved at Nassau because President Kennedy evidently thought that the partnership was worth preserving. Britain was seen to be a close ally whose advice and actions were generally to be much valued by President Kennedy.[79] Even during the Cuban missile crisis in October 1962, which is often cited as an illustration of the decline in British influence in Washington, it now appears that Britain played an important part in the American decision-making process. Evidence now exists that Britain was 'not merely consulted but, by the regular telephone talks between Kennedy and Macmillan and the presence of Ormsby-Gore, was intimately involved in the decisions taken'.[80] Mr Macmillan was apparently consulted two or three times a day during the crisis and British officials were responsible *inter alia* for various crucial decisions, including not calling a NATO alert and the shortening of the 'interception line' of the blockade from 800 to 500 miles, to give the Russians more time to reflect on the consequences of their actions. So closely, in fact, was he involved that Prime Minister Macmillan has subsequently argued that he felt as though he were 'in the battle headquarters' itself.[81]

The key to this relationship then was reciprocal assistance. Britain enjoyed close collaboration with the US and got preferential treatment, mainly because she had something to offer in return. As Mr Healey once observed, however, a nation's power in any particular sphere is dependent on its ability to help a friend (or harm an enemy).[82] As that ability declines, so the cohesion of the relationship is likely to be affected. To a great extent this is what seems to have happened in Anglo-American relations during the 1960s. As David Nunnerley has suggested, from 1963 onwards the simple fact was that the two countries did not 'have the same kind of business to transact' as they had previously.[83] Britain's declining power meant that she was increasingly less useful to the United States. The convertibility of sterling in 1958 and Britain's continuing economic problems in the mid-1960s, culminating in devaluation in November 1967, took place at a time when American foreign policy was in the process of reorientation.[84] On the one hand, the growing importance of the Common Market meant that American Presidents began to focus their attention on the more prosperous West European states, like West Germany, rather than on ailing Britain.[85] At the same time, the deterioration of the situation in Vietnam and the commitment of American ground troops in 1965 focused the attention of the United States Administration on Asia rather than on Europe. The changing strategic balance also necessitated the search for an agreement with the Soviet Union to slow down the arms race. These changing patterns of international relations meant that Anglo-American relations were no longer as important to the American administration as they had been in the past.

Although the declining cohesion of the 'special relationship' has been continuous since the mid-1960s, however, the process has never-theless been a gradual and uneven one. Despite Britain's declining power and the divergence of policies in some fields there have been other areas in which common interests have prevailed. President Johnson was particularly concerned to retain a British presence east of Suez during the Vietnam War. In return for certain diplomatic support, the British Prime Minister, Harold Wilson, was able to perpetuate the partnership with the United States in the defence field (as well as in the economic field).[86] Aubrey Jones even went as far as to argue in Parliament on 3 March 1965 that the 'Wilson government was using the East of Suez presence rather than the nuclear deterrent to perpetuate the "special relationship" with the United States and to keep a seat at the international top-table.'[87]

The relationship remained close in certain other areas of defence as
well. The services in particular retained their close ties with their counterparts in America. Despite promises to the contrary, the Polaris programme also was continued by the Labour Government and with the
growing Soviet interest in the Indian Ocean a secret deal was signed by
the two countries to develop jointly a naval base at Diego Garcia.[88]
Even in the nuclear field scientific co-operation continued and Britain
accepted dependence on the United States in the mid-1960s for
materials such as tritium and enriched uranium, so vital in the production of Britain's nuclear warheads. Collaboration between the two
defence establishments also remained close in the chemical and biological warfare field, as it had done for the entire post-war period. A certain amount of controversy arose in Britain in 1968 when it was
revealed that work carried out at Porton Down was being put to practical use in Vietnam. The Commons Select Committee on Science and
Technology set up to investigate the matter significantly went out of its
way to emphasise the value of the connection with the United States in
this field in the report which it produced on 7 May 1969.[89]

Despite these areas of collaboration, however, the direction of the
relationship in the late 1960s and 1970s is plain. There is little doubt
that the degree of co-operation between the two countries in the diplomatic and defence fields has declined considerably. The British withdrawal from east of Suez and concentration on Europe as well as
American preoccupation with Watergate and superpower relations all
helped to loosen the ties. During the Heath administration in particular,
differences of outlook on such issues as the Indo-Pakistan War, Malta
and arms for South Africa severely strained relations between the two
countries. Similarly, the lack of consultation over the American New
China policy, the economic crisis measures of 1971, and especially the
clash of interests brought about by the oil embargo in the aftermath of
the Yom Kippur War in October 1973 further signified the growing divergence. As one, usually sympathetic observer of the Atlantic partnership concluded at the time, 'there can be no doubt at all that the Anglo-
American alliance is, in early 1974, in some disarray.'[90] Although some
attempt was made by the new Labour Government in 1974 to improve
relations between the two countries, the alliance has subsequently appeared
in many ways to be no more 'special' than America's relations with a number of her other allies; in some cases perhaps even less 'special'.[91] Despite
the continuing willingness to listen to each other in particular circumstances,
such as southern Africa, and the very close relations between President

Carter and Prime Minister Callaghan, the underlying assumption that policies will be automatically aligned, which has traditionally been a feature of the partnership between the two states, no longer seems to exist.

A strong case can perhaps be made therefore that it is now time to drop the term 'special relationship' from our vocabulary,[92] at least as far as contemporary Anglo-American relations are concerned. The use of terms like the 'natural' or 'close' relationship by British and American leaders would seem to suggest that they, at least, no longer see the relationship as being 'special'[93] in the sense that it once was. Anglo-American relations remain, as they always have been, multidimensional in nature. Undoubtedly there are still vestiges, especially in the defence field, of the close and intimate co-operation of the past. Although the much publicised preferential treatment characteristic of the 1950s seems in large part to have disappeared, the partnership in some areas of defence, particularly behind the scenes, still continues. The joint targeting system, for example, which presupposes close co-operation between the military intelligence establishments, appears to have remained unimpaired. Professor Coral Bell sees this relationship between the intelligence communities as representing a particularly important dimension of the continuing relationship between the two countries. 'No doubt', she argues, 'the CIA and the Special Intelligence Service (SIS) compete in many areas . . . but it is clear from such scraps of knowledge as the outsider can gather that there is also a considerable "pooling" of information in Washington and London.'[94] This she estimates has been closer between the two allies and continues to be closer than with any third power, even Australia or Canada. Much the same is no doubt true of the continuation of links between the services in both countries. A very close liaison has been built up over the years both in the formal arena of NATO and on a more informal level between the respective armed forces and defence departments, and these remain an undramatic but nevertheless significant manifestation of the continuing alliance between the two countries.[95] Even in the nuclear field collaboration continues. In 1973 the 1958 treaty between the two countries on the exchange of nuclear materials and information was renegotiated and Britain also continues to use the American underground test site in Nevada in order to perfect new warheads for her Polaris missiles. Whether all this adds up to a 'special relationship', however, is doubtful. The contemporary relationship, although remaining close, seems to lack both the breadth of co-operation and intimacy which would warrant the use of such a phrase to describe either the wider relationship or even perhaps that in the defence field. The British

decision not to buy Poseidon and the American decision not to offer it
to Britain at special rates; the decision by the British Government in
April 1976 to produce tritium in Britain to ensure self-sufficiency in
the manufacture of thermonuclear warheads;[96] and the increasing collaboration between Britain and other West European states on weapons
systems, all symbolise the general loosening of ties which is taking place,
even in the security field. Not unnaturally, Britain's retreat from world
power and the diverging interests of the two states have progressively
eroded the exceptional intimacy of the 1940s and 1950s at the height
of the Cold War, when Britain made a significant contribution to
American defence policy. Sentiment may retard the process but it
alone is unlikely to reverse it. Only a change in Britain's position in the
world and heightened threats to Western interests are likely to do that.

In making an assessment of Anglo-American relations in the defence
field, one important question remains to be answered. What impact has
the 'special relationship' had on British defence policy in the post-war
period? Has it been overwhelmingly beneficial or, as some would argue,
has it been generally detrimental to Britain's security needs?

Despite the generally held assumption that the Anglo-American
alliance has served British interests well, especially in the defence field,
a case can certainly be made in support of the opposite point of view.
It could be argued, for example, that the 'special relationship' with the
United States, particularly the help given to Britain in the strategic
weapons field, significantly contributed to the maintenance of the
harmful illusion of great power status in Britain for much of the
period.[97] The belief that Britain was a world power lasted until the
aftermath of Suez and in some degree even up to 1967. It was this belief in large part that discouraged Britain from shedding her widespread
responsibilities, despite the declining resources available to support
them. The result was the serious divergence between capabilities and
commitments which characterised British defence policy in the early
part of the 1960s in particular.

It was in many respects this belief in Britain's status as a world
power predicated on American technological and financial support
which constrained Britain's choices, particularly as far as Europe was
concerned. The alliance helped create a framework of assumptions
which prevented consideration in Britain of other alternatives; particularly that of Europe. Andrew Pierre, for one, argues that the nuclear
partnership in particular has probably been 'injurious' to her long-term
interests 'to the extent that it encouraged Britain to feel that she could
avoid Europe'.[98] The possession of nuclear weapons and the close ties

with the United States helped produce something of a 'superiority complex' in Britain towards the other European states. Britain saw herself as a world power rather than a European power. The Anglo-American alliance was seen as the sheet anchor of Britain's foreign policy and as such helped divert attention away from the European option.[99] De Gaulle in particular saw the alliance in general, and especially the preferential Nassau deal, as a clear manifestation of the lack of genuine British commitment to Europe. Had Britain not enjoyed such close ties with the US it could be argued that she might have recognised the reality of her position sooner than she did and joined the European Community before 1973.[100]

Another detrimental effect which resulted from the close alliance, especially in the security field, is the threat of destruction which the link with the United States brought. In 1948 the 'Airstrip One' relationship undoubtedly put Britain in the forefront of any future war between the USA and USSR.[101] Conflict between the superpowers from then on would inevitably bring with it the direct threat of the total destruction of Britain. The vulnerable, slow-reacting Thor missiles with their first-strike potential which were deployed in Britain after the 1957 Bermuda agreement would seem on balance to have increased rather than decreased the danger of nuclear war.[102] It is very doubtful whether their presence was in Britain's best interest. Similarly, a great deal of concern was expressed in Britain from 1960 onwards when it was announced that the US had been allowed to set up a Polaris submarine base in Holy Loch. Like the 1948 Bases agreement, the presence of American strategic delivery vehicles in Britain meant that the Soviet Union had *added* reasons for targeting Britain. Britain would inevitably be drawn into any future war regardless of the issues at stake.

Another important effect of the 'special relationship' which is often noted is that Britain has lost a great deal of independence in the vital area of security policy.[103] Despite periodic attempts to prevent too great a dependence on the United States, collaboration in atomic energy and strategic delivery systems in particular has bound Britain closely in with American policies. It is this very same dependence which French defence policy has attempted to avoid. There have been many leading British politicians, who, over the years, have been unhappy about this growing dependence. Harold Wilson, for example, writing in 1952, complained that 'more and more American aid is being voted on conditions which involve British acceptance of American strategic decisions and control not even by Congress, but by the Pentagon, HQ of the U.S. Chiefs of Staff.'[104] Andrew Pierre has also argued that Britain in the

1960s 'tied herself to the American order of priorities in research, development and production and became dependent on American satellite intelligence and radio communications systems'.[105] In so doing, he argues, 'she has undoubtedly lost a measure of her strategic independence.'[106] This dependence is particularly evident in the case of Polaris. Besides using the data from US space satellites, the Polaris launching system, fire-control system, components of the inertial navigation system, some of the communications equipment and even the high-stress steel for the submarine hulls have to be purchased from the USA.

More recently it has been argued that various unpublished agreements with the United States signed in the 1950s have been responsible for Britain giving up important military inventions to the Americans which may be to Britain's commercial disadvantage. Under a 'Memorandum of Understanding' deriving from the Burns-Templar Agreement of 1950, it has been revealed that Britain gave the secret of Chobham armour to the Americans in 1972. Because of this, some commentators argue that the United States and West Germany may dominate the production of tanks and their guns in future, leaving Britain billions of dollars worse off.[107]

While accepting the validity of some of these arguments on the harmful aspects of the alliance, it would nevertheless be difficult to conclude that the partnership has not had some beneficial effects as well. Professor Bell, for example, highlights the very real advantages which have accrued to Britain from access to American research effort in weapons development.[108] Across the whole spectrum of military equipment the close partnership with the United States helped to cut corners in development and, especially important for Britain, to cut costs. Britain undoubtedly acquired weapons from the US that she probably would not have been able to afford or produce alone. Under both the Skybolt and Polaris deals for example, Britain was promised the most modern and sophisticated American missiles. Through these agreements Britain would be able to retain her position as a major nuclear power at relatively low cost. The Nassau agreement of 1962 was claimed by the government to have saved Britain about £1,000 million. Much the same is also true of the assistance Britain received in submarine technology from the 1954, and even more valuable, the 1958 agreements with the United States. Largely through close co-operation with the US, Britain has been able to build up a nuclear deterrent which, although not totally independent or perhaps wholly credible on its own in all circumstances, does nevertheless provide a reasonable insurance cover at a low premium.[109] Even the most powerful putative aggressor would need to stop and think carefully about the consequences before launching an attack on Britain.

In the conventional field also, American financial assistance has been of great help to Britain. The revolutionary Hawker Harrier project in particular benefited from American aid. The lack of government support for the project in Britain compelled the Hawker and Bristol companies to begin the VTOL P1127 and its engine as private ventures. They were able to do this and eventually succeed in developing the project through the substantial help they received from the American Mutual Development Programme Agency which provided 75 per cent of the funds for the engine.[110] Much the same has been true in other fields as well. Financial help as well as collaboration with the US has enabled Britain to develop and purchase many of the most up-to-date weapons systems which economic restraint at home would almost certainly have prevented, had she gone it alone.

Over much of the post-war period American economic help has also been important in enabling Britain to continue to perform her many commitments. The struggle to balance capabilities with commitments would almost certainly have been even more difficult than it was, without such help. As C.J. Bartlett has pointed out, the American loan and Marshall Aid in the 1940s in particular at a time of very severe economic troubles helped to ensure that Britain continued to perform her numerous occupation and other military duties all over the world.[111] Even when the strain became too much, as it did in Greece and Turkey in 1947, the United States stepped in to continue the commitment and to take over the responsibility from Britain. The ten-year rule of 1946 left a vacuum in British defence policy in the late 1940s and early 1950s when the Soviet threat emerged sooner than many political leaders had expected. Once again it was American military aid through such agencies as the Mutual Defence Assistance Programme which was largely instrumental in filling the void in Britain's defences.[112] American financial assistance during the 1950s similarly helped to reduce the strain of world-wide defence duties and escalating weapons costs. Between 1951 and 1958 American (and Canadian) defence aid significantly contributed to the costs of the Korean, Malayan and Mau Mau campaigns in which British forces were engaged. Without such help it is debatable whether Britain would have been able to deal with these emergencies as patiently and successfully as she did.

It would also be hard to deny that Britain benefits greatly, like other members of NATO, from the presence of American forces in Europe as well as from the protection provided by the nuclear um-

brella.[113] The withdrawal of substantial American forces from the
Continent advocated by Senator Mansfield and others would both
jeopardise British security interests and necessitate a vast increase in
defence expenditure by Britain as well as by other European NATO
countries, if a credible defensive system was to be maintained in
Europe.

Although the argument is not as clear-cut as some would assume, it
would appear then that, on balance, Britain has been 'a net beneficiary'
from the partnership with the United States. Certainly that has been
the view of most leading political, as well as military, leaders in Britain
for most of the post-war period. Both Conservative and Labour governments since the war have recognised the advantages of the alliance in
the security field and gone out of their way to foster the relationship.
Given the growing disparity of power, it is perhaps not surprising that
British leaders have seen the alliance as being more vital to their
national interests than political figures in the United States. As Andrew
Pierre has observed, 'the Anglo-American relationship has been more
important to Britain since World War Two and for this reason, primarily, it is the British who usually undertook the burden of keeping it
"special".'[114] In a way the United States has had 'special relationships'
with most of its allies; 'special' in the sense that each ally fitted a different niche in the structure of the American security system. The
difference between these other 'special relationships' and the partnership with Britain, however, is that the US has had more common interests with Britain for most of the period since 1945 than with any of her
other allies. Because of these common interests both capitals have
generally seen the benefits of working closely together. It is this 'capacity to see the elements of common interests in whatever international
storms the time may bring' which has been the great strength of the
'special relationship', according to one influential observer of Anglo-
American relations.[115]

It is the weakening of this 'capacity', however, brought about by the
growing divergence of interests and the decline of the bilateral partnership which has increasingly diluted the 'special relationship' in general
as well as specifically in the security field. The changing kaleidoscope
of international relations and the reduced circumstances of Great
Britain have removed the incentives for the web of interdependency
woven between the late 1940s and early 1960s. Common interests in
'the rational management of world politics' and in the prevention of the
expansion of Soviet power, especially in Europe, remain. Interests
which give rise to a continuation of a number of important formal and

informal links in the defence field are based on 'habits of trust' and a
certain amount of mutual esteem that has grown up between the respective governments over the years. The relationship, however, is no longer
'special' in the sense that it was in the past. The American connection
is still important and is likely to remain so for some time to come, but
it is no longer the all-pervading feature of British defence policy which
it once was.

Notes

1. Atomic energy was perhaps the main exception until the 1954 and 1958 amendments to the McMahon Act. Since then it has played a very impor-tant symbolic role in Anglo-American relations.
2. See Andrew Pierre, *Nuclear Politics* (London, Oxford University Press, 1972), p. 316.
3. For a discussion of the 'special relationship' in general see H.G. Nicholas, *The United States and Britain* (Chicago, The University of Chicago Press, 1974); H.C. Allen, *Great Britain and the United States: A History of Anglo-American Relations (1783-1952)* (London, Odhams Press, 1954); C. Bell, *The Debatable Alliance* (London, Oxford University Press, 1964); H. Kissinger, *The Troubled Partnership* (New York, McGraw-Hill, 1965); R.B. Manderson-Jones, *The Special Relationship* (London, Weidenfeld and Nicolson, 1972).
4. See in particular R. Rosecrance, *Defense of the Realm* (New York, Columbia University Press, 1968), and R. Dawson and R. Rosecrance, 'Theory and Reality in the Anglo-American Alliance', *World Politics*, vol. 19, 1966-7, pp. 21-51.
5. See F.S. Northedge, op. cit., p. 173.
6. H.C. Allen, op. cit., p. 781.
7. Quoted in D. Maclean, *British Foreign Policy since Suez* (London, Hodder and Stoughton, 1970), p. 37.
8. See Robert Rhodes James (ed.), *Winston S. Churchill. His Complete Speeches 1897-1963*, Vol. VII (New York, Chelsea House Publishers, 1974), pp. 7289-93. Churchill talked of the need for 'the continuance of the intimate relationship between our military advisers . . . a common study of potential dangers, similarity of weapons and manuals of instructions, interchange of officers . . . and joint use of all Naval and Air Force bases'.
9. For further discussion of this breakdown in wartime relations see H.G. Nicholas, op. cit., p. 104.
10. Under the Quebec agreement Britain and the US promised never to use the bomb against each other; not to use it against a third party without consent; not to communicate information except by mutual consent; post-war industrial and commercial advantages were to be dealt with on terms specified by the President to the Prime Minister; arrangements were to be made to ensure the full and effective collaboration in bringing the project to fruition through the setting up of a Combined Policy Committee. The Hyde Park *aide-memoire* between Churchill and Roosevelt, which was filed away and lost until many years after the war, agreed on full collaboration for military and commercial purposes after the defeat of Japan unless ter-

minated by joint agreement. See A. Pierre, op. cit., p. 60.

11. For a detailed discussion of the Washington talks and the Groves-Anderson Memorandum see M. Gowing, *Independence and Deterrence: Britain and Atomic Energy 1945-52*, Vol.1 (London Macmillan, 1974), pp. 73-86.

12. A. Pierre, op. cit., p. 120.

13. See M. Gowing, op. cit., pp. 179-84.

14. Lord Sherfield, 'Britain's Nuclear Story 1945-52', *Round Table*, April 1975, No. 258, pp. 193-204. See also David Carlton, 'Great Britain and Nuclear Weapons: the academic inquest', *British Journal of International Studies*, Vol. 2, No. 2, July 1976.

15. Professor Gowing, in particular, expresses this judgement.

16. Ibid., p. 94.

17. Lord Sherfield, op. cit., p. 194.

18. Ibid., pp. 102-4.

19. Ibid., p. 94.

20. See R. Osgood, *The Entangling Alliance* (Chicago, University of Chicago Press, 1962) and F. Williams, *Ernest Bevin* (London, Hutchinson, 1952), p. 267.

21. M. Gowing, op. cit., p. 95.

22. Montgomery, *The Memoirs of Field Marshal Montgomery* (London, Collins, 1958), p. 443.

23. Despite the value of these discussions there were no consultations on the American Strategic Air Plan until at least 1952. In 1948 at a meeting of the Chiefs of Staffs of the two countries Lord Tedder complained of the separation in Strategic Planning. Churchill apparently secured the promise of joint discussions on the Strategic Air Plan from Truman at their meeting in January 1952. See Gowing, op. cit., p. 413.

24. Ibid., p. 117.

25. R. Rosecrance, op. cit., p. 51.

26. See *The World Today*, Vol. 16, No. 8, August 1960, pp. 319-25.

27. Sir Stafford Cripps, the British Chancellor of the Exchequer, told the Secretary of Defense James Forrestal that Britain must be regarded as 'the main base for the deployment of American power' on a visit to Washington in October 1948. Quoted in H.G. Nicholas, op. cit., p. 127.

28. Quoted in *The World Today*, op. cit., pp. 319-20. See also Millis (ed.), *Forrestal Diaries* (London, Cassell and Company, 1952), pp. 428 and 460.

29. See *The World Today*, op. cit., pp. 322-3 (author's emphasis).

30. See Millis, op. cit., p. 428. The Americans were clearly aware of the advantages to them of sending the B29s to Britain. 'We have the opportunity *now* of sending these planes, and once they are sent they would become something of an accepted fixture, whereas a deterioration of the situation in Europe might lead to a condition of mind under which the British would be compelled to reverse their present attitude.' Ibid., p. 430.

31. Quoted in *World Today*, op. cit., p. 320.

32. See Gowing, op. cit., p. 320.

33. See footnote 10.

34. See D. Acheson, *Present at the Creation* (London, Hamish Hamilton, 1970), p. 164.

35. See A. Pierre, op. cit., p. 132.

36. R.G. Hewlett and F. Duncan, *The History of USAEC, Vol II, Atomic Shield, 1947-52* (Pennsylvania, Pennsylvania State University Press, 1969), p. 279 and *passim* (author's emphasis).

37. See A. Pierre, op. cit., pp. 128-31.

38. See George Liska, *Nations in Alliance: The Limits of Interdependence*,

(Baltimore, 1962), pp. 12, 26 and 54-5. Traditional alliance theory would suggest that 'calculation, not sentiment, determines original combinations; thereafter, ideology, cultural ties and common historical traditions may buttress the connection achieved. Interest governs the breakdown of alliances; cultural affinities can only be retarding factors.' See Dawson and Rosecrance, op. cit., p. 21.

39. See R. Rosecrance, op. cit., p. 48.
40. Dawson and Rosecrance, op. cit., p. 48.
41. 'The British also saw the [Springfields] stockpile as a bargaining counter, and had even suggested privately in Washington that, failing a satisfactory general agreement on technical co-operation, the British attitude on Congo stocks in the United Kingdom "might change".' Gowing, op. cit., p. 361.
42. '. . . failure to revamp the agreements would have a disastrous effect on Congressional consideration of the Marshall Plan.' See Arthur H. Vandenburg, Jr. (ed.), The Private Papers of Senator Vandenburg (Boston, 1952), p. 361.
43. For the advantages of the agreement to Britain see Gowing, op. cit., p. 250.
44. As the Chairman of the American Atomic Energy Commission, David Lilienthal warned in early 1947, US production was on 'thin ice' because of raw material shortages. See The Journals of David Lilienthal. Vol. II, The Atomic Energy Years (New York, 1964), p. 185.
45. The Chiefs of Staff in Britain wanted a stockpile of 20 bombs in Britain.
46. See Neal Stanford, Christian Science Monitor, 27 April 1948 and Dawson and Rosecrance, op. cit., p. 26.
47. Ibid., p. 30.
48. The rearmament plan in 1950 to spend £3,400 million over three years was increased in 1951 to £4,700 million.
49. When a Conservative Government came to power in October 1951, many economic experts thought that Britain was on the verge of bankruptcy. Churchill reduced the rearmament bill and extended it over a longer period.
50. See C.J. Bartlett, The Long Retreat (London, Macmillan, 1972), p. 64.
51. T. Geiger and H. van B. Cleveland, Making Western Europe Defensible, quoted in Barlett, ibid., p. 269 n. See also Barlett's chapter in this book, p. 36.
52. Senator Hubert Humphrey also emphasised that 'Britain is the keystone to our North Atlantic defense system.' Congressional Record, Appendix, 81st Congress, 1st Session. p. A5690 (7 September 1949).
53. As R.B. Manderson-Jones points out, 'NATO was fashioned around the Anglo-American alliance and effectively rested on Anglo-American power.' Op. cit., p. 76. General Eisenhower became SACEUR and Lord Ismay, Secretary General of NATO.
54. J. Alsop, Washington Post, 22 July 1949.
55. Letter from Peter Kellner, Sunday Times, 17 November 1976. See also the Sunday Times, 7 November 1976. This agreement is apparently still in force. See footnote 107.
56. For a fuller discussion of the EDC crisis see H.G. Nicholas, op. cit., p. 152.
57. Ibid., p. 155.
58. 'American submarines suddenly were detected all over the ocean. Finally the Commander of the British Mediterranean Fleet had to ask his Sixth Fleet counterpart to bring them to the surface. There was a distinct possibility that the British might inadvertently destroy an American submarine. There seemed little doubt that the Sixth Fleet had orders to obstruct the operation by all peaceful means.' Dawson and Rosecrance, op. cit., p. 40. For a discussion of the vital importance of American financial pressure, see C.J. Bartlett, op. cit., p. 125.

59. D. Eisenhower, *Waging Peace, 1956-61* (New York, Doubleday, 1965), p. 124.
60. Quoted in D. Maclean, op. cit., p. 66.
61. There was also an amendment to the Atomic Energy Act in July 1951 which was purely to the benefit of the United States. See Gowing, op. cit., p. 304.
62. *Agreement for Co-operation Regarding Atomic Information for Mutual Defence Purposes,* Cmd. 9555.
63. In June 1956 Britain received information on the nuclear submarine Nautilus. See H.L. Nieburg, *Nuclear Secrecy and Foreign Policy* (Washington, Public Affairs Press, 1964), p. 67.
64. See A. Pierre, op. cit., p. 141.
65. *Public Law* No. 85-479, 85th Congress, 2nd session; Senate Report 1654, House Report 1859, 85th Congress, 2nd Session, p. 12.
66. Cmnd. 657.
67. *Amendment to Agreement between the Government of the United Kingdom of Great Britain and Northern Ireland and the Government of the United States of America for Co-operation on the Uses of Atomic Energy for Mutual Defence Purposes of July 3, 1958.* Cmnd. 859.
68. Letter to the author from Air Vice-Marshall S.W.B. Menaul, CB, CBE, DFC, AFC, 2 April 1976.
69. Ibid.
70. Especially in the manned aircraft versus missile controversy and the attempts to keep the Skybolt project alive. (Dawson and Rosecrance, op. cit.)
71. Op. cit., p. 51.
72. As Coral Bell suggests, 'Probably the personal factor is more often over-rated than underrated, but it ought never to be disregarded.' 'The Special Relationship', in M. Leifer (ed.), *Constraints and Adjustments in British Foreign Policy* (London, Allen and Unwin, 1972), p. 114.
73. The common language, the interpenetration of the two cultures, the wide network of friendships, intermarriages and other personal ties makes for easier understanding and greater responsiveness. See Maclean, op. cit., pp. 43-4. The 'special relationship' is seen here as resulting from both sentiment and interest – the two cannot be totally separated. The point being made here, however, is that of these two major influences in Anglo-American relations the calculation of national interest has been more powerful as a determinant of policy in both capitals.
74. For the advantages to the United States see C.J. Bartlett, op. cit., p. 151.
75. Ibid., p. 73.
76. Ibid., p. 109.
77. Ibid., p. 156.
78. Britain could withdraw her Polaris missiles from the NATO multilateral nuclear force under paragraph 8 of the Nassau Agreement when her 'supreme national interests were at stake'. Britain remained dependent, however, on the United States for satellite information, certain vital materials and on replacements from the US of the missiles themselves. The MLF concept was later revived as a means of furthering control over the 'independent' nuclear deterrents but was rejected by both France and Britain. Wilson's ANF concept effectively ended American pressure for the acceptance of an MLF in 1964/5.
79. See D. Nunnerley, *President Kennedy and Britain* (London, Bodley Head, 1972), p. 128. It was perhaps just as well that Kennedy felt this way and Macmillan was able to portray Nassau as a great success. Failure would certainly have weakened further his already tarnished image.

80. See H.G. Nicholas, op. cit., p. 165.
81. H. Macmillan, *At the End of the Day* (London, Macmillan, 1973), p. 220.
82. Quoted in C. Bell, 'The Special Relationship', op. cit., p. 110 (author's brackets).
83. D. Nunnerley, op. cit., p. 189.
84. R. Maddock highlights the importance of changing economic relations in a paper entitled 'Economic Rationality and the Anglo-American Alliance'. I am indebted to him for a number of very useful discussions on the subject.
85. The importance of Britain in Western security overrode the American interest in pressurising Britain to join the European movement for much of the period according to Manderson-Jones, op. cit., p. 131. As Britain's power declined, however, the US was less concerned to treat Britain separately from the Continent.
86. In the economic field American assistance for sterling in the mid-sixties was of great assistance to Britain. By the 1970s, however, the reduced importance of sterling has been paralleled by a declining economic relationship with the United States.
87. Quoted in C.J. Bartlett, op. cit., p. 219
88. The original agreement seems to have been signed in 1966 and Britain's contribution to the project was offset against the 1963 Polaris agreement (in which Britain had to pay 5 per cent of the American costs for further research and development of the missile).
89. C.J. Bartlett, op. cit., p. 253.
90. P. Lyon, 'Britain and the United States', *Current History*, March 1974.
91. For a discussion of the close relationship between Jim Callaghan and Henry Kissinger, see *The Times*, 4 March 1975, 'Patching up Anglo-American Relations: the big hurdle is whether we stay in Europe'.
92. For a critical view of the continuing usefulness of the term see P. Lyon, op. cit.
93. Prime Minister Heath talked of the 'natural' relationship and Prime Minister Wilson of the 'close' relationship. President Nixon and Carter, however, have on occasions revived the use of the term.
94. C. Bell, 'The Special Relationship', op. cit., p. 112.
95. Both C. Bell and P. Lyon emphasise the importance of Anglo-American relations within the North Atlantic Alliance. C. Bell, ibid., p. 106; P. Lyon, op. cit.
96. See the *Sunday Times*, 2 May 1976, 'Why Britain has do-it-yourself Bombs'.
97. See H. Kissinger, *The Troubled Partnership* (New York, McGraw-Hill, 1965), p. 80.
98. A. Pierre, op. cit., p. 316. Professor Gowing argues that it was the hope of re-establishing the alliance in atomic energy with the US in the late 1940s which prevented Britain from collaborating with the other European countries (or other Commonwealth countries) in that field. Gowing, op. cit., p. 160. Lord Sherfield, however, has questioned whether such alternatives were in fact realistic at this time. See Lord Sherfield, op. cit.
99. For a discussion of the 'special relationship' as a constraint on policy in Britain see C. Bell, 'The Special Relationship', op. cit., p. 103.
100. There is, of course, a debatable assumption here that this would have been a good thing.
101. The phrase 'Airstrip One' relationship was coined by Professor Bell. See *The Debatable Alliance*, op. cit.
102. In the sense that because they would only be used for a first-strike attack they might alarm the Russians into launching a pre-emptive first strike of their own.
103. This dependence in strategic matters began with the 1948 Bases

'agreement'.
104. H. Wilson, *In Place of Dollars* (London, Tribune Pamphlet, 1952); see also
     L.D. Epstein, *Britain – Uneasy Ally* (Chicago, University of Chicago Press,
     1954).
105. A. Pierre, op. cit., p. 316.
106. Ibid.
107. Chobham Armour is a radically new kind of armour which is said to provide
     protection from Russia's latest generation of guns and hand-launched
     missiles. See the *Sunday Times,* 7 November 1976.
108. C. Bell, 'The Special Relationship', op. cit.
109. The total cost of the Polaris system was reported to be about £350 million
     with an annual £32 million running costs. This compares favourably with
     the £500 million spent on the V-bomber force.
110. This was estimated to be about £12½ million.
111. C.J. Bartlett, op. cit., p. 44.
112. Britain also relied on the US strategic delivery system until the V-bomber
     force came into operation in 1957. The first atomic bombs had been avail-
     able in 1953.
113. The US air force and navy continues to have bases and facilities in Britain
     in the following places: Burton Wood, Brawdy, Milden Hall, Alconbury,
     Lakenheath, Upper Heyford, Bentwaters, Chicksands, Holy Loch, Edzell,
     Thurso, Macrihanish, Londonderry, St Mawgan and London. In 1976
     Britain benefited to the tune of about 300 million dollars from this
     American presence. With the build-up of Soviet IRBMs targeted on Europe
     (the SS-20 in particular) the US has built up its nuclear strike aircraft in
     Britain in early 1977. 84 F-111 aircraft have been sent to Lakenheath to
     join the 72 at Upper Heyford.
114. A. Pierre, op. cit., p. 318.
115. C. Bell, 'The Special Relationship', op. cit., p. 119.

4 BRITAIN, NATO AND EUROPEAN SECURITY: THE IRREDUCIBLE COMMITMENT

Stephen Kirby

In the post-war world Britain has committed substantial forces and a large part of her defence spending to maintain a continuous military presence in Europe. This undertaking has been the most consistent feature of Britain's post-war defence policy but successive governments have lacked enthusiasm for it, for, until recently, the commitment to Europe has been least in harmony with Britain's foreign policy aspirations. In 1945 British defence commitments stretched from South-East Asia through the Indian sub-continent and the Middle East to Western Europe and they reflected a world role and a great power status that were unquestioned. Britain maintained forces in Germany first as an occupying power and later in the spirit of a guarantor of European security but, in the first two decades after the war, heavy emphasis was placed upon policing Empire and Commonwealth, assisting allies outside Europe[1] and upon making a significant contribution to strategic air power. But Britain has been unable to sustain all the demands of a global role and the post-war experience has been one of a hesitant and often painful recognition that of all her defence interests, only that in 'European security was, and will remain irreducible'.[2]

As the only undefeated Western European state at the end of the war, it was inevitable that Britain would play a great part in the reconstruction of a European order. At the Yalta Conference in 1945 President Roosevelt had expressed the belief that American troops would be out of Europe within two years of the end of hostilities.[3] Indeed the United States demobilised and withdrew troops from Europe far faster than did Britain. In 1945 Britain had 488,000 men stationed in Germany compared to the 391,000 of the United States,[4] and she maintained twice as many men *per capita* under arms as America.[5] This was achieved despite severe economic problems and the additional burden of a German occupation zone that was heavily dependent upon British resources for survival. Despite this effort, American relations with Europe, and especially with Britain, were strained throughout 1946. There had been sustained disagreement about occupation policy, and the Anglo-American loan negotiations often soured relations between Washington and London. The exchange of atomic technology

data also caused problems and culminated in Congress passing the
McMahon Act on 1 August 1946, which denied Britain many of the
fruits of the wartime Manhattan project.

In this period Britain struggled with the consequences of victory and
had not completed the process of establishing priorities for her foreign
and defence policies. In Europe, under the guidance of Foreign
Secretary Bevin,[6] Britain sought little more than a working relationship
with the Americans, the French and the Russians in the administration
of occupied Germany. Bevin had been embarrassed by Churchill's 'iron
curtain' speech in Fulton, Missouri, on 16 March 1946 for he, like the
Americans, had not yet fully discounted the possibility of co-operation
with Russia. In 1946 the major security problem in Europe was still
Germany and it was a regard for French fears of a revanchist Germany
that encouraged Bevin to negotiate the Anglo-French Treaty which was
signed at Dunkirk on 4 March 1947. Even at this time Bevin sought to
allay Soviet suspicions and to prevent a partition of Europe by
announcing that the treaty did not amount to a 'Western bloc'.[7]

Throughout 1947 several issues began to be more clearly defined in
British defence policy. It became clear that the rate of demobilisation
would have to be rapid to relieve the burden of defence spending and
that this would necessitate a reduction in the programme of overseas
military assistance. In February Bevin sent two notes to Washington
warning that if United States aid were not forthcoming, British military
assistance to Greece and Turkey would end within six weeks. These
notes set in train a series of negotiations between President Truman and
leaders of the Congress and on 12 March 1947 the Truman doctrine was
announced and marked a significant shift in American policy not only
in terms of its anti-Communist tone, but also in terms of future relations with Europe. Bevin's pleas had brought home to the American Administration just how desperate was the economic plight of Europe and
stimulated a speech made by the American Secretary of State, George
Marshall, at Harvard on 5 June 1947. Marshall proposed a plan for the
economic recovery of Europe. To Bevin this offer seemed 'like a life
line to sinking men',[8] and, as he reported to Parliament on 19 June,
'when the Marshall proposals were announced, I grabbed them with
both hands.'[9] Bevin became the organising force on the European side
and he was closely involved in the creation of the institutions to ad-
minister the European Recovery Programme. The programme was
offered to all European states, but after prolonged negotiations
Marshall Aid was rejected by Russia and the East European states, and
when the Organisation for European Economic Co-operation (OEEC)

was set up in April 1948, it was in fact a Western bloc and represented
the effective division of Europe.

Bevin had by this time accepted the fact that agreement between
Russia and the other Allied occupation powers was remote and, despite
the very real advances that the Truman doctrine and the Marshall Aid
programme represented in the United States relations with Europe, he
became convinced that the Western European states should work more
closely together and that America must become directly involved in
their defence now that the major threat to Western interests emanated
from a militarily powerful Russia. In December 1947 he confided to
Field-Marshal Montgomery 'that the time had come to begin the formation of a federation or union in Western Europe, and if possible to
bring the Americans into it',[10] and on 23 January 1948 Bevin
announced to Parliament that 'we are thinking now of Western Europe
as a unity . . . We shall do all we can to advance the spirit and machinery
of co-operation.'[11]

It is important that Bevin promoted the unity of Western Europe as
the unity of co-operation and not the unity of integration. As a
response to the devastation of the war and later to satisfy Marshall's
demands that Europe should unite, most British leaders publicly pro-
tested their support for some form of European unity. Attlee is on
record as saying that 'Europe must federate or perish,'[12] and even
Churchill in Zurich on 19 September 1946 had called for Franco-
German reconciliation within 'a kind of United States of Europe'.[13]
But when opportunities became available for integration in both the
economic and the military fields, Britain rejected them on the grounds
that she was more than a European power and had world-wide interests.
Throughout 1948 Bevin steered a very fine course between organising
and stimulating the growth of a Western European bloc with enough
vigour to satisfy American demands for European integration and to
draw the United States into a more direct defence relationship, but
with enough flexibility to place only the loosest restraint on Britain's
freedom of action. This policy met with considerable success when
Britain, France and the Benelux countries signed the Brussels Treaty of
Economic, Social and Cultural Collaboration and Collective Self-
Defence on 17 March 1948, thereby creating the Western Union. Under
Article 4 of the treaty, which provided for mutual defence in the event
of armed aggression against any of the signatories, a Western Union
Defence Organisation was developed and by September 1948 it had
established permanent headquarters at Fontainebleau. Field-Marshal
Montgomery became the first Chairman of the Chiefs of Staff of the

Western Union and his office symbolised Britain's new and strong commitment to the defence of Europe, but a Europe of independent states.

The treaty did not, however, require the presence of additional
British troops on the European mainland nor did it prevent the British
Government continuing its programme of demobilisation or of carrying
out further reductions of those troops already stationed in Germany.
The American Government welcomed the Brussels Pact but remained
formally uncommitted to it or to any other defence arrangement with
Western Europe. Bevin constantly pressed the need for greater United
States involvement and his case was assisted by events. The Prague
coup in February 1948, followed by Soviet pressure on Norway in
March, and the beginning of the Berlin blockade in June combined to
accelerate the movement in America to make a more positive commitment to the security of Western Europe. As early as April 1948, and in
response to Bevin's constant encouragement, the Secretary of State
George Marshall and his Under-Secretary Robert Lovett began discussions with Senators Arthur Vandenburg and Tom Connally about
security problems in the North Atlantic area. On 11 June 1948,
prompted by the Berlin crisis, the Senate pre-empted a cautious administration by adopting Resolution 239, tabled by Vandenburg. The resolution was framed in general terms to allow the United States Government to become involved in 'collective arrangements' for defence under
Article 51 of the United Nations Charter, but it was designed specifically to meet the defence requirements of Western Europe. By July
1948 squadrons of American B29s were operating from East Anglian
airfields and it was but a short step to the signature of the North
Atlantic Treaty in Washington on 4 April 1949.

The creation of NATO owed a great deal to the work and the vision
of Ernest Bevin and represented an outcome that corresponded to many
of his aspirations. NATO linked the United States to the defence of
Europe and at the same time placed Britain's commitment to her
European allies in an expanded North Atlantic context more in keeping
with Britain's maritime and global traditions. The treaty did not
diminish Britain's independence over the levels and the deployments of
her forces. Indeed, with the European theatre regarded as more secure,
Britain's still dwindling forces could be used to bolster her extra-
European interests. Bevin's biographer notes how, 'forced by the conditions of the time', Bevin had concentrated upon security and European affairs, but once satisfied 'that he had secured the framework of
European and Atlantic security', he had turned his attention more
towards Asia.[14]

This was the first of a number of occasions when a British Government felt that it had settled the 'European question' sufficiently well to turn its attention elsewhere, and the apparent relaxation of tensions in Europe in 1949 confirmed this trend. In May the Berlin blockade was lifted and a four-power Foreign Ministers meeting in Paris made some progress on minor issues relating to trade and to Germany and Austria. In this context the major effort in the newly formed NATO alliance was directed to establishing its institutions. At the first Council meeting held in Washington in September 1949 a Defence Committee was set up to co-ordinate defence plans for the North Atlantic area. By January 1950 the Council had agreed that there should be an 'integrated defence of the North Atlantic area' but made it clear that the concept was based upon 'self-help and mutual aid',[15] emphasising that contributions towards the integrated defence would be purely national. By April 1950 the Defence Committee had worked out a 'medium term defence plan' and in May a permanent Council was established. But in essence NATO was a paper treaty in 1949 and the first half of 1950.

In this first year the emphasis among all NATO members was upon national recovery rather than rearmament, and Britain was engaged in the main upon a determined defence of its independence by staving off plans for European integration that emanated from Europe and which received strong American backing. In May 1948 the Hague Congress called for the creation of a European Assembly and urged European governments to unite. Indeed Belgium and France submitted proposals for such an assembly to the Permanent Commission of the Western Union, but the proposals floundered upon British objections and the best that could be achieved was a Council of Europe set up on 10 August 1949 with nothing but a hortative capacity. Britain also objected to, and prevented, the appointment of a director-general for the OEEC to ensure that its intergovernmental status remained unchallenged. And when on 18 September 1949 Stafford Cripps, the Chancellor of the Exchequer, announced the devaluation of sterling without consulting Britain's European allies, it was clear that Britain's commitment to European unity ran no further than prudential military co-operation, the parameters of which were determined by the need to retain a United States commitment to European security. This conclusion was reinforced by the ambiguous and later negative reaction of the Labour Government to the Schuman Plan announced in May 1950 for the creation of a European Coal and Steel Community.

These differences were rapidly overtaken and submerged by the repercussions of the attack by North Korean forces on the Republic of

South Korea on 25 June 1950. Britain supported the American initiative for a United Nations' resistance to North Korea, but it became
clear how woefully inadequate were the forces of the two most powerful states of the Western world for this task. But even greater concern
was expressed about the state of Allied force levels within NATO, for
the most common reaction among the Western allies was that Korea
might be the opening shot of a Communist offensive against the 'free
world'. The situation was summed up by Churchill in a Commons
speech on 30 November 1950, when he said, 'The sooner the Far
Eastern diversion — because vast as it is, it is but a diversion — can be
brought into something like a static condition, and stabilisation is
effected, the better it will be for all the purposes which the United
Nations have in hand. For it is in Europe that the world cause will be
decided.'[16] But in Europe the military situation was as bleak as that in
Asia. Britain, like the United States, maintained only two under-
strength divisions in Germany and only a very small air force and these
were faced by some 22 Soviet divisions in East Germany. The overall
military balance in Europe was daunting, with some 14 NATO divisions
faced by nearly 210 divisions in Eastern Europe.[17] At a NATO Council
meeting in New York in September 1950 arrangements were put in
hand as a matter of urgency to create a NATO integrated force under a
centralised command which would operate under a supreme commander
appointed by NATO. But far more significantly, the Council communiqué revealed that 'The utilisation of German manpower and resources
were discussed . . . The Council was in agreement that Germany should
be enabled to contribute to the build-up of the defence of Western
Europe.'[18] In December the Council announced that it had 'reached
unanimous agreement regarding the part which Germany might assume
in the common defence'.[19]

But the issue of Germany's defence role was far from settled and it
brought European defence once again to the forefront of British
defence planning. France was deeply concerned about German rearmament although she acknowledged that there was a patent need to tap
the resources of German manpower, especially since NATO was now
committed to forward defence on German soil. But France did not
want the recreation of an independent German Army and proposed a
solution which stemmed from an idea first proposed by Churchill in the
Council of Europe on 11 August when he had demanded 'the immediate
creation of a unified European Army subject to proper European democratic control and acting in full co-operation with the United States and
Canada'.[20] The French Prime Minister, Pleven, developed this idea and

on 24 October 1950 submitted proposals to the French National
Assembly for the creation of a European Army to be styled the European Defence Community (EDC) and which was to be linked to a European Political Community (EPC) that would exercise the necessary
democratic control. Britain publicly supported the EDC plan, but her
reaction to ideas of her own involvement was swift and predictable. At
the Labour Party Conference in September 1950 Bevin had already indicated that he had no faith in a European Army and, after the official
announcement of the Pleven Plan, Bevin replied on 29 November that
it was 'not the present policy of His Majesty's Government to contribute United Kingdom forces to a European Army' and he added rather
gratuitously that 'Europe is not enough, it is not big enough.'[21]

Britain therefore had to consider her own response to the Korean
crisis and how this would affect her contribution to NATO. At the
September 1950 NATO council meeting, Britain's contribution to
revised NATO force goals was to be 4 divisions in Germany by 1952 and
1 division earmarked from central reserve. Also in September Attlee
announced a rearmament programme of £3.6 billions for the 1951-4
period. After substantial United States encouragement, pressure and
promises of aid, the three-year programme was increased to £4.7
billions in January 1951. Britain made substantial economic sacrifices in
the attempt to meet these rearmament goals since increased armaments
manufactures would command industrial capacity that had been leading
Britain's export recovery, and the additional demands for service manpower would unsettle an economy which enjoyed full employment in
the early 1950s.

In October 1951 the Conservative Party won power with Churchill as
Premier and Anthony Eden as Foreign Secretary. Almost immediately
Churchill confirmed Bevin's rejection of the EDC concept for Britain,
but said that once the EDC was formed, 'a European Army, containing
a German contribution of agreed size and strength, will stand alongside
the British and United States Armies in a common defensive front.'[22]
Eden and Churchill visited Paris on 17 and 18 December 1951 for discussions with Pleven, Schuman and the new Supreme Allied Commander,
Eisenhower. After the meeting a statement was issued that declared
Britain's resolve to 'maintain armed forces on the continent of Europe
to fulfill their obligation in the Common cause'. Also Britain 'would
associate [herself] as closely as possible with the European defence
community in all stages of its political and military developments'.[23]
This was a disappointment to the United States, which felt that
Britain's unwillingness to join was jeopardising the prospects of success

for the EDC and was delaying the rearmament of Germany. This pressure on the Conservative Government was increased when the NATO council meeting in Lisbon in February 1952 approved a resolution for the creation of a 50-division NATO army and a 4,000 strong air force by the end of 1952 and an army of 96 divisions by the end of 1954. These force goals and the proportion to be provided by the United Kingdom shocked the Conservative Government, but they agreed to them. But from this point the British Government began to develop two policies in respect of NATO. The first was to give every assistance to the EDC negotiations short of membership to resolve the German rearmament question and relieve NATO's demand for manpower. The second was to examine NATO strategy in the light of its requirement for conventional forces.

The EDC Treaty was signed on 27 May 1952 but it had to be ratified by the member governments. To increase the chances of ratification Britain and America signed a joint declaration on the same day which said that they would regard any threat to the integrity or unity of the EDC as a threat to their own security. The intention was to discourage the secession of Germany from the EDC after German units had been created and armed. Despite this and other guarantees a major political controversy dissuaded successive French governments from presenting the treaty to the Assembly for ratification. By December 1953 the new American Secretary of State, John Foster Dulles, was threatening an 'agonizing reappraisal' if progress were not made on German rearmament. Britain responded in April 1954 by offering even greater guarantees to the French, but to no avail. On 30 August and without the courtesy of a debate, the EDC ratification proposal was defeated in the National Assembly.

The rejection threatened America's continued involvement in Europe's defence, which was one of the pillars of Britain's European policy. Eden played a leading part in resolving this crisis. He developed the idea of expanding the Brussels Pact to include Italy and Germany, who would make agreed numbers of forces available to the Pact for assignment to NATO. By implication the existing members of the Pact would also have to assign a proportion of their forces to be placed under NATO command. Eden convened a Nine Power Conference in London between 28 September and 3 October, where this plan was formally agreed. The price of success was high for the United Kingdom, who undertook to maintain the four divisions and the tactical air force she then had in Germany. But more important was the agreement 'not to withdraw those forces against the wishes of the majority of the

Brussels Treaty Powers'. Only two caveats were inserted to say that these procedures may not be complied with in the event of an 'acute overseas emergency' or a 'heavy strain on the external finances of the United Kingdom'.[24] Eden emphasised the far-reaching nature of this undertaking when in the closing speech to the London Conference he said, 'my colleagues will realise that what I have announced is for us a very formidable step to take. You all know that ours is above all an island story. We are still an island people in thought and tradition.'[25] The Nine-Power Agreement announced the end of the occupation status of Germany and invited Germany and Italy to join the NATO alliance.

At the same time that the long debate about Germany's rearmament was going on, an internal review of Britain's defence obligations laid the foundation for a revision of the NATO strategy implicitly endorsed by the Lisbon council meeting in 1952. The goal of 96 divisions by the end of 1954 was an attempt to match the conventional might of the Soviet Union and its implication for Britain was an obligation to maintain the vast majority of its forces-in-being in Europe. The alternatives of increasing the armed forces and defence expenditure were rejected by the Churchill government. The Defence White Paper of 1952 announced that it had been necessary to 'adjust' the rearmament programme inherited from the Labour Government by spreading the expenditure planned for a three-year period over a longer term. The White Paper reflected Churchill's belief that the deterrent capacity of atomic weapons had been underestimated in favour of conventional forces in both Britain and NATO. In 1952 the firm orders for the V-bomber fleet were placed and they had to be partially offset by a cut in the rate of production of Canberras, an aircraft more suited to the NATO role.[26] The emphasis on strategic weapons in Britain became even more pronounced in 1954, when the EDC proposals were coming to a head. Although Britain's world-wide commitments were increasing, the Defence White Paper of 1954 noted that 'still greater emphasis' was to be placed on the strategic role of the RAF and said that it was the aim of the Government 'gradually to reduce the total size of the army'.[27] This would be compensated by the creation of a strategic reserve at home. Thus at the very time that Eden was accepting an obligation to maintain some 80,000 men in Europe, Britain was initiating policies that made her capacity to fulfil those obligations very doubtful.

However, the logic of the changes in British defence policy was not lost on the NATO allies. The Lisbon force goals had not taken into account the deterrent effect of America's atomic weapons, and by 1954 it was clear that Britain would not be alone in failing to meet the targets set at Lisbon. Added to this the main stream of American defence policy after Dulles's announcement of 'massive retaliation' in January 1954 ran counter to meeting like with like when dealing with Soviet power. In December 1954 the growing gap between the military policies of Britain and her NATO partners was closed when the NATO council scaled down the Lisbon force goals and agreed that US tactical atomic weapons could be used in the defence of NATO Europe. For the Conservative Government these decisions once again reduced the priority of NATO in British defence planning and after December 1954 greater priority was given to developing an independent deterrent and meeting Britain's extra-European 'cold-war' commitments. The demand for industrial manpower that followed the 1955 economic boom reinforced the decision taken in 1954 to cut the armed forces, including those in NATO.

Eden became Prime Minister in April 1955 and was acutely aware of the economic pressures to cut defence spending. The results of a long-term defence review ordered by Eden in the summer of 1956 showed that 'the United Kingdom had attempted too much in too many spheres of defence, which had contributed to the economic crisis which every administration had suffered since 1945.'[28] But what Eden found of even more significance in the review 'was the reappraisal of NATO's strategy and of the doctrine of reliance on the nuclear deterrent'. In a telegram to President Eisenhower on 18 July 1956 Eden accepted the need to retain some British and American ground troops in Europe under NATO command but added, 'A "shield" of conventional forces is still required, but it is no longer our principal military protection.' Conventional forces need only hold a Soviet offensive 'until the full impact is felt of the thermo-nuclear retaliation'.[29] Clearly the arguments of Eden, and Churchill before him, had an important impact on the development of NATO's sword and shield strategy, but the decisive shift in NATO policy came after the launching of Russia's first Sputnik in October 1957 followed by a NATO Council meeting in December which decided that intermediate-range ballistic missiles should be put at the disposal of SACEUR.[30]

But the very important contribution that Eden made to British and Allied defence policy has been overshadowed by the débâcle of Suez in November 1956. The impact on national pride was immense, but the implications for Britain's role in the world were more far-reaching and serious. The crisis demonstrated the economic and military weakness of Britain. She had been unable to mount a swift operation against even

the modest resources of Egypt. Several months of re-equipping and re-
training preceded the ill-fated attack, demonstrating that an operation
of even these limited dimensions was not an option readily available to
Britain without excessive cost. The crisis revealed how fragile was
Britain's economic independence and also demonstrated the febrile
nature of the 'special relationship', even with Eisenhower as President;
a man well-disposed to Britain, if less so to France. Even in Europe
there were consequences, for Britain's friendship and assistance as an
asset for influencing Washington were now valued less by European
governments. Suez severely shook British confidence and called into
question her world power status. Clearly a major review of Britain's
defence role was required, but this fell to Eden's successor Harold
Macmillan, who took office in January 1957.

The authors of the review published as the 1957 Defence White
Paper *Defence, Outline of Future Policy* believed that it involved 'the
biggest change in military policy ever made in normal times'.[31] Many
striking decisions were taken and, on the basis of the argument that
there could be no effective defence against nuclear attack, more energy
was to be devoted to deterrent forces than to defensive forces. Yet the
major effect was to construct a new balance in the structure of British
forces, mainly by reducing manpower, and the review left the range of
defence obligations unchanged. The role of the V-bomber was confirmed and the decision that they would be 'supplemented by ballistic
rockets'[32] announced. Fighter command aircraft were to be
substantially cut and were to be replaced by ground-to-air missiles.
National Service conscription was to be phased out by the end of 1960,
when the armed forces manpower levels would be stabilised at a level of
some 375,000 personnel. To make these forces rapidly available for
overseas emergencies there was to be an expansion of RAF transport
command, but at the same time there had to be a reduction of forces
posted overseas, especially in NATO. In March 1957 Macmillan had
negotiated with the WEU partners a reduction in the strength of BAOR
from 77,000 to 64,000 men and this was announced in the White
Paper, along with a decision to cut the 2nd Tactical Airforce stationed
in Germany by half. It was also announced that 'subject to consultation with the Allied Governments in the autumn, further reductions
will be made thereafter'.[33] In January 1958 a reduction of BAOR to
55,000 men was announced and, after the May NATO council meeting
had struggled with the vexed question of support costs, the British and
German governments signed an agreement which anticipated no more
than 45,000 British troops in Germany by April 1961. The Berlin crisis,

provoked by Khrushchev's announcement on 10 November 1958 that
Russia wished to terminate the Four-Power Agreement on the status of
Berlin, prevented Britain carrying out these troop reductions and
BAOR force levels were maintained at something over 50,000 troops
until the crisis subsided in late 1961. It is notable however that, despite
American pressure, the Macmillan government did not reinforce BAOR
during the Berlin episode.

Throughout this period Macmillan seemed to be far more concerned
with Anglo-American relations and with Britain's independent deterrent
than with either Berlin or NATO. Britain's influence in the world and
with Washington declined sharply after the Suez crisis and was compounded by the dominant roles played by the United States and Russia
in the Berlin crisis. This demonstrated the decline of the tradition of
four-power summitry and was graphically illustrated by the collapse of
the summit meeting organised by Macmillan in May 1960. Although the
'special relationship' was never to be restored fully, Macmillan succeeded
in patching up Anglo-American relations very well and the most notable
successes concerned strategic weapons. On 22 February 1958 Macmillan
and Eisenhower signed an agreement on the stationing of American
IRBMs in the United Kingdom and in July the McMahon Act was
amended to allow America to share nuclear information with allies. An
agreement to establish a United States Polaris submarine base at Holy
Loch was signed on 1 November 1960. This decision coincided with the
cancellation of Britain's own Blue Streak missile programme and served
to demonstrate the fiction of an 'independent' British deterrent as
well as an ever deepening British dependence on the United States for
nuclear weapons. The crowning episode in this period of Anglo-
American *rapprochement* followed the cancellation in December 1962
of the Skybolt missile after which the hastily convened Nassau Conference produced an agreement for the supply of American Polaris missiles
to the United Kingdom.

The Nassau Agreement affected British-European relations in several
important ways. It provided ammunition for and helps explain President
de Gaulle's rejection in January 1963 of Britain's first attempt to join
the European Economic Community. With some justice de Gaulle
argued that Britain's commitment to the European idea was overshadowed by her links with America and the Commonwealth. The
second effect was that at Nassau Britain agreed 'that in normal circumstances we would regard our nuclear power as available to NATO'.[34]
This was designed to put some substance into the Multilateral Force
concept proposed by the Americans to try and solve the intra-alliance

conflict over the control and use of nuclear weapons in NATO. This decision strengthened de Gaulle's conviction that Britain was an 'Anglo-Saxon' rather than a European state. The last paragraph of the Nassau Communiqué recorded the agreement of Prime Minister and President that 'in addition to having a nuclear shield it is important to have a non-nuclear sword. For this purpose they agreed on the importance of increasing the effectiveness of their conventional forces on a world-wide basis.'[35] This reflected the new 'graduated and flexible response' policy that had been developed by the American Secretary of Defense Robert McNamara to deal with the new strategic situation in which the superpowers had the capacity for mutual nuclear destruction. This undertaking encouraged Macmillan to maintain BAOR strength virtually unchanged until the end of his administration, but Britain's defence commitment to Europe, like her application to join the EEC, remained hedged around with pretentions of a global role and qualified by world-wide interests and responsibilities.

When the Labour Party won office in October 1964, they inherited a defence policy still global in dimensions but lacking in authority and in substance. On assuming office the Labour Government oscillated between a root and branch criticism of their predecessor's global defence policies and a willingness to devise formulas to give a British world role a new lease of life. Harold Wilson was unrestrained in his assumptions about Britain's place in the world. In December 1964 he told Parliament that Britain could not 'afford to relinquish a world role'[36] and in November he informed an audience at the Guildhall: 'We are a World Power and a world influence or we are nothing.'[37] One of the first Chequers weekend conferences, 21 and 22 November 1964, was devoted to defence, where it was decided to retain the independent deterrent, to remain east of Suez, and to make new initiatives in NATO. These decisions were taken despite Wilson's recognition 'that British defence forces were over-stretched almost to breaking point' and a decision to make 'a sharp cut' in the defence budget and hold defence spending at £2,000 millions at 1964 prices.[38] In the Defence White Paper of 1965 allegations were renewed that the Labour Government had 'inherited defence forces which are seriously overstretched and in some respects dangerously under-equipped', and that there had been 'no real attempt to match political commitments to military resources, still less to relate the resources made available for defence to the economic circumstances of the nation'.[39] Yet at best the 1965 White Paper looked at the resources made available for defence, but did very little to examine political commitments. It was above all a cost-effectiveness exercise to

make a world role less expensive and therefore more acceptable. But
the world role was of a rather different kind to the one that had
attracted previous governments. Wilson argues that his government was
'moved more by thoughts of a contribution to international peacekeeping than by considerations of imperial splendour'.[40] Yet even this
more modest role was rendered suspect by the inability of Britain to
deal militarily with the Rhodesian UDI in November 1965.

Some important decisions concerning commitments were made in
February 1966 when *The Defence Review*[41] announced that Britain
was to leave the Aden base by 1968 and her presence in the Middle East
was to be confined to the Persian Gulf. Forces in the Far East were to
be substantially cut after the end of confrontation and Britain's carrier
force was to be phased out in the 1970s. The government also deemed
it impossible to conduct major operations overseas unless assisted by
allies, or to retain overseas bases against the wishes of host nations.
Again the government had devised a new formula to support commitments that were diluted but not reduced. It has been suggested that the
Foreign Office rendered the 1966 Defence Review banal and insubstantial because 'it refused to establish a more realistic foreign policy'.[42]
There is certainly evidence to suggest that foreign and defence policies
were not well co-ordinated. The 1966 Review justified Britain's extra-
European military commitments in terms of the political benefits that
would accrue from them. But in November 1966 the government
announced its intention to reapply for membership of the EEC on the
grounds that, although the economic case for entry was arguable, the
political case was overwhelming.[43]

These policy statements were directly contradictory and in the event
both were to be frustrated. Outside Europe, Britain's inability to intervene in Rhodesia in 1965 soured Commonwealth relations and her
refusal to assist in Vietnam angered America. These, combined with
Wilson's failure to engineer a peace settlement in Vietnam during
Kosygin's visit to London in February 1967, demolished the argument
that Britain would receive political advantages by having forces outside
Europe. Inside Europe, it was the economic weakness of Britain rather
than the strength of her political commitment to the EEC that was the
decisive argument used by de Gaulle when he vetoed Britain's second
application for membership.

In the summer of 1966 Britain suffered its worst economic crisis for
many years and in a statement to Parliament on 22 July Wilson
announced a range of budgetary cuts that would include defence. The
repercussions of this decision were far-reaching and Wilson recalls that

in late October 1966 Denis Healey, the Secretary for Defence, was
ready to propose a terminal date for the east of Suez role.[44] But as the
Defence White Paper of February 1967 revealed, the east of Suez role
was retained, much to the anger of Labour left-wingers, 63 of whom
abstained from voting on the policy. Yet again events conspired to
question the validity of a defence policy decision, for when some of the
Arab states employed oil sanctions against Britain and the West
following the Arab-Israeli War of June 1967, Britain's forces in the Gulf
were powerless to affect the situation.

The political and economic consequences for defence of the June
War were summarised in a supplementary statement on defence in July,
which announced that the state of the economy provided a 'more
pressing need to reduce overseas expenditure'.[45] The major decision was
that there would be a 50 per cent reduction in forces committed to the
east of Suez role by 1971 and the role terminated between 1973 and
1976. More modest cuts would be made elsewhere, including the rede-
ployment to Britain of one brigade of BAOR and one squadron of RAF
Germany, despite what the White Paper described as 'the evolution of
Government policy towards Europe' and 'progress in revising NATO
strategy'.[46] Government policy towards Europe was still uncertain but
there had been progress in revising NATO strategy, and it was largely
the work of Denis Healey. The Labour Government had acquired, along
with the Nassau Agreement, an implicit undertaking to support the
American MLF proposals which by 1964 were the subject of an acrimonious debate in NATO. Healey was largely responsible for promoting
the idea that what was essential in alliance nuclear affairs was not
physical arrangements for participation, for these would always be
dominated by America, but political arrangements for consultation
where arguments could be treated on their merits. To give substance to
this approach NATO set up a Nuclear Planning Group in December
1966 to formulate plans for the control and use of nuclear weapons in
Europe. Healey was also instrumental in getting more realistic NATO
planning by basing strategy upon actual NATO force levels instead of
planned force levels.

The defence cuts of July 1967 had still to be implemented when the
pound sterling was devalued on 18 November. The devaluation alone
added some £50 millions to the cost of the overseas defence bill and
precipitated the speed and the range of the defence cuts agreed in principle in late 1966 and early 1967. On the 16 January 1968 the end of
the east of Suez role was announced, and from 1971 British defence
forces were to 'be concentrated in Europe'.[47] The weakness of the

British economy and the difficulty of maintaining a high enough rate of
voluntary recruitment to the armed services to support the world role
were important considerations and weighed heavily upon the government. Certainly these considerations were far more important than the
estimated benefits of a greater military effort in Europe, and it was
only after the decision to end the east of Suez role, which Healey had
tried to delay, that Healey devoted his energies towards developing a
more viable Eurocentric defence policy. Indeed, Europe was a very un-
attractive prospect in early 1968. American interests were heavily
engaged elsewhere, and the EEC was still struggling to regain momentum
after de Gaulle's seven-month boycott over the financing of the
common agricultural policy and his rejection in December 1967 of
Britain's application for membership. And after several years of post-
Cuban stability, NATO was suffering a period of torpidity marked by
the gradual diminution of NATO force levels by European members in
the face of North American demands that they should carry even more
of NATO's defence burden. After the adoption of the Harmel Report in
December 1967, which identified the future task of the Alliance to be
the pursuit of *détente* as well as defence, the overwhelming opinion of
the European NATO members was that European security was stable,
despite a considerable and growing imbalance between the conventional forces of NATO and the Warsaw Pact.

This view evaporated in the face of the invasion of Czechoslovakia
in August 1968. This action by the Warsaw Pact rather than the fore-
sight of British defence planners was to give substance to the decision
of January to concentrate Britain's defence effort in Europe. In September all NATO members agreed to halt any further reduction of
Western forces and in November the NATO Council announced the
decision to improve ground forces 'in order to provide a better capability for.defence as far forward as possible'.[48] If this policy was to be
made viable it was essential that NATO members, especially the European ones, improve the quality and the numbers of conventional forces
assigned to the Alliance. Until the end of its administration, the Labour
Government improved its military contribution to NATO.

Of even greater significance than the purely military implications
of the Czechoslovak crisis were the political and diplomatic ones. The
United States and Russia had been deeply concerned by the potential
military dangers of the crisis at a time when their own strategic relationship was becoming less stable with the introduction of ABM and MIRV
weapons. In such a strategic context the superpowers were less tolerant
of political developments that might provoke a crisis in Europe, es-

pecially if it were precipitated by one of their own allies. It became
clear that the superpowers preferred the *status quo* in Europe to a programme of political change dictated by the Europeans themselves, and if
significant changes were to be made in the political relations of their
allies, the United States and Russia were to be deeply involved. Within
months of the invasion the first of a series of East-West contacts took
place to open what President Nixon described as the 'era of
negotiations'. Exploratory talks took place in late 1968 between Soviet
and American representatives laying the foundation for the opening in
Helsinki on 17 November 1969 of the preparatory talks for the limitation of strategic arms. In October 1969 Herr Willy Brandt became
Federal Chancellor in Germany and vigorously developed an *Ostpolitik*
aimed at normalising the Federal Republic's relations with Russia and
with the Eastern European states. Brandt also showed a willingness to
settle some of the outstanding border issues that had symbolised the
East-West split since 1945. A major step was taken to reconcile the two
German states when Brandt met Herr Stoph, the East German Prime
Minister, in March, and again in May 1970. Treaties signed between
Bonn and Moscow on 12 August and between Bonn and Warsaw on 7
December 1970 were major developments in *détente,* but the United
States had earlier declared its intention to retain a close supervision of
its progress by making the ratification of these treaties dependent upon
the successful outcome of the superpower-dominated talks on the status
of Berlin that began in late September 1970.

The Labour Government was extremely sensitive to these new developments and was especially concerned not just because the substance
and the pace of the new *détente* were being determined by the superpowers, but because it was happening without the depth of consultation to which Britain and many European states felt they were entitled.
Many Western European governments believed that America and Russia
were willing to settle issues vital to Europe's security over their heads if
this meant a reduction of the burden and the risks of superpower involvement in Europe's alliances. In this context NATO became an important institution through which the Western European governments
concerted their views to impress upon the United States their special
defence interests. Wilson records that he learnt a twin lesson from
Czechoslovakia: 'One was the need for vigilance and greater cohesion of
the Western Alliance. The other was the need for the greater unity of
Europe so that the view of Europe as a whole could be more strongly
concentrated on any threat to freedom in Europe.'[49] In the last year of
his administration Wilson developed the theme that a united Europe, in-

cluding Britain, could be an effective force in world politics. If Europe
chose to reject Britain again it would be 'at a devastating price for
Europe's influence in the world'.[50] It was a measure of Britain's awareness of the weakness of her own and Europe's relations with Washington
that Denis Healey became the leading advocate of a 'European defence
identity' and the development of a ten-nation[51] Eurogroup in NATO to
ensure that the European members could maximise their influence on
détente negotiations by consulting together and speaking with a single
voice.

It was therefore a heavily Eurocentric defence and foreign policy
that Edward Heath and his Conservative administration took over in
June 1970. Heath had a long-established record of Europeanism and
many of the policies of the Wilson government corresponded with his
own views. He pursued Britain's application to join the EEC and
brought it to a successful conclusion in January 1972. He accepted that
'Britain's basic security continues to depend on the strength of the
North Atlantic Alliance.'[52] But he introduced a number of significant
nuances into these policies. While accepting the political, economic and
military commitments to Europe, Heath nevertheless looked forward to
'a new era of British diplomacy'[53] and later asserted that 'the voice of
Britain in the councils of the world is going to be louder and clearer
than it has been and it will be an unmistakably British voice.'[54] This
tough and independent line was to lead to some conflicts with Washington.

During the Indo-Pakistan War in November 1971, Anglo-American
relations deteriorated and 'at Heath's instructions Whitehall briefings
became increasingly hostile to United States intervention on Pakistan's
side.'[55] Heath also resented and resisted both American and NATO
interference into Britain's disagreement with Malta following Dom
Mintoff's abrogation of the Anglo-Maltese Defence Agreement of 1964,
and this aspect of the issue was settled and Heath mollified only after
Dr Joseph Luns, NATO's Secretary-General, had made a special visit to
Chequers on 10 January 1972. The episode resulted in Britain's NATO
allies developing 'a new respect for Heath's no-nonsense qualities'.[56]
Heath's decision to supply defensive arms to South Africa was less
successful and not only strained Commonwealth relations to breaking
point, but also evoked from the United States Government a statement
formally disassociating itself from any measures to increase the flow of
arms to South Africa. Even on the issue of Britain's entry into the EEC,
which the United States had supported and encouraged for many years,
Heath 'made it clear that the larger EEC he envisaged would be giving

the USA a run for its money', and he wanted 'Britain in the van of a
West European superpower able to confront the Americans and
Russians as equal'.[57]

This new approach was reflected in the government's defence policy
statements. A supplementary statement on defence of July 1970
accepted that NATO would command the greater part of Britain's
defence efforts but said that the United Kingdom should 'resume,
within her resources, a proper share of responsibility for the preservation of peace and stability in the world'.[58] The government supported
this policy by retaining a small military presence in South-East Asia,
although the Defence Secretary recognised that it was no more than 'a
token of our continuing concern to help in promoting confidence',[59]
and extending the life of the carrier force. The Simonstown Agreement
with South Africa was maintained and negotiations were carried out to
retain troops in the Persian Gulf.

All this ran counter to the political and military conditions prevailing within the Alliance in the early 1970s. The momentum of
détente was gathering pace and it was acknowledged that if major political developments occurred in Europe, it must inevitably involve the
North Atlantic Alliance. The political and military implications of
détente were exhaustively examined by a NATO ministerial meetings at
Brussels in December 1970 and a report *Allied Defence and the 1970s*
was approved. Its major theme was that 'There is a close inter-relation-
ship between the maintenance of adequate defensive strength and the
negotiations of settlements affecting the security of member states.'[60]
It was heavily emphasised that NATO conventional capabilities should
be improved to make viable the Alliance strategy of flexible response,
to counterbalance the growing strength of the Warsaw Pact and to provide a basis of strength from which to negotiate the long-standing allied
goal of mutual and balanced force reductions.

These military requirements and the dominant role of America in the
negotiation of *détente* emphasised the special role of United States
forces in Europe as both the essential political foundation of the Allied
nuclear deterrent and as a valuable element of NATO's conventional
strength. European governments had become particularly susceptible to
American demands for co-operation in NATO as the price of preventing
United States troop withdrawals and of influencing the United States in
its conduct of superpower *détente*. In return for a pledge by Nixon not
to reduce American forces in NATO, the European member countries
agreed in December 1970 to implement a European Defence Improvement Programme which was to cost some £400 millions over a five-year

period. This decision was consistent with the Nixon doctrine enunci-
ated in February 1970, and which Nixon explained in the following
terms. 'Previous conceptions in burden sharing were that our allies
should share our burden. The thrust of the Nixon doctrine is that the
primary task of the Europeans is to shoulder their own.'[61]

The Heath government acknowledged and responded to the obvious
need to improve conventional force levels for military reasons and also
to ensure that the United Kingdom could exert the maximum possible
influence through NATO on the *detente* process. The government also
recognised that the increased defence burden of each European member
could be reduced and their defence interests better served if there were
greater co-operation between them. Lord Carrington and Helmut
Schmidt, the West German Defence Minister, became the moving forces
behind the transition of the Eurogroup from an informal after-dinner
gathering of defence Ministers initiated by Denis Healey into a more
business-like but still informal arrangement to assist the European
members to work out the implications of burden-sharing and to maximise
their political weight in the alliance. Carrington described the value of
the Eurogroup as its ability to

> help towards framing a distinctive European approach to major
> defence issues on which European interests may not wholly coincide
> with those of the U.S.A. Secondly, it can publicise what Europe is
> doing in its own defence. The third area for the Eurogroup . . . is in
> encouraging measures of practical co-operation to ensure that they
> get the maximum value from individual national defence
> programmes.[62]

These themes were reiterated in the Defence White Paper of 1972
which said that 'Europe needs both to exert more influence on the
major issues affecting Western security and to assume increased responsibility for its own defence.'[63] This approach reflected Heath's wish to
see Europe, particularly after the expansion of the EEC in January
1972, exert more influence on the major issues of the East-West dia-
logue. But the tide of events was running against these aspirations as the
superpowers came to determine more and more issues vital to the military and political interests of Europe. In February 1972 an interim
agreement on SALT was signed, in November preparatory talks for the
Conference on Security and Co-operation in Europe opened and in
January 1973 multilateral exploratory talks on mutual and balanced
force reductions were inaugurated in Vienna. All these negotiations had

implications vital for the European members of NATO, but a feeling
persisted in many West European capitals that the United States was
not fully consulting its allies, and this was matched by an attitude in
Washington that the lack of unity in the European camp prevented
them giving support to the United States in the way that they should.
The mood of the British Government was captured in the Defence
White Paper of 1973 which said, 'The pace of change has quickened as
the political alignments of the post-war world have become less rigid:
this development and the period of collective negotiations ahead will be
a test of the solidarity of the Alliance.'[64] It was a test that the
Alliance survived but only after a considerable buffeting.

In April 1973 Henry Kissinger proposed a new Atlantic Charter in
which he sought to link defence,political and economic issues. America
was concerned that the Europeans demanded consultation with
America on military and security affairs but were inspired by 'economic nationalism' in their trade and fiscal affairs. NATO's Secretary-
General noted that although NATO was not the forum for economic
matters, it was 'vitally concerned with their outcome. If these problems
are not promptly solved by Americans and Europeans alike the tensions
which may develop between the two sides of the Atlantic would undermine the Alliance's solidarity and furthermore affect the availability of
resources needed for a sustained defence effort'.[65] The European
nations resisted this attempt and strove to keep their economic and
defence roles separate to prevent Kissinger achieving for the United
States an added leverage in EEC affairs by exploiting the European dependence on American troops in NATO. Intra-alliance relations became
strained but reached their lowest point with the outbreak of the Middle
East war on 6 October 1973. Once more the superpowers moved to
settle this crisis bilaterally, which angered the Europeans and they
became even more distressed by Nixon's order on 25 October for a
world-wide 'Defence Condition 3' alert without consulting NATO
allies. The situation became even more strained when some NATO
members refused facilities to America for the transport of arms to
Israel. Kissinger was later to complain that the Europeans acted as if the
Alliance did not exist.

The Middle East war had two major effects on NATO. The first was
to underline the need for better consultation and co-operation within
the alliance. An *Atlantic Declaration* signed in Brussels on 26 June 1974
to celebrate NATO's 25th year did something to paper over the cracks and
to improve intra-alliance relations. The second effect of the war was to
make even the modest attempts by the European members to accept

more of NATO's defence burden insupportable. By November 1974 the
Chairman of NATO's Military Committee reported that even the European Defence Improvement Programme was 'already heavily in arrears
and although we can observe some improvement in our military capabilities, the past year or so has been a time of reduction by some member nations in defence expenditure with probable economies to
come'.[66] Britain was particularly hard hit by the economic repercussions of the October War and, despite the return of a Labour administration in March 1974 more committed to co-operation with the
United States and with NATO than had been Heath, a gradual diminution of Britain's efforts in NATO became a priority.

Economic pressures lay heavily upon the Labour administration,
which suffered one of the worst rates of inflation in the developed
world and a rate of unemployment reaching its highest post-war level.
As a minority government between March and October 1974, and with
painfully small majorities throughout 1975 and 1976, the Labour
Government had to be more receptive to the demands of the Labour
Party's left wing, which was calling for substantial defence cuts. In
December 1974, a £4.7 billion cut in defence spending over 10 years
was announced and all Britain's remaining extra-European commitments were to suffer major reductions. These included Singapore, Gan,
Mauritius, Brunei, Simonstown, Hong Kong and Cyprus. These cuts not
only allowed a run-down of manpower to be made, but ended any pre-
tence of a global defence policy. The attempt was made, however, in
1974 to maintain Britain's obligation to NATO, even though Northern
Ireland required considerable numbers of British troops.

The economic problems continued to worsen in 1975, as Britain's
recovery was substantially less than that of most of her NATO partners.
The cost of military manpower and equipment was driven up by
inflation and in March 1975 Britain announced defence cuts to achieve
a reduction of defence expenditure as a proportion of GNP to 4½ per
cent over ten years. There was also to be a reduction of 38,000 troops
over the next four years and a withdrawal of naval forces from the
Mediterranean, a decision that caused considerable disquiet in NATO
headquarters. Although the need to establish a healthy economy was a
major factor in this decision, it was supported by a number of developments in the European security and political situation.

Britain was typical among European states in believing that the risks
of a European conflict were very low, although the government added
the proviso in 1975 that 'this is a political judgement which neither
alters the military facts nor necessarily holds good for ever.'[67] By

1976 the government was more confident when it said 'there is no evidence that the Soviet Union and its allies are contemplating a military attack upon the West. Such an attack would not, in present circumstances, succeed . . . '[68] There has also been a decline in the heady optimism about the potential gains from *détente* that existed in the early 1970s. This has been frustrated not just by the relative exclusion of the European powers from the *détente* process, but by the limited results of the 'era of negotiation'. Much of this pessimism was typified by reactions to the Final Act of the Conference on Security and Co-operation which was signed on 1 August 1975 at Helsinki. The major feature of the Final Act emphasised by most European states is that it recognises the post-war frontiers of Eastern Europe and Soviet domination there. European capitals have ambiguous views about this; many see it as the reinforcement of the *status quo* and superpower domination in Europe, others as the necessary foundation of stability for some future development in *détente*. Much will depend upon the follow-up conference to be held in Belgrade in June 1977. This conference itself symbolises the current problem of *détente*, for it was a compromise between America and Russia who wished to terminate CSCE with the Final Act, and the European states who want to see *détente* as an ongoing process in which they are involved.

Until Belgrade and under continuing economic pressure it is likely that European governments with Britain foremost amongst them will simply mark time in NATO. Military expenditure will continue to compete unfavourably against other public expenditure programmes so long as military risks are judged to be low and the political benefits of a large defence role in Europe are small. Britain will remain committed to European security, but in the years ahead the Government must judge how much of our limited resources can be devoted to a defence effort in Europe that is retained to ensure that if the military risks or political opportunities in Europe increase, Britain will have a voice in how Europe and the West responds to them.

Notes

1. The main exception was aid to Greece from 1947.
2. Denis Healey, 'British Defence Policy', *The Royal United Services Institution Journal*, Vol. CXIV, No. 656, December 1969, pp. 15-20.
3. See G. Goodwin, 'British Foreign Policy since 1945: The Long Odyssey to Europe', in M. Leifer (ed.), *Constraints and Adjustments in British Foreign Policy* (London, George Allen and Unwin, 1972), p. 36.

4.   *NATO Facts and Figures* (Brussels, NATO Information Service, 1969),
      p. 14.
5.   R.N. Rosecrance, *Defense of the Realm: British Strategy in the Nuclear
      Epoch* (New York and London, Columbia University Press, 1968), p. 35.
6.   Prime Minister Attlee was uninvolved in defence and foreign affairs to a
      surprising degree: in his autobiography he says 'Foreign Affairs are the
      province of the Foreign Secretary and it is . . . a mistake for a Prime
      Minister . . . to intervene personally.' *As it Happened* (London, Heinemann,
      1954), p. 169.
7.   Elizabeth Barker, *Britain in a Divided Europe 1945-70* (London, Weidenfeld
      and Nicolson, 1971), p. 66.
8.   Francis Williams, *Ernest Bevin: Portrait of a Great Englishman* (London,
      Hutchinson, 1952), p. 265.
9.   Noted in D.N. Pritt, *The Labour Government 1945-51* (London, Lawrence
      and Wishart, 1963), p. 122.
10.   Field Marshal the Viscount Montgomery, *The Memoirs of Field Marshal
      Montgomery* (New York, Signet, 1958), p. 67.
11.   House of Commons Debates (23 January 1948), Vol. 466, col. 397.
12.   Attlee, op. cit., p. 172.
13.   See James Barber and Bruce Reed (eds.), *European Community: Vision
      and Reality* (London, Croom Helm, 1973), pp. 23-4.
14.   Williams, op. cit., p. 270.
15.   *NATO Final Communiqués 1949-74* (Brussels, NATO Information
      Service), p. 52.
16.   Footnoted in M.A. Fitzsimons, *The Foreign Policy of the British Labour
      Government 1945-51* (Notre Dame, Indiana, University of Notre Dame
      Press, 1953), p. 137.
17.   *NATO Facts and Figures*, p. 30.
18.   *NATO Final Communiqués*, p. 60.
19.   Ibid., p. 61.
20.   *Summary of the Debates in the Consultative Assembly of the Council of
      Europe*, Vol. 1, 1950, cols. 59-61.
21.   House of Commons Debates (29 November 1950), Vol. 481, col. 1173.
      Quoted in Rosecrance, op. cit., p. 147.
22.   House of Commons Debates (6 December, 1951). Vol. 494, cols. 2591-7.
23.   Part of the statement is reproduced in *Notes on Current Policy*, No. 1,
      21 January 1952.
24.   See Cmd. 9289, *Final Acts of the Nine Power Conference held in London
      September 28-October 3*, 1954.
25.   Ibid., Annex II B.
26.   See Rosecrance, op. cit., p. 167.
27.   Cmd. 9075, *Statement on Defence*, 1954, p. 5.
28.   Anthony Eden, *Full Circle* (London, Cassell, 1960), p. 371.
29.   Ibid., pp. 272-3.
30.   *NATO Facts and Figures*, p. 64.
31.   Cmnd. 124, *Defence Outline of Future Policy*, April 1957, p. 9.
32.   Ibid., p. 3.
33.   Ibid., p. 4.
34.   Harold Macmillan, *At the End of the Day* (London, Macmillan, 1973),
      p. 359.
35.   *Statement on Nuclear Defence Systems*, 21 December 1962. The Nassau
      Communiqué is reproduced in ibid., pp. 553-5.
36.   Quoted in Christopher Mayhew, *Britain's Role Tomorrow* (London,
      Hutchinson, 1967), p. 131.

37. Quoted in F.S. Northedge, *Descent From Power: British Foreign Policy 1945-1973* (London, George Allen and Unwin, 1974), p. 296.
38. Harold Wilson, *The Labour Government 1964-1970: A Personal Record* (London, Weidenfeld and Nicolson, 1971), p. 42. See also Mayhew, op. cit., p. 131.
39. Cmnd. 2592, *Statement on the Defence Estimates 1965*, p. 5.
40. Wilson, op. cit., p. 212.
41. Cmnd. 2901, *Statement on the Defence Estimates 1966. Part I: The Defence Review,* February 1966.
42. Bruce Reed and Geoffrey Williams, *Denis Healey and the Politics of Power* (London, Sidgwick and Jackson, 1971), p. 270.
43. Wilson, op. cit., p. 687.
44. Ibid., p. 297.
45. Cmnd. 3357, *Supplementary Statement on Defence Policy 1967*, p. 1.
46. Loc. cit.
47. Cmnd. 3515, *Public Expenditure 1968-69 and 1969-70*, p. 2.
48. *NATO Final Communiqués*, p. 214.
49. Wilson, op. cit., p. 554.
50. Ibid., p. 705.
51. Belgium, Denmark, Germany, Greece, Netherlands, Norway, Portugal, Turkey and the United Kingdom.
52. Cmnd. 4592, *Statement on the Defence Estimates 1971*, p. 1.
53. *Sunday Times*, 11 October 1970.
54. *The Times*, 18 November 1970.
55. Andrew Roth, *Heath and the Heathmen* (London, Routledge and Kegan Paul, 1972), p. 227.
56. Ibid., p. 219.
57. Ibid., p. 211.
58. Cmnd. 4521, *Supplementary Statement on Defence Policy 1970*, p. 1.
59. The Rt. Hon. Lord Carrington, 'British Defence Policy', *The Royal United Services Institution Journal,* Vol. CXV, No. 660, December 1970, p. 6.
60. *NATO Final Communiqués*, p. 250.
61. Quoted in Dr Joseph Luns, 'NATO in the 1970's', *RUSI Journal for Defence Studies,* Vol. 117, No. 4, December 1972, p. 5.
62. The Rt. Hon. Lord Carrington, 'British Defence Policy', *RUSI Journal for Defence Studies,* Vol. 118, No. 3, September 1973, p. 5.
63. Cmnd. 4891, *Statement on the Defence Estimates 1972*, p. 3.
64. Cmnd. 5231, *Statement on the Defence Estimates 1973*, p. 1.
65. Luns, op. cit., p. 6.
66. See Sir Peter Hill-Norton's lecture to the RUSI printed in the *RUSI Journal for Defence Studies,* Vol. 120, No. 1, March 1975, pp. 14-21, especially p. 16.
67. Cmnd. 5976, *Statement on the Defence Estimates 1975*, p. 8.
68. Cmnd. 6432, *Statement on the Defence Estimates 1976*, p. 9.

5 THE BRITISH DETERRENT

A.J.R. Groom

Much of Britain's post-war history — in foreign and defence policy, in its economic and social difficulties — has been reflected in the quest for, the achievement of, and the maintenance of a British nuclear deterrent, its warheads and delivery systems. This reflection is but partial, although its implication is that the policy of successive British governments towards the deterrent cannot be seen in isolation either from defence policy as a whole or from wider considerations. Britain's role in the world, its self-image and the evaluation of others have changed radically in the last few decades. From standing alone against the Axis Powers in 1940 to victory in 1945 as one of the Big Three, from a great imperial power to devolution and the European Community, from a fairly rigid class system to a permissive society, from a relatively high standard of living among advanced industrial powers to a relatively low one, from a market economy to a mixed economy and a welfare state, the change has been rapid and fundamental. Sometimes the change has also been far-sighted and controlled, while sometimes it has been chaotic and dependent on chance. Occasionally, the change has been judged 'for better' but more often it has been accepted by the British Government and people as 'worse', if inevitable. Yet Britain has survived, and although the change has been radical and general, it has been evolutionary — a remarkable phenomenon. Such is the background to the British deterrent.[1]

In this chapter our main consideration will be the activities of the government of the day, but it is as well to recall that of the nuclear and near-nuclear powers, only Britain has had a mass public active in debating nuclear issues, albeit for a rather short period in the late fifties and early sixties. Otherwise, as in other countries, discussion of these issues has been restricted to an informed élite. The thinking of this élite and the policy of the government of the day has been influential in the United States and in France, particularly in the fifties and early sixties. British ideas and policy have also been influenced massively by the debate in and policy of the United States and to a lesser extent, but significantly and increasingly, by those of France. Indeed, although the strategic and technological rationales for the British deterrent are determined essentially by Soviet capabilities (even if it is likely that a British deterrent would have come into being without a perception of a Soviet threat) the political rationale has been a function of United States policy. This rationale was both to be able to influence the United States and to be independent of the United States. The rationale to influence the United States was derived from a view of that country as the major Western power — the cornerstone, first potential then actual, of the defence of Western Europe and a potential source of 'know-how' for the development of the British deterrent. But there was also a need for influence in order to restrain the United States on such occasions when it may have been tempted to use nuclear weapons unjustifiably in British eyes, as in Korea. The rationale of being independent of the United States derived from the need to protect those areas where Britain felt it had vital interests which the United States Government was unlikely to sustain, as in the Middle East in the fifties, or it was seen as an insurance in case of a resurgence of isolationism in the United States or, latterly, of a Soviet-American 'deal' inimical to the interests of Western Europe. Anglo-American relations are thus of crucial importance in understanding the evolution of Britain's deterrent policy. Since they form an important part of another chapter they will only be touched upon lightly here, but they are fundamental. The influence of France was more in its espousals of arguments in favour of an independent deterrent. The British were not unsympathetic towards such arguments, for they too were worried about the decline in the credibility of the United States nuclear guarantee for Europe in a situation of mutual deterrence, but they were willing to keep such doubts to themselves. More recently the French have set a standard in nuclear forces below which the British would not like to fall.

If the physical requirements of the British deterrent have been set by the capabilities of the Soviet Union and the political requirements have been determined by the need to influence or to act independently of the United States and to keep in step with France, a fourth major factor cannot be ignored, namely, the need not to overburden the British economy and tax-payer. Until the end of the fifties decisions regarding the British deterrent were taken, for the most part, without any real consideration of cost. This was partly a matter of political conviction — that Britain as a first-class power had to have nuclear weapons — and partly it was because the cost was unknown. This meant that decisions were inevitably 'irresponsible' and that a crisis arose in the late fifties and early sixties because of the gap between costs and commitment. The commitment to an atomic bomb and later to a hydrogen bomb was finite and so, therefore, were the costs, even if they were unknown, albeit likely to be high. However, the commitment to a first-class delivery system and associated warheads was infinite since technology was and is still advancing rapidly. The costs were therefore not finite and while the GNP increased and with it the amount of re-sources available for defence in general, such increases were not commensurate with a long-term commitment to the latest relevant delivery systems. Thus either the commitment had to be altered or more resources had to be made available for the deterrent. Mr Macmillan's government failed to make a clear choice and so it was left to the Wilson-Healey régime to resolve the crisis, in effect until the 1980s, although due to the dictates of forward planning it is with us in less acute form once again.

The threat (German and later seen as Soviet), great power status, the Anglo-American relationship, the French connection and cost are the principal factors moulding successive British governments' policies to-wards the deterrent. To these must be added bureaucratic factors and the civilian programme which tended to give rise to a situation in which the deterrent was no longer questioned in a radical way. Once a nuclear power, always a nuclear power of one sort or another. The infra-structure, the budget, the physical capacity remain unless positive action is taken to change them. When such a momentum is created with the tremendous degree of commitment — psychological, political and economic — as it was in the British case, it is difficult to reverse. It can slowly slacken or be deflected but bureaucratic processes alone strongly militate against its reversal. This was particularly the case in Britain, where the deterrent was buttressed during the build-up of momentum by the civilian nuclear programme. Thereafter the two programmes went their separate ways but the deterrent had reached cruising speed bureaucratically, from the budgetary viewpoint and politically from which the tugging of the Campaign for Nuclear Disarmament and the crisis engendered by the cost of a second-generation delivery system did not, in the event, slow it appreciably. It is with an account of the build-up of momentum that we begin our chronological narrative.[2]

The War and the Post-War Labour Governments[3]

Britain was the world's first nuclear power in aspiration if not in fact. In the summer of 1941 a committee that had been set up to consider 'the possibilities of producing atomic bombs during the war, and their military effect . . . ' concluded that such bombs were possible and that, 'In spite of this very large expenditure we consider that the destructive effect, both material and moral, is so great that every effort should be made to produce bombs of this kind.' It added that ' . . . no nation would care to risk being caught without a weapon of such decisive possibilities.'[4] Their recommendation was accepted and work began. Although Britain briefly held the lead, the United States was keen to co-operate and when it became apparent that the scale of the United States programme and its resources would dwarf the British effort, together with the greater security of the North American continent, then with some misgivings, the British accepted American terms and the British efforts were integrated into the United States programme to which the Canadians, Belgians and French also contributed.

At the end of the war Britain was a nuclear power of sorts. Although it had neither weapons nor installations it did have knowledge, access to uranium and, above all, an immense psychological and political commitment to the possession of nuclear weapons. For example, Sir John Anderson, the British Minister in charge of the wartime project, had conceived of nuclear weapons as giving 'control of the world to whatever country obtains them first'.[5] Britain had been a founder-member of the nuclear club. With the end of the war it could, of course, have opted out but, given its wartime experience and the overwhelming importance attached to nuclear weapons by British decision-makers both during and after the war, this was unlikely. Moreover, the outlook was sombre.

The grand alliance that had won the Second World War did not survive the peace. Mr Attlee's post-war government was profoundly suspicious of Soviet intentions and could find little comfort in Soviet actions. As the Soviet Union established its hegemony in Central and Eastern Europe, often at the expense of indigenous social democrats of the Attlee ilk, the British Government, with the support of the Opposition, determined to meet what they considered to be the Soviet threat. They were effectively alone since in the immediate post-war years the United States was anxious to disengage from Europe and an element in their decision-making élite was both sanguine about Soviet and suspicious of British intentions. Moreover, France was beset by internal difficulties (as was Italy), and, like Britain, colonial questions diverted French attention from Europe. The Commonwealth countries were beginning to demand the fruits of their wartime co-operation in terms of independence, access to sterling balances or aid in the case of the non-white territories and hegemonial areas such as Egypt, and the Old Dominions had pressing concerns of their own and neither the will nor the resources to join Britain in confronting the Soviet Union. To make matters worse, the British economy required renewal, reconversion and reconstruction. Moreover, it had to help to sustain the world economy as it moved to a peacetime footing and Britain needed to re-establish its role in it. In addition, the British people demanded what their leaders had pledged to give them and wished to give them — a social revolution and a welfare state. Britain was broke, broken-down and bereft of effective allies in a hostile and threatening environment. Tremendous demands were being made on its reduced resources both internally and internationally. Its armed forces were dispersed in penny-packets around the world and they were often over-stretched and low in morale as the colonial world erupted. Not only did they have to re-establish themselves in British colonies but they were also in temporary control of Dutch and French colonies which were in great ferment. Thus Britain faced an unenviable task in seeking to parry the perceived Soviet threat. Although this analysis of threat was challenged by a few it was, rightly or wrongly, the dominant and forthrightly held view of both the major political parties.

There were only two ways in which Britain could hope to dissuade or to parry a Soviet threat. If it could not match the Soviet Union in the men and equipment it was prepared to put in the field then the British Government could both seek to envelop the United States in the economic recovery and defence of Western Europe and pursue the atomic bomb project with the highest priority. The British Government chose to follow both courses as the opportunities presented themselves. By seizing upon an encouraging but general invitation in a speech by General Marshall, the United States Secretary of State, the Foreign Secretary, Ernest Bevin, and his French colleague acted as mid-wives to the Marshall Plan and the economic recovery of Western Europe. By inveigling the United States into an active role in Greece and Turkey, by organising the Western European liberal democracies into an alliance framework and thereby encouraging the United States to think of joint defence by this display of resolve, by allowing units of the USAF to deploy in Britain and by deciding to obtain its own deterrent either in co-operation with the United States or independently, the British Government struggled to enhance its security and that of the Western world in the face of what it viewed as hostile and threatening Soviet behaviour. It is thus to the genesis of the British deterrent that we now turn — Anglo-American or independent?

Successive British governments have faced this problem. Full independence for the British deterrent has been deemed desirable but not practicable. Thus British governments have tried to have their cake and

eat it by seeking the benefits of interdependence in order to be independent. Not surprisingly they have run into difficulties. During the
war years the British programme was incorporated into that of the
United States. The British thought that they had safeguarded their post-
war position both militarily and commercially. However, in the changed
circumstances of post-war domestic politics in the United States, the
assurances given to Mr Churchill by President Roosevelt did not prevent
the passage of the McMahon Act through the United States Congress on
1 August 1946, whereupon the atom was nationalised and co-operation
with the United States was no longer possible. The British felt betrayed
and subsequent attempts to re-establish co-operation failed until the
late fifties despite British protests, British progress and the North
Atlantic Alliance. Post-war decision-makers in the United States were
ill-informed, uncomprehending and concerned with domestic factors,
so that the British got a raw deal. The British deterrent was perforce independent of the United States, but this enforced independence gave it
a further rationale — by demonstrating British competence in the field
the United States Administration might be induced to reconsider
Anglo-American nuclear co-operation — a British hypothesis that was
later to be vindicated.

With the termination of the American connection the British bomb
project got under way (in January 1947) in a secretive manner and with
the utmost priority. However, the same degree of alacrity and priority
did not characterise the provision of the delivery system — the V-
bombers. Indeed, it may be an indication of the British view of nuclear
weapons as a political instrument as much as an active military weapon
that this was so. The political aspect was particularly dominant after
the signing of the North Atlantic Treaty and the establishment of
NATO, since the international security situation had changed significantly. Although the British Government felt the full rigours of the
Cold War it considered the security position to be better, despite the
tense international situation, since the United States was firmly committed to the defence and economic well-being of the Western liberal
democracies which were themselves now stable politically. However,
after the establishment of the North Atlantic Alliance was there any
pressing need for a British deterrent which was such a run on scarce resources and manpower? The question was debated seriously but the
project was too well-established for it to be abandoned. However, it
could have been integrated with that of the United States, but efforts
to achieve this failed. On the other hand, there was an additional
rationale which grew out of the United States commitment to Europe:

there was now a need to exert influence more generally over United States foreign and defence policy since it had become so important for European security. Moreover, other rationales remained such as the view that possession, and better still manufacture, of nuclear weapons was an indication of and a passport to great power status. Significantly the United States deterrent did not come under NATO control and so the British hoped to cement a 'special relationship' with the United States and thereby to influence its nuclear policy (notwithstanding the failure to re-establish integration) through the creation of an independent British deterrent, also outside of NATO control. Britain as a world power and as a nuclear power claimed a special role in the determination of Western policy. However, Britain had still to produce nuclear weapons and this was not accomplished by the time that Mr Attlee's government was defeated in 1951 despite herculean efforts by those concerned and great political determination by Mr Attlee and his senior colleagues. It was not until after Mr Churchill had returned to office that Britain became a military nuclear power in fact as well as in aspiration. How did the Conservatives manage Britain's hard-earned nuclear status?

The Evolution of Conservative Policy

Mr Churchill could find little fault in his predecessor's conduct of nuclear affairs. On 3 October 1952 the first British atomic weapon test took place but the kudos that accrued to Britain had already been diminished by the first Soviet test in September 1949, thus making Britain not the second nuclear power, as had been anticipated, but the third. It was subsequently diminished still further by the United States and Soviet hydrogen bomb tests a few months later. Nevertheless, Britain was to get atomic weapons in the near future and this, along with Soviet progress, gave a new urgency to the consideration of strategic problems. Two notions dominated the government's thinking: that of deterrence and that of 'broken-backed' warfare. The latter proved to be somewhat ephemeral but the Prime Minister explored the idea that since all states would be vulnerable to the hydrogen bomb the strategic issue of the day was prevention of war rather than its conduct after a strategic interchange had broken the backs of the adversaries.

Mr Churchill remarked that 'I have sometimes the odd thought that the annihilating character of these agencies may bring an utterly unforeseeable security to mankind'[6] — a theme that marked all his thoughts on the deterrent. In the 1955 Defence White Paper these sentiments were translated into a government policy of massive retaliation.[7] In

defending the White Paper in Parliament Mr Churchill stressed the onset
of mutual deterrence in which 'it may well be that we shall by a process of sublime irony have reached a stage in this story where safety will
be the sturdy child of terror, and survival the twin brother of annihilation . . . '[8] The British hydrogen bomb project had also been announced
in the White Paper, although the decision to proceed had been taken in
1952. This raised the question of whether Britain needed to play a role
in the Western deterrent. The Prime Minister told the House that it did
need to do so in order to ensure that targets of cardinal importance to
Britain would be dealt with as and when Britain so desired and to
strengthen British influence both generally and particularly on the
United States. Moreover, in the short term the question of abandoning
the deterrent was somewhat academic, since Britain was now a fledgling
nuclear power with the commencement of the deployment of British
bombs in the V-bombers and the promise of the hydrogen weapon and
with a new delivery system – Blue Streak – to come. It was, however,
soon to become a question of pressing actuality in so far as future
delivery systems were concerned. Meanwhile, as Sir Anthony Eden took
over as Prime Minister in 1955, Britain was entering its age of nuclear
plenitude as a first-class nuclear power, one which was to last but a
decade or thereabouts.

The new Prime Minister was quickly forced to come to terms with a
fundamental strategic problem. Britain's nuclear establishment had
been superimposed upon its conventional warfare structure. But with
the advent of mutual deterrence, what was to be the role of conventional forces, especially in Europe? Moreover, could Britain afford to
remain a first-class military power in both domains? In answer to the
first question, Sir Anthony told President Eisenhower that conventional forces were

> to deal with any local infiltration, to prevent external intimidation
> and to enable aggression to be identified as such. It may be that it
> should also be capable of imposing some delay on the progress of a
> Soviet land invasion until the full impact is felt of the thermonuclear
> retaliation which would be launched against the Soviet Union.[9]

Yet despite this limited role for conventional forces Sir Anthony, as
Foreign Secretary, had committed substantial numbers to the Continent
in 1954 in order to secure French acquiescence to German rearmament.
Moreover, Britain's colonial policing also required a major conventional
effort. As Sir Anthony and his colleagues reviewed the economic impli-

cations of future developments in deterrent and conventional forces
they came to the realisation that economies would have to be made and
determined that they would be made in conventional forces. The implications of such cuts were either that the use of nuclear weapons would
be made at a relatively early time in a war in Europe, despite the ability
of the Soviet Union to retaliate in kind, or that the Western powers
would be forced to cede. It was in answer to such a dilemma that
critics of the government advocated graduated deterrence with the
limited tactical use of the new small-yield nuclear weapons that were
being developed. Thus, while its critics and NATO moved towards a
doctrine of graduated deterrence and, later, flexible response, the
government emphasised increasingly a strategy of massive retaliation. In
their colonial policing role British forces would have to get by as best
they could. For in truth the government had no alternative if it wished
to economise by cutting expensive conventional forces and court electoral popularity by abolishing conscription. Moreover, it believed,
erroneously, that to nuclearise Britain's armed forces would be to get a
viable defence policy and political prestige on the cheap.

The Suez experience only served to strengthen these trends. Britain's
conventional forces had not proved equal to the demands made upon
them, whereas Marshal Bulganin's question, 'In what position would
Britain have found herself if she herself had been attacked by more
powerful states possessing every kind of modern destructive weapon?'
only served to underline the need to have a deterrent to resist nuclear
blackmail and also to pursue an independent foreign policy. Moreover,
United States policy over Suez raised questions regarding its commitment to the defence of Europe, although President Eisenhower made it
clear that, despite his opposition to the Anglo-Israeli-French operation
and the growing vulnerability of North American cities, the United
States would respond in kind if Marshal Bulganin implemented his
threats. Britain's failure to achieve its goals in the Suez crisis was due
to many factors and they were exacerbated by its failure to bring its
conventional forces to bear in adequate strength at the right time and
in the right place. For example, when the crisis first broke the conventional forces available were not sufficient for a *coup de main*, should
the government have so wished. The eventual expeditionary force was
ponderous in the extreme, thus adding to the government's political
difficulties. While the deterrent was not called into play except silently
to resist Marshal Bulganin's nuclear blackmail, the conventional forces
were unable to fulfil the demands that the government would have
liked to have made on them. Yet perversely, the government drew the

conclusion from this that it should put its resources where it felt itself
already to be strong, that is, on the deterrent, rather than where it was
manifestly weak. The motivation was political, economic and electoral
rather than strategic, but it ignored the fact that there were considerable demands on the existing conventional forces and that such
demands were not likely to diminish. Thus, when graduating to the
status of a first-class nuclear power the British Government was at the
time running the risk that its conventional forces would not be able to
meet the demands made upon them. Commitments were not reduced
in a manner commensurate with the reduction of conventional forces
with consequences fraught with the dangers of either defeat or nuclear
escalation. As Mr Macmillan took over from Sir Anthony Eden in early
1957, he appointed Mr Duncan Sandys to be his Minister of Defence
with a remit and the political support necessary for a fundamental
reshaping of the armed forces with an emphasis on the nuclear deterrent.

The Sandys Plan

Suez marked the end of the post-war period so far as Britain was concerned. Britain was no longer one of the Big Three, the economy was in
relatively good trim and the ration books had been finally consigned to
the waste-paper basket, a new post-war generation — the first fruits of
the welfare state — was beginning to make itself felt and a new burst of
decolonialisation was about to begin. It was a difficult time since there
was no real conception and certainly no consensus on what should be
Britain's future role. Nevertheless, in the government's eyes, the need to
economise on defence to satisfy the growing consumerism in British
society was clear beyond doubt. Yet, equally, the need for a strong
defence and foreign policy to salvage Britain's wounded *amour propre*
was evident to the government. The government thought that an
emphasis on the deterrent would accomplish both those goals, besides
being popular with the electorate and giving Britain considerable influence with the United States and in alliance affairs. In the Defence White
Papers of 1957 and 1958[10] Mr Sandys went about his reshaping of the
armed forces.

The starting point was that 'it is . . . in the true interests of defence
that the claims of military expenditure should be considered in conjunction with the need to maintain the country's financial and economic
strength'[11] and, therefore, that these claims would have to be reduced.
Mr Sandys proposed the possession of 'an appreciable element of
nuclear deterrent power of [our] own'[12] which would strengthen the

alliance, reassure the continental allies and provide a means of assurance should the United States revert to isolation. But the price of this was the reduction of the personnel of the armed forces from 690,000 to 375,000 by 1962. The following year, in acknowledging the import of Sputnik for Soviet-American mutual deterrence, Mr Sandys argued that invulnerable second-strike forces meant that there was 'no military reason why a world conflagration should not be prevented for another generation or more through the balancing fears of mutual annihilation. In fact, there is no reason why all this should not go on almost indefinitely.'[13] Mr Sandys passed over the likely vulnerability of Blue Streak, Britain's successor to the V-bombers, to a Soviet first strike to remark that 'when fully equipped with megaton weapons, the British bomber force will in itself constitute a formidable deterrent.'[14] Moreover, in his mind there was no doubt about the use to which such a force would be put — massive retaliation. After surveying the Soviet Union's conventional capability he stated that

> The West, on the other hand, relies for its defence primarily upon the deterrent effect of its vast stockpile of nuclear weapons and its capacity to deliver them. The democratic Western nations will never start a war against Russia. But it must be well understood that, if Russia were to launch a major attack on them, even with conventional forces only, they would have to hit back with strategic nuclear weapons. In fact, the strategy of NATO is based on the frank recognition that a full-scale Soviet attack could not be repelled without resort to a massive nuclear bombardment of the sources of power in Russia. In that event, the role of the allied defence forces in Europe would be to hold the front for the time needed to allow the effects of the nuclear counter-offensive to make themselves felt.[15]

The policy was audacious and convenient, and what is more it could not be dismissed on the basis of empirical data. It was a policy based on the conjecture that if the sanction was sufficiently catastrophic for the target actor, it would be dissuaded, whatever the likelihood of the sanction being applied. But if the application of the sanction meant *mutual* catastrophe, was it credible? Such was the counter-conjecture and, happily, we have no experience of inter-state nuclear war to say who is right nor do we know whether, if his bluff had been called, Mr Sandys meant what he wrote. However, in terms of NATO strategy Britain's policy meant that the nuclear threshold in Europe was very low, given the crucial position of BAOR on the Central Front, even though, in supplying low-yield limited-range nuclear weapons to their allies, the United States was striving to ensure that, in the first instance at least, it would be transversed in a tactical way.

The motives for Mr Sandys' policy were far from being essentially strategic. Mr Macmillan had decided that defence should have a lower claim on national resources than hitherto and that an emphasis on the deterrent was better value for less money than an emphasis on conventional forces. But commitments demanding conventional forces outside Europe were not reduced so that besides the risk of lowering the nuclear threshold in Europe, there was also a risk of being overwhelmed elsewhere. That Britain's extra-European commitments did not entail disaster is a tribute to the ingenuity of the services, and great good fortune, for it was at least a decade before the commitments were reduced to a level that the forces available could adequately fulfil. Mr Sandys was both thorough and ruthless in implementing his policy and the conventional forces, once disbanded, were never likely to be reformed except in the most dire circumstances. Britain's defence policy and obligations involved much crossing of fingers, and it remained to be seen whether the emphasis on the deterrent would achieve its purpose of economy and enhancing prestige.

One immediate result of Britain's growing nuclear capability was a breakthrough in co-operation with the United States. Britain now had something to offer the United States in the nuclear sphere and was being very co-operative in allowing the United States to base the controversial 'first strike' Thor missiles in the United Kingdom and subsequently the less controversial (since clearly second-strike) Polaris submarines. The British were also willing to accept a considerable degree of co-ordination in the operation, deployment and targeting of their deterrent with that of the United States. In return the United States modified the McMahon Act in Britain's favour and, in 1958, information began to flow in quantity across the Atlantic, especially for the Blue Streak missile and the nuclear propulsion units for submarines of the hunter-killer variety.[16] Britain's concern was now with delivery systems rather than weapons as such. The British deterrent was fully independent, if co-ordinated with that of the United States, but its future was becoming heavily dependent on continued co-operation with the United States for delivery systems.

The Independent Deterrent and the United States

Mr Sandys' chickens soon came home to roost as the deterrent proved to be neither cheap nor, in the eyes of many, prestigious. In the mid-

fifties the British Government had decided to develop Blue Streak, a
liquid-fuelled unhardened ground-to-ground missile, to succeed the V-
bombers as the principal delivery system for the deterrent. The Royal
Navy had never exhibited any great interest in providing the delivery
system for the deterrent, whereas the proponents of Blue Streak were
keen and there was a good prospect of help from the United States.
Although there were alternatives, the British Government felt that it
had to concentrate on one delivery system and there was little disagreement when that choice fell on Blue Streak. Nevertheless, although
United States help was forthcoming, Soviet advances were such that
Blue Streak would have been obsolete before it could be deployed,
since with only four minutes' warning of a Soviet attack Blue Streak
could only be used as a first-strike weapon. While the British Government may have contemplated it in such a role the Opposition, the
British public and Britain's allies did not. The Conservative Government
thus found itself in a dilemma.

In 1957 the Conservatives had committed themselves to a policy of
massive retaliation as the basis of Britain's defence policy. In the three
years that followed the Labour Opposition had repeatedly pointed to
the weaknesses of Blue Streak. In April 1960 the government acknowledged these weaknesses when it cancelled the military version of the
missile. Thereupon the bi-partisan policy on the deterrent ended, for
both the Labour and Liberal parties favoured the ending of the independent deterrent posture, the deterrent's integration into an alliance
setting and no attempt being made to develop future delivery systems.
Labour even toyed with the idea of a non-nuclear club with Britain as a
founder-member, but this notion had much to do with taking the steam
out of the Campaign for Nuclear Disarmament. However, if the government had relinquished the independent deterrent it would then have
been forced to admit that it had been an error to put all its eggs in the
nuclear basket or, at least, that in choosing Blue Streak it had not made
the best choice since in the United States the submarine-launched
system, Polaris, was making great progress — an option that the British
had never considered seriously. More fundamentally it was becoming
clear that the Sandys goals of economy and prestige were seriously
compromised: a future delivery system would be inordinately expensive if developed by Britain alone, and the symbol of Britain's first-
class status — the deterrent — would be seriously tarnished if Britain
became dependent on the United States for the supply of its delivery
system. Yet to reverse the Sandys plan when it was well on the way to
completion and develop a new defence policy would have had grave

political implications for the government — not to mention the havoc that it would have wrought on the armed forces. The government in fact chose to maintain its belief in an independent deterrent, but to see seek a delivery system from the United States, in the face of strong public criticism both inside and outside Parliament. The choice fell on Skybolt, and it was made by the new Defence Minister, Mr Watkinson, who, not being hostage to Mr Sandys' strategic doctrine, also began to modify the rigidity with which the government clung to the notion of massive retaliation.

The government had to justify both its pursuance of the independent deterrent concept and the choice of Skybolt. The 1960 Defence White Paper said little about doctrine, but in his White Paper the following year, Mr Watkinson justified Britain's 'contribution to the nuclear deterrent forces of the West' by arguing that:

Making full allowance for the growth of nuclear powers in the world our contribution still provides a valuable degree of strength and diversity to the Western forces as a whole. It increases dispersal and reduces reaction time. It provides powerful backing for our alliances. The government believes that it is in the national interest that we should continue to share the burden and responsibility of maintaining this important element in the total power of the Western deterrent. Our contribution also substantially increases our influence in negotiations for a nuclear test agreement, disarmament and the reorganisation of NATO strategy.[17]

While much of this may have been true of the V-bomber force, would it also hold for a Skybolt force technologically dependent on the United States? The Prime Minister's justification was more emotional. In the context of an 'interdependence' speech in the United States he pointed out that

we have always been ready in the last resort to fight alone . . . Our determination to make our own contribution was in a sense instinctive. And perhaps with the Atlantic Ocean between us it has been no bad thing for the people of Europe to see that at least one European member of NATO shares the nuclear power with you . . . [18]

although he warned other European Powers not to follow suit in 'wasteful duplication'. The 1962 White Paper affirmed that the British deterrent was 'by itself enough', but would it remain so? Indeed, the

debate was becoming fudged by the government's refusal to differentiate clearly between 'an independent deterrent', which would have all
the attributes it claimed, and 'an independent contribution to the
deterrent' which, given the plenitude of United States nuclear power,
would serve chiefly as a catalytic force to trigger the United States
deterrent. Ironically, the British Government was asking the United
States Government to supply it with a delivery system to be used by
the British to force an unwilling American hand, that is, to use United
States weapons systems to force United States participation against its
better judgement. Of course, the British offered bases and operational
co-operation in return, but there was little wonder that Mr McNamara,
the in-coming Secretary of Defense, asserted the need for central
United States control of nuclear weapons in the alliance.

The British had a choice of Skybolt or Polaris. Skybolt was an air-to-
ground missile which would have prolonged the life of the V-bomber
force, and it was highly regarded by the RAF and USAF, not to mention the British aircraft industry, which was hoping for more orders.
Although it was not yet ready, the scientific reports were reassuring and
the cost to Britain was not overly daunting. Moreover, it could be
supplied to the RAF before the V-bombers' ability to penetrate to
Soviet targets would be in question. This was not the case of Polaris,
although it was clear in 1960 that the United States would itself deploy
the Polaris while doubts remained over Skybolt. However, there was no
strong pressure group in favour of Polaris in Britain. The Royal Navy
was lukewarm since it did not want a fight with the RAF, the demands
for skilled personnel would be hard to meet, the hunter-killer programme
would be disrupted, and the Polaris programme might have to be fin-
anced out of existing funds. The government could, of course, have
delayed taking a decision, but its political situation and the debate on
the deterrent were such that it felt it prudent to shout, 'The King is
dead, long live the King.' It therefore favoured Skybolt despite the
Polaris option and the latter's superiority in long-term cost, in invulner-
ability and in probability of completion – the decision whether to
proceed with Skybolt lying entirely with the United States on the basis
of criteria acceptable to the United States alone.

Skybolt, as far as the government was concerned, and to its great
relief, meant the continuation of the British independent deterrent. But
the government was blind to numerous indications that all was not well
with the programme. Perhaps this was because there was no opposition
to the missile in the government, the services or the arms industry.
Moreover, warnings from the Labour Party's spokesmen could be dis-

counted as the normal machinations of an opposition party. When it finally realised, towards the end of 1962, that the United States was going to drop the project, as it had every right to do, there was great consternation and the Prime Minister and the President met in the Bahamas in an atmosphere of a major crisis in Anglo-American relations. The arguments, political and strategic, for an independent deterrent which were made in 1960 to justify the replacement of Blue Streak with Skybolt were used again in 1962 to justify the exchange of Skybolt with Polaris. If the government had not sought a replacement for Skybolt in 1962 it would have been tantamount to admitting its error of judgement in 1960 in replacing Blue Streak, which was further compounded by its unfortunate choice of Skybolt rather than Polaris when both were available in 1960. The British position *vis-à-vis* the United States was based on the notion that to offer Polaris in 1962 was little different from offering Skybolt in 1960. The British rejected other alternatives such as sharing the future development costs of Skybolt with the United States or accepting Hound Dog – a less sophisticated and shorter-range air-to-ground missile. But on the United States side things were different. President Kennedy had taken over and appointed Robert McNamara as Secretary for Defense, who quickly made his views crystal clear in a speech at the University of Michigan:

relatively weak national nuclear forces with enemy cities as their targets are not likely to be sufficient to perform even the function of deterrence. If they are small, and perhaps vulnerable on the ground or in the air, or inaccurate, a major antagonist can take a variety of measures to counter them. Indeed, if a major antagonist came to believe there was a substantial likelihood of it being used independently, this force would be inviting a 'pre-emptive' first strike against it. In the event of war, the use of such a force against cities of a major nuclear power would be tantamount to suicide, while its employment against significant military targets would have a negligible effect on the outcome of the conflict. Meanwhile, the creation of a single national nuclear force encourages the proliferation of nuclear power with all its attendant dangers. In short then, limited nuclear capabilities, operating independently, are dangerous, expensive, prone to obsolescence and lacking in credibility as a deterrent. Clearly, the United States nuclear contribution to the Alliance is neither obsolete nor dispensable. At the same time, the general strategy I have summarised magnifies the importance of unity and planning, concentration of executive authority and central direction.

There must not be competing and conflicting strategies to meet the
contingency of nuclear war. We are convinced that a general nuclear
war target system is indivisible, and if, despite all our efforts, nuclear
war should occur our best hope lies in conducting a centrally controlled campaign against all of the enemy's vital nuclear capabilities,
while retaining reserve forces all centrally controlled . . . We expect
that our allies will also undertake to strengthen further their non-
nuclear forces and to improve the quality and staying power of these
forces.[19]

The United States had moved away from the doctrine of massive
retaliation but Britain escaped the full force of Mr McNamara's strictures because it met the requirements of central control. Yet if central
control was tantamount to United States control then how independent was Britain's deterrent? Moreover, if Britain's megatonnage was
not a necessity, would not Britain have furthered the cause of the
alliance as a whole by concentrating its efforts on those conventional
forces the lack of which worried Mr McNamara? As the parties met in
the Bahamas the British were stressing the independence of their deterrent and asking the United States to help them to maintain that independence, whereas the United States deplored independent deterrents
and did not consider the British one to be independent. Clearly the
British Government would be hard pressed to proclaim independence
to the world and promise central control to the United States as a condition for the substitution of Polaris for Skybolt.

In a brilliant diplomatic *tour de force* Mr Macmillan succeeded.
Besides Mr Macmillan's diplomatic skills the President may have been
influenced by other factors. The British were ready to concede co-
ordination to a degree tantamount to integration in all circumstances
but those considered by the United States to be extremely unlikely.
Moreover, the British Government had accepted without demur the
Thor and Polaris bases even though the former, being first-strike
weapons, might have invited a Soviet pre-emptive blow, and despite the
latter proving to be grist to the nuclear disarmers' mill in British domestic politics, Mr Macmillan therefore had some claim for a political *quid
pro quo*. Nor were the British empty-handed, for they could offer the
United States useful information in the nuclear field and more generally ease the burden of the United States by fulfilling major security
roles in various parts of the world which might otherwise devolve on
the United States. Moreover, with Franco-American relations far from
happy, President Kennedy could hardly have looked with equanimity

upon the prospect of strained relations with a second major ally. The
British negotiators could also point to a quarter-century of nuclear
partnership during which Britain had given much and had not always
received its due. Finally, President Kennedy liked Mr Macmillan, and
he was a friend of the British Ambassador in Washington so that he was
sensitive to and knowledgeable about the importance of the meeting to
Mr Macmillan's political fortunes in Britain.

In the event the United States agreed to 'make available on a continuing basis Polaris missiles (less warheads) for British submarines . . .
[and] study the feasibility of making available certain support facilities
for such submarines'. The submarines and missile warheads would be of
British construction.[20] The submarines 'would be assigned as part of a
NATO force and targeted in accordance with NATO plans . . . except
where Her Majesty's Government may decide that supreme national
interests are at stake.'[21] For the President this exception ' . . . was a
recognition . . . [that] every nation is conscious that there may be a
moment when it is isolated and when national interests are involved'[22]
while for the Prime Minister, 'This agreement preserves both the concepts of independence and interdependence.'[23] It also forms the basis
of the present British deterrent. By reconciling independence and interdependence the Prime Minister fulfilled his own immediate political
need, kept the deterrent a viable economic proposition, and looked to
its long-term preservation. That on one side of the Atlantic the British
force was hailed as independent and on the other as interdependent was
something both the British Government and United States Administration were able to accept. In practical terms the British deterrent henceforth had two roles: one was purely British and the other was as an
integral part of the alliance forces in Europe. In the former Polaris is
not only British-owned and manned but also British-controlled, whereas
in the latter role it is subject to NATO decision-making processes in
which Britain plays a part. This situation has remained and it is now
common to most of Britain's armed forces.

In many respects the Bahamas meeting and the subsequent unevent-
ful implementation of its provisions regarding Polaris settled matters
until the approach of the 1980s, the only major question being whether
a Labour Government would implement it and this was quickly
decided in the affirmative. However, there was one other 'threat' to the
deterrent — disarmament and arms control — which bears consideration.

The international control of nuclear weapons did not seem a likely
prospect to British governments either during the war or in the immed-

iate post-war years. The dominant view was that the possession of
nuclear weapons was so important to governments that few would forgo
them since their possession by other powers or by an international
authority would be a serious attenuation of national sovereignty. Moreover, the absence of cast-iron verification procedures would render
nuclear disarmament perilous given the great advantages a successful
cheater would enjoy. No British government has taken British or
general nuclear disarmament seriously for these reasons. Measures of
nuclear arms control are, however, a different matter since they have
the less ambitious aim of removing irritants rather than seeking to
change the basic nature of a relationship although they may help to
reduce tension and bring an element of stability into an arms race or
make a power politics relationship safer.

In the mid-fifties public opinion in Britain became concerned at the
health hazards arising from nuclear tests in the atmosphere and the
governments of Sir Anthony Eden and Mr Macmillan responded to this
by taking an active part in the long-drawn-out negotiations which
resulted in the Partial Nuclear Test Ban Treaty of 1963. Prior to this
agreement the British Government conducted those atmospheric tests
that it thought necessary for the furtherance of the British weapons
programme, but when atmospheric tests were no longer essential and
national means of verification were sufficient, it joined the United
States and the Soviet Union in sponsoring the 1963 Treaty. Indeed,
pushed by a vociferous public opinion the British Government was
always ready to bring the Big Two together for another try and, but for
British insistence, the Treaty might have been considerably delayed.
Interestingly and paradoxically, the Conservative governments of the
day used Britain's role in the arms control negotiations as a justification
for the independent deterrent — the possession of arms was needed in
order to be able to influence the disarmament process! However, there
is little evidence to suggest that British possession of nuclear weapons
was a determining factor since more recently Britain has had no role in
SALT whereas its brokerage role in the late fifties was not so much
contingent upon its deterrent as upon its general diplomatic standing
and the world security role of its conventional forces at the time.

Although the Labour governments of the sixties appointed a Minister
of Disarmament and an Arms Control and Disarmament Research Unit
in the Foreign Office, Britain only had a modest role to play internationally except perhaps in the negotiation of the Nuclear Non-Prolif-
eration Treaty with its echoes of Labour's non-nuclear club — but this
time without Britain. The governments, Labour and Conservative, of

the seventies have done their best to promote measures of nuclear arms
control but there is little scope for manoeuvre. The debate and the
policy options are for the superpowers and the near-nuclear powers and
there is little that Britain can do to influence them. However, the situation had seemed to be somewhat different from this when Labour
came to power in 1964. How would it handle the deterrent? Would it
implement the Bahamas agreement? Would it de-nuclearise Britain as
many in the party wished? Would it internationalise the deterrent?
Would it, could it, give a great lead in nuclear disarmament and arms
control? It is to Mr Healey's reign that we now turn.

Mr Healey's Reign

Conservative Defence Ministers averaged only a little over a year in
office. Mr Healey held the post throughout Labour's period in power
until 1970. He brought about many changes, and for the better, not the
least being the adjustment of Britain's commitments to fit its
capabilities, although the manner in which it was done was often
tortuous and the timing of decisions was greatly influenced by
tumultuous changes in Britain's economic situation. Questions concerning the deterrent were an immediate concern of the new government and once they had been resolved, the deterrent excited little
attention, either governmental or public, probably to the relief of all
concerned.

Mr Healey did not come into office with *tabula rasa*. Indeed, he himself had poked fun at the Conservatives whom he had accused of regarding the independent deterrent as a national virility symbol. Although
by October 1964 unilateral nuclear disarmament was no longer a
burning issue in the Labour Party, the new government was pledged to
renegotiate the Bahamas agreements. Prominent unilateralists were in
the Cabinet but they did not have responsibility for defence matters
and, although they could put their views in Cabinet to the extent that
Cabinet discussed such matters, they could not do so out of Cabinet
since they were bound by collective responsibility. In any case unilateralist Ministers had exciting things to do in the exercise of their new
responsibilities which may have distracted them from their erstwhile
cause. Although the non-nuclear club had lost its principal protagonist
with the death of Mr Gaitskell, and its relevance with the continued
progress of France and China as nuclear powers, the party did have a
strong commitment to nuclear disarmament and arms control. Nevertheless, in the event Labour did not institute radical change but merely
altered the emphasis of the previous government's policy on the deter-

rent.

The 1965 Defence White Paper justly chastised the previous government for putting the services in a situation of being 'seriously over-
stretched and in some respects dangerously under-equipped' because
'there has been no real attempt to match political commitments to
military resources, still less to relate the resources made available for
defence to the economic circumstances of the nation.'[24] Mutual deterrence made 'deliberate aggression . . . unlikely' in Europe[25] but this
could be prejudiced by the proliferation of nuclear weapons. In order
to prevent this within the alliance the government proposed 'an
Atlantic Nuclear Force in which strategic nuclear weapons available or
to be made available to the Alliance would be subject to collective
authority'.[26] The British forces involved would be the V-bombers
(except for those required for commitments outside the NATO area)
and the Polaris submarines all of which 'would be wholly committed
for as long as the Alliance continued'.[27] However, the ANF did not
come into being, nor did the United States-sponsored Multilateral Force
to which the ANF was the British response. The commital to NATO
remained, nevertheless, since it was in accordance with the Bahamas
agreement. The British Government did not renounce the right to
withdraw the forces for matters of supreme national interest, although
presumably it could not conceive of such circumstances while NATO
remained in being. If NATO had collapsed it might have been a
different matter. Indeed, Polaris was to be entirely British-owned and
operated and, as the Prime Minister told the Commons, 'there will not
be any system of locks which interferes with our right of communication with a submarine or our right to withdraw the submarine',[28] so
that, in fact, neither the ANF nor the MLF would have altered the
Bahamas provisions in so far as the withdrawal for national purposes
was concerned.

In one respect Labour did alter the Conservatives' plans: it cancelled the fifth Polaris submarine. On coming to power Labour found
that the first three submarines were sufficiently advanced that con-
version to a hunter-killer role or simple cancellation would be very expensive. The fourth submarine would guarantee that at least one submarine would be on patrol at all times and so, on military advice, it
was retained, and with it the makings of an independent deterrent in
case of catastrophe. The cancellation of the fifth submarine was an
economy measure that was also a gesture to the anti-nuclear lobby in
the party and a token of Britain's earnestness in seeking to prevent
nuclear proliferation. There was also the additional factor that Britain

was hard put to find sufficient skilled men to sustain a five-boat force.
Nevertheless, despite this alteration the jibes of Labour's left that the
new government was following the Conservatives' policy were, in
essence, correct, the more so because the Conservatives themselves
were showing little disquiet over the government's policy. Why did the
Labour Government accept the Bahamas agreement and thus restore a
bi-partisan policy on the deterrent?

Labour claimed that their policy towards the deterrent was one of
pragmatism. It was on practical grounds that they had opposed the
independent deterrent from 1960, not on moral or political grounds.
To them the amended Bahamas arrangements in the form of the ANF
would enable Britain to play its part in checking the proliferation of
nuclear weapons in NATO and, at the same time, give Britain the
makings of a deterrent if the alliance should collapse. Mr Healey and his
colleagues were also impressed at 'the extremely low cost of the deterrent'.[29] Moreover, Mr Healey was able to make good use of Britain's
nuclear role not only in the ANF-MLF debate but also later in working
out a strategy for NATO in the European theatre. He saw strategic
advantages too, since he is reported to have remarked that 'if you are
inside an alliance you increase the deterrent to the other side enormously if there is more than one centre of decision for first use of
nuclear weapons.'[30] One further aspect was Britain's defence role east
of Suez — a role dear to the hearts of the Prime Minister and of the
services. In proposing the ANF the government had made provision for
some V-bombers to be available as a deterrent force 'east of Suez'. The
Polaris force would enable that capability to be continued and, besides
providing a foundation on which Britain's role as peacekeeper in the
area could be based, it might, in view of China's nuclear status, provide
sufficient reassurance to dissuade India from developing its own military
nuclear programme. Such arguments did not, in the event, meet with a
favourable response from India and in any case the east of Suez role
collapsed, but by then the argument over the deterrent in the Labour
Party was over.

In foreign and defence matters the Labour Government was not a
little concerned with prestige. The Prime Minister, in particular,
claimed a major role for Britain and the retention of nuclear weapons,
even in the Bahamas framework, could not be to its detriment. The
post-Bahamas deterrent still afforded Britain a modicum of influence
over the United States — an influence that was held in high regard by
the Prime Minister. Although the 'special relationship' in nuclear
affairs — always a hard-nosed matter of what Britain could offer with

perhaps the sole exception of the Bahamas agreement — was waning, the east of Suez role, with its deterrent adjunct, which was fully in accordance with the wishes of the United States Administration, did provide another 'special relationship' in the sphere of defence and foreign policy. Thus, after the Bahamas arrangements had been confirmed by the Labour Government, Anglo-American nuclear co-operation was on a firm footing, although the degree of British dependence in the field militated strongly against the deterrent in and of itself giving any great British influence over the United States. No longer were the British forces part of the Anglo-American strategic deterrent outside of NATO they were an integral part of NATO, as Mr Macmillan had been forced to concede. True, they also had a purely British role, and possibly a European role, as a catalytic force — an assurance against a United States refusal to act or even their withdrawal. Nor was the British force a function of Moscow, since the alliance had all the megatonnage it needed to obliterate Soviet targets although Soviet capabilities did set the requirements for the British forces' second-strike posture (except for a possible role east of Suez which was less demanding, given China's vulnerability and inability to attack Britain) and thus ensured that the Labour Government had to authorise technical improvements in the force. The British deterrent had no powers to enable the British to act as a mediator in East/West encounters, for with the amelioration in Soviet-American relations there was no brokerage role. Apart from being an ultimate assurance in defence matters, at a modest price, the Polaris force which the Labour Government built up along with the V-bombers (which could have both a strategic and a tactical nuclear role although many were converted to tankers or scrapped) had another important role. The British nuclear force constituted the cards on the table that enabled Mr Healey to play the leading role in revising NATO's war-fighting strategy in the European theatre, and particularly in the elaboration of guide-lines for the tactical use of nuclear weapons. The 'great debate' on the British deterrent was over. Labour instituted the Conservatives' policy and the left, conscious of the government's narrow majority, gave up the fight. The Conservatives, for their part, were muted since, although their policy was being implemented, there were plenty of skeletons in their cupboard.

During Labour's years in opposition Mr Healey had made an enviable reputation for himself as a 'defence intellectual', both in Parliament, in academia and as a journalist. It was a reputation that was not confined to Britain but was also upheld in the United States, Germany and

Scandinavia. He was one of those who had argued in favour of graduated deterrence and, once in office, he set about implementing his ideas
in the European NATO framework. British policy was no longer one of
massive retaliation, except possibly if the nuclear force was withdrawn
from NATO in defence of supreme national interests. NATO strategy
had been based on a quick recourse to nuclear weapons, but this suited
neither Mr Healey nor his United States counterpart Mr McNamara.
Mr Healey took the lead in revising it. Both NATO and Warsaw Pact
forces had ample nuclear weapons at their disposal for either tactical or
strategic use — the latter being a second-strike posture. Mr Healey
therefore set to work and he was successful in persuading his allied
colleagues 'to develop a strategy which would improve the prospects
for rational control of a military conflict in Europe while maintaining
the credibility of the nuclear guarantee'.[31] The strategy had to be based
on the resources likely to be available and it sought to arrive at a
credible balance between conventional and nuclear forces. The result,
in December 1967, was a

> new strategy designed to provide a wider and more flexible range of
> response appropriate to the nature of the threat. It recognises that,
> while NATO must be ready to use nuclear weapons if necessary, this
> must not be the only response which the Alliance can make to any
> of the threats which it might have to face and that steps must there-
> fore be taken to maximise the capability of NATO's forces in con-
> ventional conflicts.[32]

This ' . . . would allow time for negotiations to end the conflict and for
consultations among the Allies about the initial use of nuclear weapons
if negotiations should fail'.[33] Doubtless the existence of the British
deterrent lent both purpose and weight to Mr Healey's activities in this
necessary and important task in which Britain played a leading role.
    Under Mr Healey's direction the creation of the Polaris force went
forward smoothly and expeditiously. It was a major project well executed from a variety of viewpoints, not least financial. In 1969 the
Royal Navy took over responsibility for the deterrent from the RAF
and in 1970 the final Polaris submarine became operational, but some
decisions regarding the deterrent had still to be made. The British submarines were fitted with the A-3 missile with multiple re-entry vehicles
(MRV), but the government did not apparently seek the Poseidon
missile with its multiple independently-targeted re-entry vehicles
(MIRV). No reason was given: perhaps the government feared a refusal

on the part of the United States to supply them. The most weighty
factor was probably that the British force had no great need of MIRVs,
even though some research had been done on them since it was primarily a counter-city force. However, some improvements of the
Polaris A-3 were undertaken. Thus, as the Conservatives returned to
power in 1970, both the letter and the spirit of the Bahamas agreement
had been fulfilled. Mr Macmillan must have felt vindicated.

A Period of Stability

The new Conservative Government of 1970 inherited the fruits of its
own endeavours in the field of the deterrent — the Polaris force (and in
addition there were those V-bombers still operational in a nuclear role).
It also had at its disposal a considerable tactical nuclear capability
which had first been deployed in the late fifties and a NATO doctrine
on its use, together with a reasonable balance between commitments
and resources generally and between nuclear and conventional arms in
particular. Mr Heath's government made no changes in policy towards
the deterrent and its basic concern remained the same as under Labour
— NATO and European security — demanding both conventional and
nuclear forces but with some potentially dangerous east of Suez
trimmings whose demands were more likely to be in the form of conventional than nuclear forces. While the Soviet 'threat' was given
greater prominence by the Conservatives they nevertheless, if reluctant
reluctantly, did acknowledge the notion of *détente* even if they were
highly sceptical of its practical value. Although the Conservatives
accorded defence a somewhat higher priority than hitherto, this did not
lead to any dramatic changes and had no effect on the deterrent, since
its call on the defence budget was virtually insignificant. However, the
government bolstered its pretensions east of Suez by visits to Singapore
from V-bombers and a nuclear capability for action in the CENTO area
was maintained. The new government reconsidered, but continued
Labour's decision on the cancellation of the fifth Polaris submarine,
and that not to request Poseidon from the United States,[34] although, as
previously with the Labour Government, the existing Polaris force was
modernised.

Mr Heath's determination to maintain the existing deterrent was
made abundantly clear, and it was in his term of office that some
thought was given by Ministers to the post-Polaris situation. Mr Heath
had, while in opposition, suggested a future 'nuclear force based on the
existing British and French forces which would be held in trusteeship
for Europe as a whole',[35] but neither the British nor French Defence

Ministers of the day, Lord Carrington and M. Debré, considered the prospect in anything other than the long term. Mr Heath may also have discussed the long-term future of the deterrent with Mr Nixon, but there was no immediate need for a new 'Bahamas' with the United States since the ABM agreement in SALT ensured the Polaris fleet's second-strike capability well into the future. In the meantime Anglo-American agreements on various technical matters were renewed without fuss so that existing collaboration continued smoothly. Nor was there any rocking of the boat in NATO's European theatre where the Conservatives accepted the Alliance's position on the role of nuclear weapons. Indeed, the British Government continued to play a leading role in such discussions, as it had done under Labour.

The return to power of a Labour Government has not disturbed this period of stability. Labour's pre-election promise to 'seek removal of American Polaris bases from Britain'[36] was a 'cosmetic' promise, since this was only to occur in the context of multilateral disarmament. Labour's election manifesto stated that 'We have renounced any intention of moving towards a new generation of strategic nuclear weapons'[37] – a pledge that was subsequently repeated in the 1975 Defence White Paper.[38] The government's general view of the security situation was that they did 'not believe that the Warsaw Pact countries would contemplate outright aggression against the West in present circumstances . . .', however, 'Détente is not yet irreversible', and so

> Adequate defence calls for military forces capable of denying any potential aggressor the prospect of easy victory. It calls for conventional forces manifestly capable of withstanding any initial attack and backed by tactical and strategic nuclear forces which in Europe and the Atlantic only the NATO Alliance can provide. So long as the Alliance has such a capability and the will to use it if necessary, aggression of whatever sort can be deterred and the use of military power as a political weapon neutralised.[39]

Britain's contribution to the NATO nuclear deterrent was given due importance by the government. The White Paper stated that

> The Polaris force, which Britain will continue to make available to the Alliance, provides a unique European contribution to NATO's strategic nuclear capability out of all proportion to the small fraction of our defence budget which it costs to maintain. We shall maintain its effectiveness. We shall also maintain our tactical nuclear

capability in accordance with NATO strategy.[40]

This capability, strategic and tactical, was accorded the equal highest priority in Britain's contribution to NATO along with that to the Central Front, the East Atlantic and Channel and the defence of the UK home base.[41] A memorandum from the Ministry of Defence expanded upon the importance given by the Labour Government to the deterrent in the NATO context:

> This gives NATO a separate centre of decision-making in Europe which the Soviets must take into account (the French strategic deterrent is not committed to the alliance); it increases the credibility of the overall NATO deterrent; and it provides an element of insurance, and reassurance to our European allies, against any weakening of the United States nuclear guarantee.

Moreover,

> In the last resort, if the Alliance was to collapse, the possession of an independent strategic weapon provides the United Kingdom with the means of preserving national security by deterring large scale conventional or nuclear attack or of countering nuclear blackmail ... Furthermore the Polaris force has much of its active life remaining; it enables both the United Kingdom and the Alliance to derive substantially enhanced security for a relatively small annual cost.[42]

Thus, the government is prepared to argue strongly in favour of the deterrent and it is confident of its long life. The only 'threat' to the deterrent is 'multilateral negotiations on the phasing out of the Polaris deterrent force. But this depends entirely upon the progress made with CSCE and MBFR negotiations.'[43] Such progress, if any, has been slow and in any case it seems not to have any relevance for the British possession of nuclear weapons, at least for the time being. Nevertheless the final relinquishment of a British role east of Suez, in CENTO and in the Mediterranean does imply that the deterrent will no longer have even a residual role in those areas.

In 1974, as in 1964, a Labour Government came to power with some doubts in party circles as to the utility and, indeed, the rectitude of preserving a British deterrent. In both cases the new government rapidly became convinced of the usefulness of the deterrent and the

party did not demur from this. The present government has stated its
belief in the value of the deterrent in such forthright terms that the
finality of its pledge not to acquire a new generation of strategic nuclear
weapons may be questioned. Since the need for such a decision may
not be necessary before the next election and in any case may be held
over in the current financial situation such an acquisition may be made
by a future Conservative Government to be bequeathed to a secretly
happy Labour administration. Such speculation aside, the present
Labour Government has done all that is necessary to incorporate the
latest modifications into the present Polaris force. Two underground
tests have taken place, in 1974 and 1976, in Nevada but, despite press
speculation and some work in the area, there has been no official
indication that they are the prelude to MIRV-ing the British deterrent.
A flurry of interest and speculation was also aroused by the British
decision henceforth to make its own tritium for use in warheads rather
than to rely on the United States.[44] These are, however, but preludes
to a more serious debate towards the end of this decade on the future
of the deterrent. What, at present, seem to be the options?

The Future of the Deterrent

It is not our purpose to attempt an elaborate exercise in prediction but
the historical record does suggest some pointers to the future. If the
Soviet threat is perceived to be of a considerably greater order of mag-
nitude than at present, or if NATO collapses, then both political parties
are likely to find the resources necessary to refurbish the deterrent. At
the other end of the spectrum, that is, if we suppose a genuine and
multilateral movement towards nuclear disarmament, then Britain
would be likely to promote it even if this movement did not include
the two (or three) superpowers. Both parties, however, would be likely
to insist that nuclear disarmament should be accompanied by measures
of conventional disarmament. Assuming that the present international
and national political and economic environments do not change
radically, then a Conservative Government is likely to continue the
deterrent by purchasing delivery systems in either a European, Anglo-
French or Anglo-American context provided that, in certain exceptional circumstances, the British element could be withdrawn to constitute an independent deterrent and that the cost does not overwhelm
the defence budget of the period. A Labour Government is less likely to
do so, although subsequently it would probably maintain any such
force that it inherited. These speculations need to be related to the
possible options available in terms of present and future weapons sys-

tems and it is to these that we now turn.

There is a very high probability that the present British Polaris force has a second-strike capability against every other power, including the Soviet Union, its most likely target.[45] But such a situation is not immutable even if the requirements of minimum deterrence for a country such as Britain may be low.[46] Theoretically, however, the British deterrent could be relinquished at any time but since the demise of the Campaign for Nuclear Disarmament more than a decade ago and the failure of the 1964 Labour Government to act in this way there has been no effective advocacy of such an option. Moreover, no nuclear power has yet relinquished its military capability and it might prove difficult to convince potential adversaries and other interested parties of the effectiveness of unilateral nuclear disarmament without considerable on-site inspection during the course of which other secrets would willy-nilly be revealed. Moreover, the basic knowledge would remain, as would a major civilian nuclear programme and many weapons systems suitable for use with nuclear warheads. In short, Britain would perforce remain a near-nuclear power. However, the present Labour Government's policy is to maintain the effectiveness of the existing force but not to replace it. In such circumstances the deterrent could continue into the 1990s, by which time subsequent governments might not be so willing to allow the deterrent the old soldier's fate of just fading away. The fading-away process may be precipitated and speeded up by factors other than the mere wearing-out of the present boats. It could depend on advances in anti-submarine warfare (ASW), on advances in anti-ballistic missile systems (ABM), the financial situation, or changes in United States policy, to mention some of the contingencies worth considering.

At present, Soviet ASW capabilities are not a serious threat to the British submarines, although research will doubtless give rise to considerably improved capabilities in the next decade. Should such be the case, the superpowers too would wish to preserve their second-strike capability, perhaps through the creation of an ASW-free zone in the ocean from which British submarines could also benefit. While it is possible that a British submarine could, unless counter-measures are taken, be trailed over long periods of time after leaving port, such counter-measures as simple as decoys or of far greater sophistication could be employed. It is perhaps salutary to remember that a vessel only has to escape once to regain its full second-strike capability, whereas to deprive it of it, ASW has to be totally effective. Nevertheless, it is prudent not to be sanguine in such matters. While the long-

term survivability of the submarines against ASW measures needs to be
kept under review, the penetrative capability of Polaris missiles *vis-à-vis*
Soviet defences presents less of a potential problem. The ABM agreement in SALT ensures that Soviet cities are vulnerable to British
missiles and even an abrogation of that agreement is unlikely to mean
that all major Soviet cities would have the necessary protection against
the British force. In the present situation it is likely that British missiles
could penetrate the existing ABM defences of Moscow. The SALT
agreements do, however, present a potential threat to the British
deterrent, in that in accepting the limitation of numbers of submarines
and launchers, the Soviet Union unilaterally declared that it would take
into consideration British and French vessels when counting United
States submarines. Although this has little import at present, it might
conceivably cause the United States to put pressure on Britain should
either the United States or France wish to increase numbers in the
future.

The current cost of the deterrent is insignificant — some one or two
per cent of the defence budget — but in considering any option other
than immediate nuclear disarmament or 'fading away', financial limitations are of great importance. This is particularly the case of options
that require expenditure before the mid-1980s, because there is intense
pressure on the defence budget both from the government's determination to cut public expenditure generally and from the financial demands
of existing projects such as the through-deck cruiser and the multi-role
combat aircraft. In the future such pressures may ease due to a healthier
economy generally and the completion of existing projects. This problem can be seen even if the present government merely wishes to maintain the effectiveness of the deterrent — its declared policy.

Since missiles cannot be stored indefinitely, Britain's Polaris stocks
will require replenishment long before the hulls of the submarines are
worn out. Britain's reliance on the United States in this matter is total,
but there is no reason to believe that the United States will not continue to be most helpful over defence questions in the future. However,
such help may prove more costly than hitherto. The United States is at
present converting 31 of its 41 Polaris submarines to Poseidon, and
thereafter it may decide either to scrap, adapt for other purposes or
replace the remaining 10 submarines in order to remain within the
SALT limitations. At the moment the United States is bound to supply
Britain with missiles, but what will the situation be after the con-
version? It is not certain that the United States is obliged to supply
Britain and maintain the support facilities when it no longer has Polaris

submarines of its own. If it agrees to do so, would the cost of maintaining the facilities be borne by Britain, by the United States or be
apportioned between them? A possible solution to this problem might
be the purchase by Britain of all or part of the existing stocks of
missiles, which are considerable, and an attempt made to prolong their
life through refrigeration. Consideration might also be given to the
purchase of additional surplus United States boats if they are still
serviceable and if the United States is willing to sell, bearing in mind the
Soviet Union's stated views on the SALT limitations — but these are
onerous conditions to satisfy. On the other hand, if the United States
does not prove co-operative, Britain could develop its own missiles or
convert the existing missiles to a MIRV. Some work may at present be
going on for a British MIRV, or at least to be in an advanced state of
readiness should the option be chosen. This would satisfy both scientific and service desires to stay in touch with the frontiers of research.
It is also argued that it would refurbish Britain's prestige as a nuclear
military power, signify potential procurement, provide a possible *quid
pro quo* for co-operation with the French and an assurance in the event
of disengagement by the United States. In whatever way the government decides to maintain the effectiveness of the present deterrent, it
will be involved in greater expenditure than at the moment and such
decisions may be necessary before the end of the decade, perhaps
thereby giving rise to another great debate on the deterrent.

     If a future government decides to replace the existing deterrent it
may, like the United States, opt for Poseidon. The advantage of
Poseidon is that it can carry a greater number of warheads than Polaris,
it is 'mirved' and it has a slightly longer range. Moreover, having converted its submarines the United States is likely to keep them in its inventory, along with the support facilities, for a reasonable length of
time, although not necessarily as long as the hulls of the present British
boats will last. For Britain the interest does not lie in the 'mirving' or
the number of warheads, since Britain could 'mirv' the existing Polaris
and a counter-city force does not require such numbers of warheads. It
lies in the longevity of the system (which nevertheless is still in
question, given the finite limits on numbers agreed in SALT and the
desire of the United States to introduce new systems, thus obliging it
to scrap old ones due to the SALT ceilings) and in its availability.
Whether Poseidon will be treated by the United States as falling under
the original Polaris agreement with Britain or whether it will be prepared to supply it in any case is open to speculation, although the Conservative Government thought that Poseidon would fall under the ori-

ginal agreement and that the United States would therefore be obliged
to supply it. Either way the cost will be significant at a time when the
British defence budget is already under pressure. Thus, given the cost,
the limited additional military value and doubts over its continued availability, it seems that a British Government would be well advised to
look elsewhere if it is contemplating a successor to the present deterrent.

In the United States, development of the Trident I missile is continuing and it is expected to be deployed in mid-1978, when it will be
fitted into ten Poseidon boats. It could also be fitted into the British
Polaris boats and would double their range, so that they would have a
greater possibility of evading ASW measures. In addition, there is the
7,000-mile-range Trident 2, esconced in a completely new 24-tube submarine. The submarine is scheduled to be operational in 1978 with
Trident I missiles — the Trident 2 missiles not being available before
the mid-1980s. Trident 2, which cannot be fitted into a Polaris-Poseidon
boat, and the new submarine are likely to be exceedingly expensive and
not cost-effective for Britain's relatively unsophisticated needs of a
minimum counter-city force. Trident I in the present boats has the
attraction of a reasonably long-term future and obviates the problem of
the continuing supply of Polaris or the problematic period of deployment of Poseidon. There remain, however, those hardy perennials —
cost and the willingness of the United States to make the missiles available.

The possibilities of co-operation with the United States have not yet
been exhausted. A 1,750-mile-range cruise missile is under development.
It can be air-launched or fired from surface vessels or from submarines.
The cost of a missile may be no more than that of a battle tank, it flies
so low that radar detection is difficult and terminal guidance gives it
great accuracy. In short, it can be the effective vehicle of a deterrent
for a medium or small power and it is thus likely to be a great incite-
ment to horizontal proliferation. The prospect of such proliferation
may induce Britain to remain a nuclear power and it may seek to purchase cruise missiles 'off the shelf' from the United States or develop
them independently. Their cheapness, their accuracy, their penetra-
bility and their proliferation could keep Britain a member of an expanding nuclear club.

A final option does not involve the United States, but France or
other European Community countries. France's prowess in the nuclear
field and the shudder of fear that would pass through Europe if the
Federal Republic of Germany were to have unfettered access to nuclear

weapons and the reactions that might well entail suggest that Anglo-French nuclear co-operation is the more likely option. Such co-operation, if limited to targeting and deployment, could be immediate, whether within or without the NATO framework. Technical co-operation, however, is for the future and may be subject to a United States veto, since the British force has become heavily dependent on information provided by the United States and the passing of such information to third parties requires United States approval. More generally, even if Britain kept to the letter of its agreements with the United States, so long as the United States remains firmly committed to the defence of Europe, both conventionally and with its deterrent, a British Government is likely to heed the wishes of the United States. For its part, there are signs that the United States may look upon Anglo-French nuclear co-operation with greater equanimity in the future than in the past. Such a change in the attitude of the United States is important, since the United States commitment is still a cardinal aim of British defence and foreign policy. With a more permissive attitude on the part of the United States and a less Gaullist frame of mind on matters of nuclear co-operation in Paris, Anglo-French co-operation may look more promising due to the complementarity of Anglo-French skills (the former in warheads, the latter in missiles), due to the sharing of costs of future developments, and due to a common belief that it is very healthy for there to be an independent European nuclear force as a supplement to the United States nuclear guarantee of Europe. Should this United States commitment be relinquished, then Anglo-French co-operation is a real possibility. Nevertheless, the real barriers to Anglo-French co-operation are political and economic: the political will does not at present exist, although this is slowly changing, as is the perception of the economic need for such co-operation. If, however, NATO collapsed — an eventuality that Mr Mason sometimes evoked when talking of the deterrent — a joint cruise missile programme could be an eventuality in any case.

Finally mention of one other aspect of the Anglo-French nuclear relationship should be made — that most British governments would be reluctant to accede to a situation in which France remained a nuclear power and Britain did not. The cost of joint development, independent development or purchase 'off the shelf' of a future delivery system will be considerable, but a future government faced with yet another round of defence cuts might decide that if Britain cannot afford a deterrent and the three arms of the services, then it would make the best of a bad job by concentrating on the deterrent and the Royal Navy, while re-

ducing the army to a token force in Germany and an internal security
and territorial defence force in Britain, with the RAF relegated to a
supporting role. In such a situation, this perusal of options suggests that
future British governments are most likely to consider the purchase of
Polaris missile stocks and possibly submarines from the United States,
the purchase of Trident I for the present submarines, and the purchase,
independent or joint manufacture of cruise missiles. Given no increased
perception of threat and the continued commitment of the United
States to NATO, the most important variables are cost, nuclear proliferation and United States co-operation. While the present Labour Government may leave the decision to a successor, it seems probable that a
future Conservative Government will strive to maintain a second-strike
counter-city force through the purchase or manufacture of a new generation delivery system.

The arguments about the deterrent have lost their sting. The Soviet
'threat' does not appear as menacing as once it did to British governments. Britain no longer claims first-class status or even a 'special
relationship' with the United States. Bureaucratic momentum may keep
the deterrent in being, but only while the cost is modest, and the
civilian nuclear programme has for long been separate from the military
enterprise. The public debate is muted. Yet the deterrent remains and is
likely to continue to do so. It satisfies a basic urge for independence,
for a say in the holocaust – a macabre form of participation. The
possibility of acting provides an element of reassurance which governments, no matter how pragmatic in opposition, may go to considerable
lengths to preserve to a surprising degree of public approval. Interdependence in the everyday management of the deterrent when it matters
little cannot hide its principal rationale – an independent role in basic
security matters in the last resort.

Notes

1. This chapter is derived largely from my *British Thinking about Nuclear
    Weapons* (London, Frances Pinter, 1974) to which reference should be
    made for the evidence on which many comments in this chapter are based.
    In order not to clog the chapter with footnotes I have not referred to my
    earlier work in footnotes. It is, however, the principal source of further
    reading for my own views and the data on which they are based.
2. The reader is reminded that the story is partial, since important parts of it
    are covered in other chapters, particularly those dealing with the Anglo-
    American relationship, NATO and strategic thought.

3.   Professor Margaret Gowing's official histories cover this period. Mrs Gowing
      concentrates on the debate within government and the policy to which it
      gave rise. My own work starts with the outcome and then considers the re-
      action to it by the political parties and other interested groups and per-
      sons. The volumes are thus complementary. Mrs Gowing's volumes are
      Britain and Atomic Energy 1939-45 (London, Macmillan, 1964) and *Inde-
      pendence and Deterrence: Britain and Atomic Energy, 1945-52* (London,
      Macmillan, 1974), 2 volumes.
4.   For text see Gowing I, *1939-45,* op. cit., Appendix 2.
5.   Quoted in J. Pickersgill, *The Mackenzie-King Record 1939-1944* (Chicago,
      University of Chicago Press, 1960), Vol. I, p. 532.
6.   *Hansard,* House of Commons, vol. 520, col. 30, 3. ix. 53.
7.   *Statement on Defence* (London, HMSO, 1955), Cmd 9391, para. 22.
8.   See *Hansard,* House of Commons, vol. 537, cols. 1894-1905, i.iii. 55 for
      the full speech.
9.   Sir Anthony Eden, *Full Circle* (London, Cassell, 1959), p. 372.
10.   *Defence: Outline of Future Policy* (London, HMSO, April 1957, Cmnd
      124); *Report on Defence: Britain's Contribution to Peace and Security*
      (London, HMSO, February 1958), Cmnd. 363.
11.   Ibid., 1957, para. 6.
12.   Ibid., para. 15.
13.   1958, Cmnd. 363, op. cit., para. 5.
14.   Ibid., para. 31.
15.   Ibid., para. 12
16.   See *Agreement for Co-operation on the Uses of Atomic Energy for Mutual
      Defence Purposes* (London, HMSO, 1958), Cmnd. 537.
17.   *Report on Defence 1961* (London, HMSO, February 1961), Cmnd. 1288,
      paras. 6, 10.
18.   *The Times,* 6 April 1961.
19.   On 16 June 1962.
20.   *The Bahamas Meetings* (London, HMSO, 1962), Cmnd. 1915, para. 8.
21.   Ibid., paras. 6-8.
22.   *The Times,* 11 Jan. 1963.
23.   Ibid., 24 Dec. 1962.
24.   *Statement on the Defence Estimates 1965* (London, HMSO, February
      1965), Cmnd. 2592, Part I, para. 1.
25.   Ibid., para. 9.
26.   Ibid., para. 14·
27.   Ibid., para. 15.
28.   *Hansard,* vol. 704, col. 694, 17 Dec. 1964.
29.   Bruce Reed and Geoffrey Williams, *Denis Healey and the Policies of Power*
      (London, Sidgwick and Jackson, 1971), p. 167.
30.   Ibid., p. 169.
31.   *Statement on the Defence Estimates 1970* (London, HMSO, February
      1970), Cmnd. 4290, Ch. I. para. 20.
32.   Ibid., para. 22.
33.   Ibid., para. 24.
34.   Some press reports suggest that Mr Heath did raise the issue on a visit to
      Washington in January 1973.
35.   Edward Heath, *Old World, New Horizon: Britain, the Common Market and
      the Atlantic Alliance* (London, Oxford University Press, 1970), p. 73.
36.   *The Times,* 8 Mar. 1974.
37.   *Financial Times,* 2 Nov. 1974.
38.   *Statement on the Defence Estimates 1975* (London, HMSO, March 1975),

Cmnd. 5976.

39.   Ibid., Ch. I, paras. 20, 21 and 23.
40.   Ibid., para. 25c.
41.   *Second Report from Expenditure Committee Session 1974-75.* The
      Defence Review Proposals, 6 Mar. 1975 (London, HMSO), p.xi, para. 16.
42.   *Second Report from the Expenditure Committee Session 1975-76.*
      Defence Minutes of Evidence taken 13 May 1975. Memorandum by the
      Ministry of Defence (SCOE 73/1), 9 May 1975. (London, HMSO, paras.
      32-4).
43.   *Hansard,* 15 April 1975, col. 251, Mr Mason, Minister of Defence.
44.   See *The Times,* Henry Stanhope, Defence Correspondent, 3 June 1976.
45.   For greater detail on the present situation and future options consult
      Expenditure Committee (Defence and External Affairs Sub-Committee),
      Minutes of Evidence, 13 Feb. 1973, Session 1972-73, Mr François Duchêne,
      (London, HMSO, 1973) and *Twelfth Report from the Expenditure Com-
      mittee,* Session 1972-73, Nuclear Weapons Programme (London, HMSO,
      1973).
46.   McGeorge Bundy, Presidential adviser to two United States Presidents, has
      written 'In the real world of real political leaders whether here [the
      United States] or in the Soviet Union — a decision that would bring even
      one hydrogen bomb on one city of one's own country would be recog-
      nised in advance as a catastrophic blunder; ten bombs on ten cities would
      be a disaster beyond history; and a hundred bombs on a hundred cities are
      unthinkable' in 'To Cap the Volcano', *Foreign Affairs,* October 1969, p. 10
      — a view endorsed by President Nixon, who argued, 'Any nuclear attack —
      no matter how small; whether accidental, unauthorised or by design, by a
      superpower or by a country with only a primitive nuclear capability —
      would be a catastrophe for the United States, no matter how devastating
      our ability to retaliate' in 'Foreign Policy for the 1970s: A New Strategy
      for Peace', reprinted in the *New York Times,* 19 Feb. 1970.

6 BRITISH STRATEGIC THOUGHT

John C. Garnett

If, as is generally acknowledged, the capacity for violence is inherent in a world of independent sovereign states, then no one should be surprised, either by the high priority which states put upon the acquisition of military power, or by the frequency with which states threaten and use it in their relations with each other. And, equally, given its importance, no one should be surprised that military power has, over the years,attracted analysis and speculation. Strategic thought is the description usually given to the considerable body of analytical propositions which have been advanced about the use and misuse of military power.

But in Britain, those who have reflected in this way have been the exception rather than the rule. In his masterly review of the history of strategic thought,[1] E.M. Earle regarded only a handful of British strategic thinkers as being of sufficient stature to be included in his study. And if he was writing today it is doubtful whether his list would be very much longer. The British, it seems, regard force as their forefathers regarded sex — something which must occasionally be indulged but which should never be talked about. In the words of P.M.S. Blackett, one of the most influential defence commentators in the post war years, 'Traditionally, Britain has been averse to thinking about war in between fighting wars; once they are over, we tend to forget them until the next time.'[2]

And yet, a variety of specialised journals, particularly those of the armed services,[3] have always devoted themselves to military subjects; but only very rarely have their contributors lifted their heads from minor tactical issues, personal reminiscences, or chunks of military history. Soldiers were not, and are not, encouraged to express their views on subjects which inevitably have a high political content, and even today, in a much more enlightened atmosphere, the armed services contribute very little to the literature of strategic studies. Those who have something to say usually wait until retirement is imminent before putting pen to paper. Of course there are exceptions; General Sir John Cowley was one. In November 1959,in a lecture at the Royal United Services Institution,he delivered a broadside attack on the government's prevailing nuclear philosophy.[4] Cowley was only saying

156

in public what many senior officers were thinking in private, but his well reasoned analysis contradicted government policy and ruffled a few feathers. The new Minister Harold Watkinson assured the House of Commons that it would not happen again.

Since then, there have, of course, been other books, letters and comments by serving officers; but none of them has been quite so explicit in criticising the main thrust of government policy. Even today, when serving officers tread, albeit ever so lightly, on matters political, the spectre of militarism is raised in the minds of some. In 1971 F. Kitson published his *Low Intensity Operations.*[5] In essence this was an unexceptional series of reflections on counter-insurgency techniques by a soldier whose military career uniquely qualified him to comment. There were one or two controversial ideas perhaps, but nothing which justified the irrational fears of a military take-over which came in the wake of publication.[6]

In general, serving officers are discouraged from thinking aloud without prior permission. Indeed they are forbidden by army law to communicate anything but official policy to the press. But even when they are positively encouraged, through the Defence Fellowship scheme, to systematically study and write about a defence related subject, they have tended to steer away from mainstream strategic analysis. It is a matter of regret that the Defence Fellowship scheme has produced so little in the way of strategic thought, and it is an equally sad reflection on the various staff colleges, the National Defence College, and the Royal College of Defence Studies that virtually no creative strategic thinking is done there. A recent article in *The Times*[7] has commented on the way in which circumstances have conspired to breed out of the armed forces 'the unfashionable maverick who might have had the moral courage and energy to risk his career and drag the question of national security into the arena of public debate. He has been replaced by the skilful bureaucrat who does not have independent means and who has therefore learned never to rock the boat. The author, who, significantly, remains anonymous, is surely right in his view that serving officers must be encouraged to play a larger part in public debate. The value of service opinion is that it is *responsible* opinion. P.M.S. Blackett once drew attention to the point that 'the essential prerequisite of sound military advice is that the giver must convince himself that if he were responsible for action, he would himself act so.'[8] Military men do have to push buttons and pull triggers, and because the responsibility for waging war is theirs, their thoughts on the subject are usually worth listening to. Surely, we can all agree with Blackett that 'war is much too serious a matter to be left to professors.'[9]

On the whole then, with some notable exceptions, the services have proved a disappointing source for British strategic thought since the Second World War. Nevertheless, it has to be said that there is now more interest in defence within the armed forces than ever before, and even the rather staid and conservative military journals reflect this lively interest in contemporary strategic affairs. As an indication of where service interest was focused in the mid-1950s, one author analysed the articles published in the *Journal of the Royal United Services Institution* in 1954.[10] Of a total of 53, only 18 dealt with contemporary military affairs; 21 were about military history before the First World War and the rest were mainly about the history of the Second World War. All that has now changed. In 1976 only about 33 per cent of the articles published in RUSI were historical. Today all the service journals have a more professional flavour about them. Editors are less afraid of political content and there is a much greater sense of relevance to current military problems.

In the early post war years, the British defence community, that is to say, that group of individuals interested and articulate about current military problems, was very small and largely confined to officials or ex-officials in government departments, recently retired officers in the armed forces, and those scientists who had been engaged in military research during the Second World War. The men who dominated the strategic debates after 1945 were very 'establishment' figures. Amongst the scientific names which crop up most frequently in the historical record are those of P.M.S. Blackett, a Nobel prizewinning physicist who had pioneered operational research in the military field during the war, and who continued to comment on nuclear matters until well into the 1960s; Sir Henry Tizard, one time chairman of the Committee for the Scientific Survey of Air Defence, and later chairman of the Defence Research Policy Committee and the Advisory Council on Scientific policy; and Sir Solly Zuckerman, Chief Scientific Advisor to the Government from 1964 until 1971.

Amongst the service figures whose names recur in the literature, Marshal of the Royal Air Force, Sir John Slessor, and Sir Antony Buzzard, one time chief of Naval Intelligence, dominated the scene. Slessor in his *Strategy for the West* and *The Great Deterrent* made a formidable contribution to British strategic thinking, and, as an influential member of the Chiefs of Staff Committee which in 1952 produced the Global Strategy Paper, was in a very good position to influence government policy. Buzzard will be best remembered for his pioneering ideas on limited war which are most fully explained in 'Massive Retaliation and Graduated Response', *World Politics,* January 1956, and in 'The H-Bomb, Massive Retaliation or Graduated Deterrence' (a discussion between Buzzard, Slessor and Richard Lowenthal), *International Affairs,* April 1956. Another influential figure in those early years was Captain Liddell Hart, the doyen of British strategy, who in 1950 produced *Defence of the West* and in 1960 *Deterrence or Defence,* both outstandingly perceptive analyses of Western defence problems. During the 1950s, Air Vice Marshal Kingston-McCloughry was also a familiar commentator on British defence policy, and, from a pacifist standpoint, Sir Stephen King Hall developed a reputation as a highly articulate and thoughtful critic of current British thinking about nuclear weapons. Amongst the politicians it was Labour MPs who expressed most interest in the defence field. R. Crossman, D. Healey, G. Wigg and J. Strachey were all frequent commentators both in the House of Commons and in the journals and press.[11]

The most keenly felt strategic problems facing British military thinkers after the Second World War were those arising out of the development of nuclear weapons. Although there were some who believed that the atomic bomb was nothing but a 'bigger and better bomb'[12] with no revolutionary implications for the conduct of either war or peace, most thoughtful commentators recognised the dawn of a new era in warfare. The problem was how to assimilate this new weapon into military thinking. It took a little time for the deterrent implications to become clear, but by the early 1950s a deterrent strategy was beginning to emerge. The Global Strategy Paper of 1952 represents the first systematic elaboration of strategic deterrence in the world, although, as Margaret Gowing has ably documented, the British had been speculating about deterrence and arguing about the priority to be allocated to nuclear weapons production since the end of the war. 'In 1945 the Chiefs of Staff said emphatically that the best method of defence against the new weapons was likely to be the deterrent effect that the possession of the means of retaliation would have on a potential aggressor.'[13] The decision to manufacture the atomic bomb was taken in January 1947, and although there was continual debate about the priority of the nuclear programme, it survived right through the 1950s as a high priority project.[14]

The central thesis of the Global Strategy Paper was that with the development of nuclear weapons, 'total war had abolished itself'. The Western powers should, therefore, concentrate on acquiring a nuclear

deterrent sufficiently powerful to make Soviet aggression an unprofit-
able venture. The paper, which remains classified, recommended that
the Western powers 'should openly declare that Soviet aggression would
be met not only at the local point of conflict, but would be punished
by nuclear retaliation at the Russian heartland'.[15] The Chiefs of Staff
also took note of the potential importance of tactical nuclear weapons
which might make it possible to reduce British conventional forces
from the impossibly high numbers recommended in the Lisbon goals,
to the more politically practical level of about 50,000 men.

In effect, the Global Strategy Paper led the British to 'become the
first nation to base its national security planning almost entirely upon a
declaratory policy of nuclear deterrence',[16] and it gave British defence
policy a nuclear flavour which culminated in the Sandys White Papers
of 1957-8. But it is worth emphasising that Slessor and his colleagues
were much more subtle than the crude 'massive retaliation' supporters
who followed him. They never made the mistake of recklessly downgrading the importance of conventional forces. In *Strategy for the West*
Slessor explained, 'we in the West must be prepared to maintain sufficient conventional forces to deal with what are and should be limited
commitments like Korea and Indo-China by limited methods, without
having recourse to the dreadful arbitrament of atomic air power.'[17] In
short, though the Global Strategy Paper had a nuclear emphasis and
pushed Britain down the nuclear road, it none the less recognised the
continuing importance of conventional forces as well.

Not everyone agreed with Slessor and one of his first and most formidable opponents was Sir Antony Buzzard who was quick to point
out the weaknesses of the great deterrent. As he saw it, the fundamental
weakness of massive retaliation was that it was incapable of dealing
with 'medium aggression, i.e. any aggression too powerful for our small
conventional forces, but not so vital as to warrant the strategic use of
nuclear weapons.'[18] Liddell Hart, in a letter to *The Times*, had also
warned of the dangers of basing defence policy on an 'all or nothing
weapon'.[19] Buzzard therefore recommended a defence policy which,
while maintaining the deterrent against deliberate war, could also provide the local tactical strength necessary to deter limited Communist
aggression.

His strategy of *graduated deterrence*, which was explained in a number of articles, sought to establish clear distinctions between tactical
and strategic targets, between vital and non-vital areas of the world, and
between small atomic weapons and large ones, including hydrogen
bombs. He believed not only that some combination of these distinc-

tions could be translated into practical policy, but also that the Russians could be persuaded to accept them as well. The essence of his idea was that the West should *unilaterally* announce its intention to limit the use of atomic weapons to the minimum necessary to repel aggression, but should not specify in advance just what particular limits would be imposed in any particular situation. By this strategy Buzzard hoped to deter the Soviets from minor as well as major aggressions. As he saw it, the great advantage of *graduated deterrence* over *massive retaliation* was that its implementation was not 'so severe in relation to the issue at stake that the country threatened, or the allies supporting her, will shrink from employing the deterrent if need arises'.[20] Of course Buzzard was well aware that his strategy might not work; but he believed that nothing was lost by trying it since if it failed it was always possible to revert to massive retaliation.

Those acquainted with the evolution of NATO strategy will recognise that this analysis was a dress rehearsal to that of Robert McNamara in the early 1960s. *Flexible response* was the result of an American attempt to grapple with exactly the same problems that worried Buzzard, and although there are differences between *graduated deterrence* and *flexible response*, the same sort of reasoning was common to both. In Britain the notion of *graduated deterrence* was important because it initiated an era of limited war thinking in which naval and conventional forces were seen to be important. Liddell Hart, Denis Healey, P.M.S. Blackett may have disagreed in detail,[21] but in their respective interventions in the debate they all acknowledged the need for greater emphasis on conventional forces. However, the interest in *graduated deterrence* did not undermine the continuing importance of the strategic deterrent; what it did do was to help restore a balance to British defence thinking by forcing politicians to accept the possibility of war beneath the nuclear umbrella.

An examination of those who figured prominently in the *massive retaliation* versus *graduated deterrence* debate suggests that during the early post war years British defence thinking was largely a specialist 'inside' affair. Furthermore, some of those who engaged in it were fairly sceptical of the value of contributions from those who had not been 'positively vetted', and who did not have access to the latest scientific information. A typically 'insider' view was the opinion that 'the raw materials of official strategic decision had become so intricately specialised and so inaccessible that outsiders were no longer able to make intelligent judgements on strategy.'[22] The difficulty with 'in group' debates in a virtually closed system is that they may become iso-

lated from creative criticism. Some years ago, in a discussion of the
Sandys era of defence thinking, L.W. Martin drew attention to the
importance of debating strategic ideas 'in a market wide and open
enough to offer every possible assurance of conceiving and evaluating
alternatives'.[23]

The market for strategic ideas in the United Kingdom is now much
wider. One of the reasons for this is that it has become apparent that in
the nuclear age the traditional identification of strategy with war and
battle was mistaken. Purely military definitions of strategy have now
disappeared because they failed to convey the essence of a subject
which straddles the activities of peace and war and which is as much
concerned with statesmanship as it is with battle. Once the subject was
expanded to include broader aspects of government and national
policymaking at the highest level, it was quickly realised that direct
military experience and classified scientific knowledge about weaponry
were much less important qualifications for studying strategic affairs
than a trained analytical mind grounded preferably in one of the social
sciences or history.

Civilians, particularly American academics, began to be involved in
strategic analysis in a major way, and it is probably true that most of
the present output of strategic analysis and commentary is produced by
civilians working mainly in universities and comparable research institutions. Certainly the foundations of contemporary strategic thought were
laid in a handful of universities and research institutions in the United
States. The contribution of these academic experts was considerable
and is now almost universally acknowledged.

Inevitably, their ideas spilled across the Atlantic and influenced
thinkers in Europe. In Britain 'Strategic Studies' has been a minor
growth industry since the late 1950s. A growing number of academics,
journalists and commentators absorbed and assimilated the American
strategic ideas which have now become the intellectual orthodoxy of
Western strategic thought. However, in the early 1960s at least one
American student could still detect a distinctive flavour about British
strategic thought. Armstrong, in his analysis of British bases,
commented that 'The British strategist . . . treats concrete situations
within a context; he is most reluctant to generalize about the same
situations in the abstract.'[24] And later he says 'In strategy as in law the
Briton prefers the particular to the general, the precedent that is
known to work to the more encompassing general rule.'[25]

There is some truth in this observation. Whereas there is a fundamental, almost timeless quality, about some American strategic theory,

its British counterpart is very firmly related to specific problems facing
the British Government. The theoretical formulations of deterrence
analysis by G. Snyder or A. Wohlstetter[26] have no counterpart in the
British literature. Nor is there any British equivalent to the theorising of
T.C. Schelling on threats and bargaining, or H. Kahn on 'escalation'[27] –
theorising which is at such a fundamental level of enquiry that it can be
applied in any historical time scale. One is tempted to make a distinction between 'pure' and 'applied' strategic thought, and to comment on
a British tendency to avoid the former. Whether this is a strength or
weakness in British strategic thought is a moot point.

American influence effectively widened the discussion of military
affairs, and although there is still no British equivalent of the RAND
Corporation or the Institute for Defence Analysis, strategic thought in
Britain is no longer a purely 'official' activity. The creation of the
Institute for Strategic Studies (now the International Institute for
Strategic Studies) was a major milestone in the evolution of the subject,
and the Institute in Adam Street is now rightly regarded as an international centre of strategic excellence. Its steady output of monographs
and books makes a formidable contribution to strategic thought; and
because it is respected by both 'insiders' and non-government analysts,
it has served as a bridge between the two communities.

Of course there are some who would still argue that British strategists, though more numerous than before, have, by their particular
realpolitik assumptions and methodology, still managed to insulate
themselves from certain kinds of 'protest' criticism. The 'language' of
contemporary strategic thought effectively protects the strategist from
the attacks of those who refuse to consider strategic questions in the
strategist's terms. For all strategists the central 'given' fact of international life is that states use military power both in their relations with
other states and also in an internal security role. As strategists – but
not necessarily as individuals – they neither approve nor disapprove of
this fact. They simply accept it, and this means that for them the
arguments of those who are morally outraged by the use to which military power is put, are at best irrelevant and at worst dangerous. That is
why the arguments of the CND movement, and to a lesser extent those
of Sir Stephen King-Hall,[28] never cut any ice with the strategic community. The strategists simply do not look at the world in that way,
and hence, their receivers are not tuned to the frequency on which a
good deal of criticism is beamed.

And, there are some who are not entirely persuaded that the virtually one-way traffic in strategic ideas from the United States has been

beneficial. P.M.S. Blackett expressed a typically British point of view when he commented on recent American strategic thinking. 'The intellectual level of much of this discussion is of the highest, so high that I find much of it very hard to understand, and I wonder sometimes whether it is all rooted in military and political reality.'[29] Sir Solly Zuckerman, in the Lees-Knowles lectures delivered in 1965, was even more sceptical about the value of contemporary American theorising. Commenting on the ideas of H. Kahn and T.C. Schelling he expressed the view that 'this kind of writing has no foundation in experience and, in particular, experience of warfare. Moreover, it is based upon assumptions about human behaviour which seem totally unreal. It neither constitutes scientific analysis nor scientific theorising, but is a non-science of untestable speculations about Western and Soviet bloc behaviour . . .'[30]

It is, perhaps, worth mentioning that the traffic in strategic ideas has not all been one way. In the early post-war years, at least one idea originated in Britain and moved across the Atlantic. Various commentators have noted that some of the ideas incorporated in the Global Strategy Paper of 1952 strongly influenced the evolution of strategic doctrine in the West, and in particular helped to originate the 'New Look' military policy of the Eisenhower years. Huntington makes the point that 'while the wealthier country was able to develop new weapons earlier than the poorer one, nonetheless, the poorer one, largely because of its more limited resources, often was first in adjusting its military policies to the new technological developments.'[31] That may have been fair comment on the alacrity with which the British recognised the advantages of a deterrent posture, but as R. Rosecrance has noted, it fails to take into account the fact that Britain hung on to its nuclear strategy long after its disadvantages had made themselves evident to other powers.[32]

And it is easy to overestimate the extent to which the 'New Look' developed from the ideas of Sir John Slessor and the British Chiefs. It is true that Slessor took the Global Strategy Paper to the United States, but there is a sense in which the 'New Look' was simply a rationalisation of the American need to reduce defence expenditure which had risen dramatically because of the Korean war. In other words, the same economic pressures which had led the British to emphasise nuclear power were also felt in the United States, and it is highly probable that the Eisenhower administration would have adopted a defence policy with a nuclear emphasis even if the Chiefs of Staff Paper had never been written. What is true, however, is that the British analysis provided add-

itional intellectual fuel for those who were already thinking along similar lines.

One of the difficulties of discussing British strategic thought lies in
distinguishing it from, and relating it to, British defence policy. The
history of British defence policy since the Second World War is clearly
not the same as the history of British strategic thought during that
period, although, obviously, the two are connected. Policy takes place
in the realm of political action. It is devised by governments to deal
with practical problems which, in the interests of good government,
must be solved. Thought, be it political or strategic, is a purely cerebral
activity which, though it is frequently prompted by the practical
problems of government, does not have any immediate policy implications at all.

In theory at least, the difference between strategic thought and
military policy is as clear as the distinction between political theory
and the behaviour of politicians. Politicians, it is hoped, justify their
actions and formulate their policies in terms of their acquaintance with
political ideas about the nature of man and his proper relationship to
other men and to society as a whole, but only rarely are politicians
political thinkers themselves. Similarly, defence planners are not
usually strategic thinkers – though in Britain there was something of
an overlap in the early post war years. But defence planners certainly
formulate their policies partly by reference to the strategic ideas which
form the intellectual climate of their professional lives.

Writing of the Sandys era, L.W. Martin makes the point that British
civil servants tended to deny that public strategic debate had much
influence on their recommendations.[33] But as he says 'one can often
trace a notion from a commentator in one year, to the lips of a parliamentary critic in the next, and to the White Paper or ministerial speech
in the third.'[34] If that was true in the 1950s it is even more true today
when strategic debate in Britain is wider and less cloaked in official
secrecy.

There is, of course, a time lag between the moment when strategic
ideas are generated by the defence community and the moment when
those ideas are incorporated in government policy. This means that
policy and thought are usually out of step with each other, and one can
see examples of this in the 1950s in Britain. In official circles the ideas
implicit in the Global Strategy Paper held sway long after the most informed commentators had either abandoned them or qualified them
beyond recognition. The 1957-58 Defence White Papers were cast in
the Slessor mould even though by that time the critics of *massive retali-*

ation far outnumbered its defenders.

The delay between the emergence of ideas in the defence community and their eventual appearance in some, usually emasculated, form in the declared policy of the government, may be regarded as inevitable and normal. It takes time for ideas to catch on, to develop the groundswell of informed support which is a necessary prerequisite for their survival in the government machine. But sometimes there is a delay in the implementation of ideas even after they have become part of government policy. This is a more puzzling phenomenon which suggests either that governments may not have much confidence in their declaratory policy and therefore set about hedging their bets by not implementing it properly, or alternatively, that operational policy, like a super oil tanker at sea, is not sensitive to light touches on the tiller in the form of government White Papers. There is a momentum about operational defence policy which cannot be quickly altered.

Thus, although the Conservative Government under Churchill accepted the overwhelming importance of nuclear deterrence, as outlined in the Global Strategy Paper, it continued to deploy substantial forces in Europe. Another curious lag in the implementation of declaratory policy occurred in the reluctance of the post-war Labour Government to designate the V-bombers which would deliver nuclear bombs a 'super-priority weapon'. In spite of the fact that the nuclear weapons programme itself had been allocated the highest priority by Attlee in 1947, it was not until 1953 — after the acceptance of the Global Strategy Paper by the Conservatives — that the decision was taken to give top priority to the delivery system for the British nuclear payload.

The same gap between official doctrine and the actual policies pursued can also be observed in the wider context of NATO strategy. The Lisbon goals were never met and so the alliance was never able to adopt a predominantly conventional strategy. Even the revised target of 30 divisions suggested by MC-70 was never met. *Massive retaliation* was never carried through to its logical conclusion of relying solely on nuclear weapons. Even the current doctrine of *flexible response* has not led to any very significant changes in manpower levels. BAOR, for example, still operates at a strength of about 50,000 men, which is more or less what it was at the end of the 1950s. In the defence field implementing change is a slow process. Hence, the most plausible explanation for any policy in a given year is that that is the way it happened the previous year.

There is usually a delay in the acceptance of strategic ideas by governments; there is frequently a delay between the acceptance of ideas and their implementation; inevitably, sometimes there is a delay in both, and the fluctuating fortunes of the idea of 'strategic mobility' is an excellent example of this. This idea had been around in defence circles at least since 1946 when Liddell Hart advocated the replacement of ordinary infantry divisions by airborne divisions which could draw their heavy equipment from regional depots.[35] Since the late 1940s various defence commentators floated the idea of constituting an air portable ground force as a strategic reserve to act as a 'fire brigade', ready to fly off at the first whiff of smoke. It is perfectly true that the logistical problems implicit in this idea were underestimated, as also were the difficulties of 'overflying' certain Middle Eastern countries; but in spite of the difficulties, the creation of a mobile strategic reserve became official policy in 1954. However, it was not until the 1960s that the policy began to have any practical significance. As Phillip Darby puts it, 'Some twelve years after the idea of an air-lifted strategic reserve had first gained currency in defence circles, and about four years after the scheme had become government policy, the provision of transport aircraft began to obtain the firm backing of the government and of the Air Staff.'[36]

The connection between strategic ideas and strategic policies is a complicated one, and it is not always the case that policies bestow official recognition, however belated, on ideas which have already gained currency in the defence community. Sometimes strategic thought, instead of stimulating policy innovations, merely rationalises existing policy. In the NATO context, for example, it is difficult to escape the conclusion that the NATO strategy of 'flexible response' represents an answer to the question 'Given our present force levels and defence policies, what is the most coherent strategy we can pursue?' It is not an answer to the question, what in the face of the Soviet threat, is the best strategy for NATO? In the British context much strategic theorising since the Second World War has been a justification of economic necessity or special interests.

A classic case is provided by the idea of 'broken-backed warfare' which was incorporated in the Global Strategy Paper largely because it suggested a role for the navy and for conventional forces already in being. The idea, in essence, was that after an initial nuclear exchange, nuclear forces would be exhausted and a period of broken-backed warfare would follow, during which the opposing sides would seek to recover their strength, carrying on the struggle as best they could. Most people thought the idea was obsolete even before it was formulated, but it was included in the Paper in order to placate the navy and because Slessor believed that at worst it was harmless, and at best, that it kept options open in a time of uncertainty.

Although the British were quick to recognise the significance of nuclear and thermo-nuclear weapons and spent a good deal of intellectual energy on thinking through their military implications, they were much less successful in analysing or even identifying the other major change in the circumstances facing Britain in the post-war world. From the point of view of British defence policy, the erosion of empire, initially signalled by the independence of India in 1947, was at least as important as the development of the atomic bomb, and yet far less attention was paid to it by the defence community.

One of the reasons for this was that whereas atomic weapons were a dramatic innovation, the erosion of empire was a much slower process which was scarcely appreciated at the time. In spite of the loss of India, which, in retrospect at least, had profound strategic implications, pre-war assumptions about Britain's imperial role and responsibilities continued to hold sway in Whitehall until long after the Suez crisis initiated a slow re-examination of Britain's east of Suez role.

After the war, traditional military bases were re-established except where a post-war change in sovereignty made it impossible; but no one asked what the bases were for or whether the traditional imperial role was sustainable in the post-war world. In a sense, victory had disguised the reality of British weakness, so that when the shooting stopped the British Government was able, without thinking about it, to resume the imperial tradition of a world power. And because this policy was never challenged, it continued to survive long after the power base which made it possible had disappeared.

Of course, a few perceptive analysts recognised the problem, but they were a small minority. In the House of Commons in 1953 John Strachey made their point.

> We must concentrate. We must stop stationing all our available
> forces — land forces, at any rate — all over the world . . . what this
> means is a radical revision of the tradition of our world defence
> policy. It means ceasing to try to behave as if we are still the leading
> world empire. From the date . . . of India's assumption of independence a re-orientation of our whole attitude was absolutely necessary.[37]

But in 1953 not many agreed with Strachey. Even after Suez, Britain's involvement was staunchly defended in terms of traditional commit-

ments, legal alliances, peacekeeping operations and the preservation of
economic interests. According to Phillip Darby, behind these rational-
isations lay deeper explanations of British policy. First, 'British troops
were already deployed East of Suez; they supported a preferred pattern
of world order; and the government required very good reasons to
withdraw them.' Second, the British had an ingrained sense of responsibility towards their ex-colonies — what Darby calls 'an element of
straight idealism'. And third, 'there was the continuing influence of the
pattern of thinking that Britain was a world power.'[38]

During the early 1960s, the British actually developed an expanded
conception of their 'peacekeeping' world role and there was a decided
east of Suez emphasis in Britain's defence policy at a time when one
Asian emergency after another occupied the government's attention.
The authors of the 1962 White Paper while acknowledging Britain's
obligations to Europe, went out of their way to emphasise its role in
contributing 'to the defence of freedom and the maintenance of peace,
not only in Europe but also in the Near East, the Middle East and the
Far East, all areas of vital interest to the Free World as a whole'.[39] In
1964 Harold Wilson claimed that 1,000 men east of Suez were prefer-
able to another 1,000 in Germany,[40] and Healey endorsed this view
with his comment that

> our most important and worthwhile job in the 10 or 20 years we can
> foresee . . . will be . . . the prevention of anarchy and war in those
> areas of the world, many of them newly independent, in Asia, the
> Middle East and Africa and perhaps in Central America.[41]

Not until the late 1960s did the call for withdrawal from Arabia, the
Persian Gulf and the Far East become an irresistible pressure, and even
then it was the constraint of reduced economic circumstances and
balance of payment difficulties rather than strategic reasoning which
produced the change. On the subject of Britain's world role, thinking
was of a responsive rather than anticipatory character. Throughout the
post-war period no British government succeeded in synchronising
Britain's defence policy outside Europe either with the process of decolonisation or the relative decline in British power.

One of the unforeseen consequences of meeting the obligations
arising out of a world role was that British soldiers, almost inadvertently,
built up a wealth of experience of small wars, policing, and counter-
insurgency operations. Between 1947 and 1967 British forces were involved in maintaining order in British Guiana, British Honduras, Kenya,

Aden, the Gold Coast, Hong Kong, Jamaica, the Cameroons, Zanzibar, Tanganyika, Uganda and Mauritius. And in Malaya and Borneo British soldiers fought protracted anti-terrorist campaigns for years on end.

Unfortunately, the techniques for handling small wars and insurgencies received very little consideration by British strategists in the early post-war years. It was left to the practitioners under the guidance of experienced soldiers like Lieutenant General Sir Harold Briggs and General Sir Gerald Templar to generalise from their practical experience and to develop effective techniques for countering insurgents. General Templar's *Conduct of Anti-Terrorist Operations in Malaya* was first produced in 1952,[42] and it soon became the official handbook for soldiers whose initial training was almost irrelevant to 'irregular warfare'.

But there was very little attempt to reflect in a systematic way about the kind of operations British soldiers found themselves engaged in until the 1960s when a spate of writing about guerrilla warfare prompted a parallel interest in counter-insurgency techniques. In a number of books and articles, Sir Robert Thompson, a veteran of the Malayan emergency, attempted to distil his experience into a coherent counter-revolutionary strategy.[43] He identified five principles of successful counter-insurgency. First, that the government should have a clear political aim; second, that it should always operate within the law; third, that it should have an overall plan that included political, social, economic, and police measures as well as military measures; fourth that it should give priority to defeating political subversion; and fifth, that it should secure its 'base areas' first.

There is a discernible difference between the kind of strategic analysis engaged in by Blackett, Buzzard and Slessor in the early post-war years, and much of what is produced today. The early British writers were laying intellectual foundation stones upon which those who followed could build; they were involved, albeit in a minor way, in the process of formulating those ideas of deterrence, arms control, limited war and crisis management which are now the main organising concepts of contemporary strategic thought.

By the mid-1960s — and largely as a result of American scholarship — that framework of analysis was virtually complete, and, in addition, the main lines of Western strategy were drawn. To the extent that the early writers were successful in providing an intellectual apparatus which stood up to the test of time and proved adequate for analysing and comprehending current policies and problems, the scope for further inventiveness diminished. Creative strategic theorising tended to give way to the refinement of established ideas, to sophisticated commentary on military problems, and to a highly professional 'micro' analysis of very specific topics. In other words, the bare bones of the subject were created in the 1950s and early 1960s, and the flesh has been added since that time.

A glance at recent Adelphi Papers[44] will confirm the professional and detailed nature of current military research, and an examination of the writings of such scholars as Hedley Bull, Laurence Martin, Michael Howard, and the late Alastair Buchan, will confirm both the sophistication and the lucidity of strategic commentary and criticism from this side of the Atlantic. Mercifully, all of these commentators have been free of the jargon which has bedevilled much American scholarship, and their clarity of thought and expression has, in itself, been a major contribution to strategic thought.

There is perhaps a further explanation for the diminution of mainstream strategic theorising in Britain. The United Kingdom is no longer a great power and in consequence no longer has the strategic responsibilities which spur new thought. Britain's decline may not have been appreciated after the Second World War, but it is certainly accepted now. One of the consequences of this is that strategic initiatives have been increasingly monopolised by the United States with Britain cast in a supporting role.

And in so far as strategic thought is developed in the wake of developments in weapon technology, it was inevitably the American inventors who first reflected upon the strategic implications of such developments as anti-ballistic missiles, cruise missiles and new weapons of mass destruction. Although these weapons undoubtedly affect the security of the British they are fundamentally beyond Britain's control, and the incentive to think about them is therefore diminished. Certainly there has been no British equivalent to the ABM debate or the current debate in the United States about SALT and the the cruise missile.

In Britain, interest in strategic matters has not suffered the fluctuating fortunes of its American counterpart. There has been no mushrooming growth comparable to that which occurred in the late 1950s and early 1960s, but, equally, there has been no dramatic decline either. This country has witnessed a steady, if unspectacular, quickening of interest in military affairs as a growing number of journalists, civil servants, members of Parliament, serving officers and ordinary members of the public involved themselves in debate. This interest has been buttressed by the attention of a handful of universities, some supported by grants from the Ministry of Defence, who now take seriously the study of strategy at both the undergraduate and postgraduate level, and whose involvement has given the subject a tenuous academic foothold.

Perhaps one of the explanations for this interest in strategic subjects is a growing public awareness that we live in a dangerous world in which our chances of survival may be marginally improved by some intelligent strategic thought. But whatever the explanation, it is probably fair comment that in the United Kingdom, reflecting on the role of military power is a less neglected subject than it used to be.

Notes

1.   E.M. Earle, *Makers of Modern Strategy* (Princeton, Princeton University Press, 1943).
2.   P.M.S. Blackett, *Studies of War* (London and Edinburgh, Oliver and Boyd, 1962), p. 115.
3.   *Journal of the Royal United Services Institute; The Army Quarterly; The British Army Review; The RAF Quarterly; Navy International; Brassey's Annual.*
4.   See 'Future Trends in Warfare', *JRUSI* 105/617, February 1960, pp. 4 -16.
5.   F. Kitson, *Low Intensity Operations* (London, Faber and Faber, 1971).
6.   In his book Kitson suggests that the army should involve itself in the identification, definition and monitoring of subversive threats as well as in the countering of them. Since this sounds very much like a military involve-ment in a *political* activity, criticism was predictable. The flavour of left-wing reaction is conveyed in an article entitled 'The Guru of the New Army', by B. Page and L. Chester in the *Sunday Times*, 14 May, 1972.
7.   *The Times*, 31 March 1977 ' Giving the Khaki bureaucrats their marching orders.'
8.   P.M.S. Blackett, 'Tizard and the Science of War', Tizard Memorial Lecture delivered at The Institute for Strategic Studies, 11 February 1960.
9.   Ibid., p. 116.
10.   Armstrong III, de Witt Clinton, *The Changing Strategy of British Bases* (Unpublished Ph.D. thesis, Princeton University, 1960), p. 182.
11.   Sir John Slessor, *Strategy for the West* (London, Cassell, 1956); *The Great Deterrent* (New York, Praeger, 1957). Sir Anthony Buzzard, 'Massive Reta-liation and Graduated Response', *World Politics*, January 1956. Sir A. Buzzard, Sir J. Slessor and R. Lowenthal, 'The H-Bomb, Massive Retalia-tion or Graduated Deterrence', *International Affairs*, April 1956. B.H. Liddell Hart, *Defence of the West* (London, Cassell, 1950); *Deterrence or Defence* (London, Stevens, 1960). Air Vice Marshall Kingston-McCloughry, *Global Strategy* (London, Cape, 1957); *Defence; Policy and Strategy* (London, Stevens, 1960). S. King-Hall, *Defence in the Nuclear Age* (London, Gollancz, 1959); *Power Politics in the Nuclear Age* (London, Gollancz, 1962).
12.   H.G. Thursfield, 'The Lessons of the War', *Brassey's Annual* (London, William Cloves, 1946) p. 10.
13.   M. Gowing, *Independence and Deterrence, Britain and Atomic Energy*

1945-52, Vol. I, Policymaking (London, Macmillan, 1974), p. 164.
14. Ibid., pp. 224-236.
15. A.J. Pierre, *Nuclear Politics* (London, Oxford University Press, 1972), p. 87.
16. Ibid., p. 87.
17. Sir J. Slessor, *Strategy for the West* (London, Cassell, 1956), p. 155.
18. Sir A. Buzzard *et al.*, op. cit., *International Affairs*, April 1956, p. 149.
19. B.H. Liddell Hart, *The Times*, 29 August 1955.
20. Sir A. Buzzard, 'The Crux of Defence Policy', *International Relations*, April 1956, p. 202.
21. See B.H. Liddell Hart, op. cit.; P.M.S. Blackett, *Atomic Weapons and East-West Relations* (London, Cambridge University Press, 1956), chapter I; D. Healey, 'The Atom Bomb and the Alliance', *Confluence*, April 1956.
22. Armstrong, op. cit., p. 81.
23. • L.W. Martin, 'The Market for Strategic Ideas in Britain: The "Sandys Era"', *The American Political Science Review*, Vol. 56, March 1962, p. 23.
24. Armstrong, op. cit., p. 32.
25. Ibid., p. 33.
26. G. Snyder, *Deterrence and Defence: Toward a Theory of National Security* (Princeton, Princeton University Press, 1961). A. Wohlstetter, 'The Delicate Balance of Terror, *Foreign Affairs*, January, 1959.
27. T.C. Schelling, *Arms and Influence* (New Haven and London, Yale University Press, 1966); H. Kahn, *On Escalation* (London, Pall Mall, 1965).
28. S. King-Hall, op. cit.
29. P.M.S. Blackett, 'Tizard and the Science of War', op. cit., p. 115.
30. Sir Solly Zuckerman, *Scientists and War, The Impact of Science on Military and Civil Affairs* (London, Hamish Hamilton, 1966), p. 63.
31. S. Huntington, *The Common Defence* (New York and London, Columbia University Press, 1961), p. 118.
32. R.N. Rosecrance, *Defense of the Realm: British Strategy in the Nuclear Epoch* (New York and London, Columbia University Press, 1968), pp. 20-21, 285.
33. L.W. Martin, op. cit., p. 38.
34. Ibid., p. 38.
35. B.H. Liddell Hart, *The Revolution in Warfare* (London, Faber and Faber, 1946), p. 89.
36. P. Darby, *British Defence Policy East of Suez 1947-68* (RIIA for Oxford University Press, London, 1973), p. 180.
37. Quoted, ibid., p. 49.
38. Ibid., pp. 155-156.
39. *Statement on Defence 1962*, The Next Five Years, Cmd 1639 (1962) para 4.
40. *U.K. H.C. Debates*, Volume 687, cols, 449-50 16 January 1964.
41. Ibid., Vol. 690, cols. 469-70, 26 February 1964.
42. General Sir G. Templar, *Conduct of Anti-Terrorist Operations in Malaya*, 1952.
43. Sir R. Thompson, *Defeating Communist Insurgency* (London, Chatto and Windus, 1966), pp. 50-57.
44. Adelphi Papers are short monographs on strategic subjects which are published and distributed by the International Institute for Strategic Studies. Well over a hundred titles have been published so far and many are still in print.

7 DEFENCE AND NATIONAL PRIORITIES SINCE 1945

David Greenwood

Defence is an economic activity because establishing and sustaining armed forces involves the commitment of resources to fulfilment of a purpose. The resources are productive capacities of various kinds: the 'factors of production' of familiar parlance. The purpose depends on circumstances. In war the operational aim is easy to define: victory, or at least avoidance of defeat, in order to maintain existing order or create some new one. In peacetime the object is more elusive: some sense of security, 'absolute security' being self-evidently unattainable. Preservation of freedom is the fundamental goal, from threat of conquest or capitulation on the one hand, fear of coercion or constriction on the other.

Resources enter the process as inputs of manpower, *matériel*, technical competence and industrial facilities. The outputs which their application yields — military capabilities embodied in warships, field force formations, aircraft or missile squadrons supported by logistic, administrative and training elements — serve the purpose. The inputs are real resources. Thus the true cost of defence is the forgone opportunity of their use elsewhere; counting the money outlay for the inputs as the price the nation pays is just a customary convenience. Nor does the actual expenditure on outputs measure their true value; this is related to the priority of the purpose, which will be high (and over-riding) when national disaster threatens, but a matter for more complex calculation in times of relative tranquillity. Yet in all conditions the value must be set against the cost. Much may be foregone — and foregone readily — when society's survival is at stake. When threats are less immediate and urgent, popular sentiment may judge even minimal provision dearly bought.

This cryptic formal argument exposes the central questions with which defence economics is concerned. Government is about choice and in this context the statesman's problem is: what provision for security is called for, given the claims of other societal goals? Or put another way, it is the riddle: how much (or little) is enough? It follows that an economist's analysis of the United Kingdom's defence policy, posture and provision in the post-war period must focus on two main features.

174

These are, first, the share of national resources allotted for 'security'; or the allocation of resources to defence. And second, the configuration of military capabilities to which money, men and *matériel* have been committed; or the allocation within defence. Facts do not speak for themselves, however. It is necessary to elucidate them by reviewing the experience they record, paying particular attention to evident continuities and significant changes, whether in defence's place in national priorities or among defence priorities themselves.

Such is the frame of reference for the present essay. The themes to be considered do not, of course, exhaust the economic content of defence analysis. There are straightforward descriptive questions which could be posed. What resources have been assigned to military uses and to what specific functions? How have the inputs been acquired and with what consequences for the economic system? At a more particular and detailed level one might ask: what is the ASW cruiser programme costing, what balance of payments burdens has the Hong Kong garrison imposed or how was development of the V-force managed? Numerous more explicitly analytical problems invite attention too. Has the defence effort assisted or impaired the economy's growth rate or industry's capacity for innovation? Has the procurement of equipment been 'efficient'? Has the geographical incidence of defence spending ameliorated or exacerbated regional disparities of income and employment? Finally, there is an economic dimension to policy evaluation, presenting tough normative questions like, 'Was the Suez intervention worth the candle?' or, 'Was the expenditure on (for example) assault ships and Argosy transport aircraft money well spent or not?'

All of these topics lie within the domain of 'the economics of defence'. But they are all incidental to the central themes which arise because *the allocation of resources to security purposes in the light of national and defence priorities* is the core policy issue. In a summary analysis specific microeconomic matters — technical, institutional or operational — merit passing mention. The emphasis, however, must be on the generalities of macroeconomics and political economy.

War and Post-War Adjustment: 1939-49

For the United Kingdom the Second World War was total war. To policy-makers and public alike the conceivable outcomes were death or victory. Allocation problems were therefore comparatively uncomplicated. No resources could be spared for maintaining or improving the capital stock for civil uses (private homes and vehicles, industrial plant for consumer goods). And private consumption, normally an end in itself, became purely instrumental. In fact, personal welfare was important only for operational reasons; if people were not in good health and good heart, the conduct of war might be endangered. Beyond that point, in the 'calculus of hell-fire and desperation' of Lord Robbins' vivid phrase, the value of additional individual welfare was zero. Thus settling the division between private and public uses of resources was surprisingly straightforward.

> You have to ask what is the minimum which will keep people alive and fighting fit and having made sure that enough resources . . . are devoted to this end you can push everything else into the war sector . . . The determination of the minima . . . is by no means an easy matter; the doctors do not always agree what is necessary for health; the politicians debate endlessly how much austerity is tolerable. But the fact remains that . . . the simplification of the allocation problem is so great as to be virtually a change in its nature.[1]

Within the public sector there was an analogous situation. Once decisions had been taken on broad strategic plans, the rest was consequential. Day-to-day problems of allocating scarce labour, materials, transport and industrial capacity were formidable and engaged a large bureaucracy. 'But in the last resort they were matters for the Defence Committee; it was the big strategic decisions which really governed everything else.'[2]

Thus in an exact sense from 1939 to 1945 the defence effort enjoyed over-riding priority. And the extent of the commitment was colossal. For present purposes a selection of salient statistics must suffice to illustrate its scale. The national accounts show that in 1938 the value of the United Kingdom's national product was c. £5,000 million, of which personal consumption accounted for some 75 per cent and public consumption around 13 per cent. In 1944, with the war effort at its peak, the proportions were 56 per cent and 50 per cent respectively, which is to say the country was consuming *more* than the value of current output by living on its capital. More detailed data on national expenditure and income — such as those in Table 7.1 — illustrate something of the character and phasing of the economic transformation that was involved. This analysis does not identify 'war expenditures' explicitly, however, not least because of definitional problems. But it has been calculated that over the three-year period from mid-1942 to mid-1945, when the economy was on a total war footing, these accounted for some 54 per cent of national income. Information on

Table 7.1: *The War Economy: National Income and Expenditure 1938-44* (Expenditure generating national product: factor incomes arising from national product)

£millions at current prices

Expenditure	1938	1941	1944
Personal consumption	4,304	4,933	5,562
Public consumption	724	4,239	5,076
Investment (net)	700	-729	-615
Gross national expenditure (at market prices)	5,728	8,443	10,023
Less: Indirect taxes, net of subsidies	640	1,114	1,384
Gross national expenditure	5,088	7,329	8,739

Income	1938	1941	1944
Wages and salaries	2,845	3,750	4,330
Pay etc. of armed forces	78	621	1,175
Other forms of income (UK)	1,547	2,388	2,669
Net income from abroad	168	110	50
'Net' national income	4,638	6,839	8,224
Provision for depreciation	450	490	515
National Income	5,088	7,329	8,739

Source: R.S. Sayers, *Financial Policy 1939-45* (London, HMSO and Longmans, 1956), p. 491.

manpower mobilisation indicates that this estimate is roughly right. In June 1944, for instance, 13 million people, or 55 per cent of the working population, were in either the armed forces (5.2 million, 22 per cent) or war employment of some kind (7.8 million, 33 per cent); this is compared with aggregate 'defence employment' of half a million on the eve of war. The sources of the additional manpower — some 12.5 million — are of interest. They were diversion from civil employment (8.7 million), the war-induced increase in the labour force (1.5 million) and absorption of the pre-war unemployed (13 million). Nor did the commitment involve only current domestic resources. In addition, assets were sold and massive debts incurred to gain access to goods and services from overseas. In 1939 the United Kingdom's foreign liabilities totalled approximately £500 million; by 1945 they exceeded £3,250 million. Add an estimated realisation of assets of £1,000 – £1,250 million plus a small decrease in the gold and currency reserves and the full scale of external disinvestment is apparent. It amounted to over £4,000 million on any reckoning.[3]

Needless to say, after six years spent single-mindedly exercising muscle and sinew (and drawing on fat) to provide the wherewithal to fight the war, when hostilities ceased the pressing claims on national resources were for recovery and rehabilitation, implying a reassertion of civilian priorities. The country had been 'mobilised' for war; the feeling was that 'demobilisation' should now proceed as quickly as orderly management would allow. Resource-use patterns had been distorted; more normal distributions might now be restored. So far as military provision was concerned, the expectation was that there would be a brisk run-down of service strengths, disposal of 'war surplus' for civilian uses where appropriate, and switches of production capacity to 'normal' peacetime output. The defence effort would be diminished. The army and air force could contract in due course to the pre-war form of essentially cadre forces — a mobilisation base, no more — stationed at home or garrisoned abroad. The navy could shrink too, resuming its responsibilities for safeguarding sea routes and providing 'presence'. Policy would rest on the traditional requirements of home and Imperial defence. Expenditure at 3 per cent of gross national product (GNP) — the pre-war norm — might be a feasible target.

To some extent this is what happened. Demobilisation did proceed. And major resource-use transfers were effected. But in neither the military nor the civil fields was it a simple matter of putting back the clock. In the circumstances of the immediate post-war years it was recognised that a new order of national priorities would have to be established and a new approach to defence's place within it. Similarly it became clear that an adjustment of security priorities themselves would be required.

What were the key features of these post-war circumstances which put a straightforward resumption of 'business as before' out of the question? On the domestic front — as both the nature of the problems and the attachment to military idiom made it appropriate to describe economic and social policy concerns — the legacy of the war was acutely problematical. The stock of physical capital, industrial and social, had become depleted by destruction or neglect. Its reconstruction was imperative to permit resumption of the domestic production of consumer goods and provision of social services (schools, hospitals and public housing). Until this was done private consumption would have to be restrained, partly to avoid an import build-up, partly to prevent pent-up purchasing power — the inevitable consequence of wartime deprivation — from provoking violent inflation. Yet the home capital goods industries lacked plant themselves and needed to import to refurbish, competing in the process for goods and materials made scarce world-wide by the disruption of normal production and trade which hostilities had caused. Not that the United Kingdom had the wherewithal to import at will, even if her requirements could have been readily satisfied; incurring yet further overseas indebtedness seemed inescapable, although some effort to regain export business would ease the problem (and also lay the basis for eventual restoration of balance of payments equilibrium). As if all this were not enough, no post-war government could have ignored the general expectation that, whatever the pressures on resources, a start on social policy reforms would soon be made, to fulfil promises made both during and before the war. (What, after all, had ordinary men and women fought for? Not freedom to enjoy the social and economic conditions of the 1930s!)

The pattern of national priorities was thus established on most stringent lines: investment in buildings, plant and vehicles; production for export (or import-saving); pressing social programmes in the public consumption sector; and personal consumption last, a long way last. The fruits of victory were years of austerity, with rationing intensified, tax burdens unrelieved and private living standards materially unaffected.[4]

And what of defence's place in this pecking order for claims on scarce resources? Had the domestic policy environment alone determined the answer to this question, it would have been very low, much lower even than in pre-war days perhaps, i.e. attracting less than 3 per

cent of GNP. But strategic circumstances too had altered and the last
major events of the Second World War had signalled the beginning of
'the nuclear age'. Formulation of security policy, choice of defence
posture and calculation of appropriate military provision had to take
these into account.[5]

Awareness of the full implications of Hiroshima and Nagasaki was
not immediate, in Britain or elsewhere. But fragments of evidence
suggest that two inferences were drawn, perhaps at first by intuition
rather than analysis, but nevertheless with sufficient conviction to influence the defence decision-making process. First, the strategic atomic
bombing foreshadowed eventual invalidation of the 'mobilisation base'
concept for force posture planning. Thus it was recognised that, while
mobilisation plans for men and munitions had not been made super-
fluous overnight and material stockpiles and reserve forces were still
important, the major powers were moving to an age of forces in being.
If decisive blows might be delivered in the early days or even hours of
future wars ready-standing forces would count for most. Following this
logic through, maintenance of minimal cadre force levels for security
contingencies would not for long suffice. Secondly, the A-bomb
evidently represented a significant new denomination in the currency
of military forces. Aspiration to great power rank would require possession of this capability which might indeed confer such status of itself. To be an atomic (and later nuclear) weapon state would therefore
be a necessary, and perhaps sufficient, condition for participation in
the regulation of international politics in the post-war world. For the
United Kingdom the meaning of these inferences was clear. Still
acknowledged as a Great Power, a fact to which her permanent membership of the United Nations' Security Council testified, future defence provision would have to incorporate the new strategic weaponry
if she aspired to live up to this status. Moreover, having taken part in
the wartime development of atomic armaments, this might be done
comparatively easily and cheaply. In some measure investment in this
direction might also allow the country to escape the full toll implied by
the requirement for 'forces in being' wherever military threats were
recognised. Not that this burden could be avoided altogether. The significance of economic war potential had been degraded. The size, shape,
equipment and deployment of peacetime formations would have to
reflect this new condition.

But after six years of bruising global war — 'to make the world safe
again' — how had strategic circumstances altered to preclude simple
reversion to former external policy dispositions? In the first place, after

the victory celebrations there were continuing tasks for troops in Europe: to occupy and run defeated Germany and conclude peripheral conflicts. There were also roles and missions arising from unfinished business in Palestine and turbulence further east which imposed demands beyond the accustomed norms of Imperial policing. More important, in the later 1940s events in Europe and elsewhere foreshadowed new requirements for peacetime deployment of military forces. Seeds of post-war animosity between the Soviet Union and the Western Allies had been sown in wartime disagreements. Stalin's ruthless and brutal insistence on establishing wholly malleable régimes in Eastern Europe nurtured suspicion and mistrust. By 1947-8 fear of Soviet expansionism, which may or may not have been well-founded, had taken hold. West European leaders considered it prudent to offer some show of countervailing power. Outside Europe the Indian experience suggested that Britain's Imperial disengagement might not be painless. Yet a trusteeship concept underlay the Imperial role, embodying elements of protection, advancement and eventual independence. It seemed possible that in the decolonisation programme to which politicians were explicitly committed protection responsibilities might well outrun the independence timetable. (As in the event they did: British forces were engaged in major operations on this account until the 1960s.[6])

Economic management in the early post-war years was therefore a matter of squeezing quarts from pint pots and, if possible, pulling rabbits out of hats. In the same spirit those responsible for defence and overseas policy were impelled to work their own minor miracles and turn a diplomatic trick or two. To be sure, the dismantling of the war machine proceeded — as Table 7.2 reveals. Almost 2,000,000 personnel were 'demobbed' in the year to 31 March 1947 and just under 1,500,000 in the next twelve months. But the pace of run-down slowed thereafter. Despite the pressure on resources security imperatives required forces in being. In 1948-9 the total strength of the services fell by a further 447,000 only to just over 1,000,000, and then only marginally to 896,000 in the following year. Plans to reduce the period of National Service were shelved. The once anticipated reversion to the median manpower level of the 1930s — around 325,000 — did not take place, nor had it done so 25 years later, for that matter.[7] Similarly, defence spending fell and fell dramatically, but not to pre-1938 levels. As a proportion of GNP in fact the budgets of the later 1940s never dropped below 6 per cent, or twice the pre-war figure (see Table 7.2).

To have persuaded Dalton, and later Cripps, to sanction such appropriations was no mean achievement for defence planners. Yet an effort

Table 7.2: *Military Manpower and Defence Expenditure: 1930s and 1946-50* (All personnel enlisted in the Forces)

Year	Manpower (000s)	Expenditure £m	Expenditure as % of GNP
1932-7 (annual average)	326	153	3.1
1947	3,033	930	8.4
1948	1,512	740	6.7
1949	1,065	770	6.5
1950	896	827	6.6

Source: T. Stone, *Abstract of Military Manpower Statistics 1900-75,* Aberdeen Studies in Defence Economics (ASIDES), No. 7, Oct. 1976, Table 2.1, Part I and tables for an *Abstract of Defence Budgetary Statistics 1900-75* (forthcoming) in the same series.

on this scale was manifestly not one to confer a real sense of security in the European setting or a strong sense of confidence that extra-European obligations could be effectively discharged. But here Bevin's vision and initiative came into play. More for defence would have distorted the economy again, even if the United Kingdom (with her Continental neighbours) had been physically capable of establishing a conventional force balance in Europe. So the Foreign Secretary did what *could* be done, to promote cohesion and self-confidence on the one hand and acquire the best feasible military underpinning on the other. A European alliance was composed with demanding mutual obligations, expressed in the Brussels Treaty of 17 March 1948. From the United States as specific and contractual a commitment as possible to the defence of Western Europe was sought and gained with the signing of the North Atlantic Treaty in April 1949.

Reviewing this process of transition, one identifies aspects of epilogue and prologue. During the Second World War defence enjoyed overriding priority in the competition for scarce national resources and security priorities themselves were determined by grand strategy. After the war the resource allocation problem assumed its more familiar form: how much for military purposes as opposed to other things? The legacy of war, however, complicated the calculation. There were insistent and inescapable claims for 'other things' — reconstruction and rehabilitation. At the same time there were new 'military purposes' to be considered in wholly new conditions. The outcomes of the exercise in squaring circles which this necessitated were, first, a place for defence among national priorities unprecedentedly high by twentieth-century

peacetime standards; and, second, an order of defence priorities with
unfamiliar emphasis on acquiring a nuclear capability and developing
European and Atlantic affiliations, notwithstanding the fact that
Imperial — and therefore global — commitments were still
quantitatively most important. If this was adjustment and 'aftermath'
it was also redefinition (of how large security concerns would loom in
the 'nuclear age' and Cold War world) and the beginning of a transformation of defence and overseas policy in which, over the years, Western
Europe and the North Atlantic would slowly assume more significance
and wider global aspirations steadily recede.

The Korean War Episode and After 1950-4

To elaborate this theme: it could be said that by 1949 a point of de-
parture had been reached for a predictable, logical policy progression.
In the short run, until the urgent tasks of economic restoration had
been completed and headway made towards social policy goals, only
parsimonious defence provision would be possible, just enough to give
credibility to the external policy stance. Even beyond this the preferred course would entail a stable level of military spending, sufficient
to furnish a minimum Alliance club subscription and the minimum contribution compatible with Commonwealth and colonial commitments.
For once domestic recovery was achieved, the obligation to compensate
for more than a decade of deprivation and austerity by allowing resources to flow to personal consumption would be compelling. Within
these guidelines the gradual transformation of defence posture might
proceed. Acquisition of nuclear weapon status and assumption of, if not
a mid-Atlantic, at least an 'offshore European' role under the North
Atlantic Treaty would constitute one aspect; acknowledgement of the
new currency of force and the new configuration of power in the world
would call for these. The other aspect would be contraction of the
global reach of Britain's military strength — but not necessarily of her
influence — in parallel with political withdrawal.

There is no evidence that this track was ever plotted, or even men-
tally charted by clairvoyant analysts. But these are the directions in
which policy might plausibly have evolved. That fact is worth regis-
tering because, although speculation on what might have been is
usually sterile, in this case it is instructive. In the early 1950s, under the
pressure of events, pursuit of an orderly progression proved impossible.
And for a decade after that British governments — Conservative governments, as it happens — were to show that lack of a clear sense of direction which prompted Acheson's celebrated jibe that Britain had 'lost an

Empire but not yet found a role'. In the third post-war decade, however, a coherent set of strategic priorities began to be developed, for a defence posture commensurate with the United Kingdom's stature in the contemporary world. In retrospect, which means with hindsight, the correspondence between the outcome of this process and the prospect at least imaginable in 1949 is striking.

The event which put paid to any hope of a considered approach to changing security conditions — for the United Kingdom or any other Western power — was, of course, the war in Korea. News of the all-out invasion of South Korea by North Korean forces in June 1950 evoked an immediate response from the United States and the United Nations. Battle was joined and led to a protracted conflict. However, it was not principally the demands of the fighting that prompted urgent revision of defence plans and programmes but the inferences drawn from the outbreak of war itself.

In the first place there seemed here to be confirmation that an open power struggle between the 'free world' and Communism was imminent; and that containment of the ideologically driven expansionism of Moscow and the new masters in Peking would require a large military effort mustered on the frontiers as unambiguous expressions of commitment. That the invasion had followed closely on the withdrawal of United States troops from Korea and ill-advised American statements about where her defensive perimeter ran afforded some justification for this view.[8] More clearly pertinent to the United Kingdom's calculations were the specific corollaries. If the establishment of Communist régimes world-wide were now on Stalin's (and Mao's) agenda, any idea of defence contraction and political withdrawal from Empire proceeding hand in hand required revision. And nearer home the sequence of questions raised was obvious. Might 'the enemy' have in mind a foray in Europe too? Would the zonal boundary in Germany be respected any more than the 38th parallel had been? To make sure that it was, should not the North Atlantic Treaty Organization (NATO) acquire some military muscle to match Soviet strength disposed in Eastern Europe?

Doubtless the politicians agonised about these things and over the likely popular reaction to demands for more economic sacrifice to permit rearmament. At the end of the day, however, there was a 'magnificent governmental and public response'.[9] Despite anxieties about inflation, chronic payments problems and continuing capacity difficulties, plans to increase arms spending were made at once. There could be no question of putting the economy on a war footing yet again. But the rearmament programme *was* granted the prior claim on national output.

The *Economic Survey for 1951* made its fulfilment the 'first objective'. Gaitskell said he would see that 'the particular resources are released which are needed for defence and exports' and backed his words with massive tax increases and cuts in civil spending.[10]

In fact the programme mapped out, because of its emphasis on re-equipment (implying a heavy load on engineering and allied industries whose own restoration had been delayed by lack of machine-tools and materials), proved over-ambitious. Some Labour politicians perceived this at the start. To Bevan the public expenditure distribution proposed by his colleagues embodied 'the arithmetic of Bedlam'; and he resigned. But it is noteworthy that not even he opposed in principle the assignment of high priority to rearmament. The essence of his ob-jection was not — as folklore has it — to the reimposition of Health Service charges but to the sheer *scale* of the defence effort now pro-posed. He thought the plans 'unrealisable'. And, as it happens, he was right.[11]

Yet for a year and more the effort of will was made, which was im-portant. Not until 1952 was the programme drastically modified as the burden on metal-using industries became apparent. Moreover, even at this juncture, the new Conservative Government insisted that the adjust-ment did not imply downgrading of defence's place in national prior-ities. The essence of the argument was that 'any further substantial diversion . . . from civil to military production would gravely impair our economic foundations and, with them, our ability to continue with the . . . programme'.[12] To underscore the point, whereas procurement plans were stretched, actual expenditure on arms continued rising. The strengths of the services also increased to 1953. So too did total spending and defence's share of GNP stayed high (see Table 7.3). At the same time, in their initial recasting of inherited expenditure pro-grammes as in later reassessments, the Conservatives were doubtless mindful of their commitment to a revision of policy priorities in favour of higher personal consumption. Butler promised a 'doubling of the standard of living' to be pursued by checking all public sector claims on national resources. There was political pressure to validate the claim — 'Conservative freedom works'.

Defence priorities during the 'Korean' crisis and immediately after were confused; and understandably so, for several strands of develop-ment interwove in a way which it took an heroic intellectual simplifica-tion to unravel; and then only when hard times and great expectations provided the motive and the opportunity to make it.

In a concise account it is impossible to capture the complexity.

Table 7.3: *Military Manpower and Defence Expenditure 1950-4*
(All personnel enlisted in the Forces)

Year	Manpower (000s)	Expenditure £m	Expenditure as % of GNP
1950	896	827	6.6
1951	890	1,102	8.0
1952	932	1,465	9.9
1953	958	1,548	9.7
1954	957	1,543	9.1

Source: T. Stone, *Abstract of Military Manpower Statistics 1900-75; Abstract of Defence Budgetary Statistics 1900-75.*

Suffice it to say that fears of a 'Korea in Europe' prompted the NATO members to (1) improvise a forward strategy, (2) express their determination to furnish force levels adequate to deter aggression and (3) establish a central command and control apparatus (under American leadership). It was recognised that to implement the first and provide the second would entail rearmament of Germany. To make this acceptable, and to facilitate the command task, proposals for an integrated European force were formulated, to function under the aegis of a European Defence Community (EDC). The United Kingdom faced the problem of deciding what contribution it was incumbent to make and whether it should be made inside or outside the EDC arrangement. The question 'how much?' was complicated by the fact that its perspectives and responsibilities stretched beyond Europe, including territories which might be vulnerable to 'liberation' movements. The question 'in or out' was complicated by, first, this self-same global reach of interests and commitments; and, second, by a self-image which intimate entanglement with Continental states might tarnish. In addition she was aware of an imminent change of status, which might legitimise a 'less than the others' option on the quantitative issue and a 'with but not of' position on the organisational one.

Atomic weapon status was the 'great expectation' which in the spring of 1952 — that is, some months before the first British nuclear device was exploded off the Monte Bello Islands — Churchill directed the Chiefs of Staff to incorporate in a new assessment of strategic policy and posture. He also counselled them to have in mind 'hard times'; for the rearmament experience had indicated that to sustain large, balanced, well equipped, conventional forces was incompatible with the internal and external stability of an economy still convalescing.

The result of the new assessment was the Global Strategy Paper of 1952. Its 'heroic intellectual simplification 'was to advocate nuclear deterrence as the central tenet of declaratory policy. Andrew Pierre has summarised the argument as follows:

> nuclear weapons had revolutionized the character of war. The most effective deterrent would be recognition by the Soviet Union that aggression on its part would bring an instantaneous atomic reprisal. The paper therefore recommended that the Western powers should openly declare that Soviet aggression would be met not only at the local point of conflict, but would be punished by nuclear retaliation at the Russian heartland. Reliance on such a strategy of nuclear deterrence would permit a reduction in conventional ground forces.[13]

Thus at a stroke, it seemed, the policy dilemmas might be resolved. As for force structure planning, the obvious message was: take care of the nuclear capability and the rest will look after itself. Accordingly the Churchill government at once decided to order V-bombers in quantity and officially accorded 'super-priority' to their production.[14]

The dilemmas would not, however, go away. Nor did the simple order of priorities implicit in the Global Strategy Paper turn out to be remotely tenable. In 1953-4 the EDC scheme ran into trouble and finally foundered in France's *Assemblée Nationale* on 30 August 1954. By a rich irony the United States' Secretary of State Dulles, who with his President (Eisenhower) had wholly embraced the British formulation of deterrence, threatened West Europeans with the famous 'agonizing reappraisal' of America's commitment to their defence if some alternative framework for co-operation (and German participation) were not found; and in order to create that framework the British Government had to undertake a binding obligation to maintain four divisions and a tactical air force − or 'equivalent fighting capacity' − on the Continent, the one really substantial, firm contractual commitment in Britain's post-war defence experience. Meanwhile in the wider world general-purpose forces occupied attention and resources in conducting operations for which the core precepts of the Chiefs of Staff paper were monumentally irrelevant. What is more there seemed no likely prospect that involvements such as these would rapidly recede.

Were there, then, any clear defence priorities? The most instructive answer is that of Richard Rosecrance. From 1952, he argues, there was an underlying tension between British doctrine and British practice.

Doctrine emphasised strategic air power, reliance on nuclear weapons, a smaller army. Practice most frequently demanded battalions, airlift and conventional naval forces. Indeed at the very time when preparations were being finalised to deploy the 'great deterrent' requirements for conventional forces were beginning to increase. 'The British had a marvellous new doctrine for other people; but they applied it to themselves,' he writes. Or rather they tried to, but it wouldn't work.[15]

Defence and National Priorities Since 1955

Security purposes were assigned overriding priority in the competition for national resources in the Second World War. They were assigned as low a priority as prudence would allow in the immediate post-war years. In the 'Korean' period and after, first a Labour Government asked, 'How much is necessary?' and seemed prepared to sacrifice economic stability and cherished social welfare aspirations in a determined effort to produce it; later a Conservative administration recast the question to, 'How little might be enough?' given a convenient doctrinal formula, but showed a good sense of political proportion by refusing to press the logic of the answer when it came.

Thus in a certain way, by the end of the first post-war decade, the United Kingdom had run the gamut of extreme, even eccentric, approaches to the formal resource allocation problem. The year 1955 is therefore notable as a landmark in the course of policy development: the point at which there was an opportunity for unconstrained judgement on the 'proper' scale and pattern of defence provision; a point where helmsmanship might have given way to navigation, so to speak.

This being so, there is some merit in surveying now, in retrospect, the general direction of the track followed in the next twenty years and noting some salient characteristics of the experience. (For the moment ignore the fact that at this juncture strong currents were flowing, that it was not clear which charts best showed what lay ahead or which weather forecasts to believe, and that the tiller was about to be taken by a strong and determined man who knew where *he* wanted to go, with whom, and how.)[16]

Contraction and Diminution or Reshaping?

Commentators who now look back on the period since 1955 are inclined to assert a generalised image of contraction and diminution. The trends they identify are adoption of less ambitious overseas aspirations and less demanding obligations, accompanied by assumption of a more modest defence posture. The statistics they quote relate to the coarse measures of arms and armed forces: the falling numbers of warships, field force formations and squadrons of combat aircraft in the national order of battle and of men and women in the services. They note too that the geographical scope of British military interests has steadily contracted and that Britain's stature, power and influence have diminished; and they readily relate one to the other.

But this image is seriously misleading. Any overview of the period should stress 'reshaping' rather than contraction and diminution, and this for two reasons. First, it is not at all clear that by contemporary standards aspirations are 'less ambitious' than before. Certainly sharing with others a determination to escape strategic intimidation by one superpower while avoiding complete domination by the other is hardly a soft option as state policies go. Nor is it obvious that obligations to help safeguard North Atlantic lines of communication, defend a Corps front in north-west Germany and preserve the integrity of NATO's air space are any 'less demanding' than former roles and missions. Second, it just is not true that the United Kingdom now disposes evidently less military might than five, ten or twenty years ago. To be sure, service strengths have fallen markedly since 1955, by 57.7 per cent to be exact (as Table 7.4 shows). But the committed 'professionals' of the 1970s cannot be counted one-for-one against the largely conscript forces of the 1950s. In any case over the years labour/capital ratios have gone down in almost all activities. If it is then argued that the stock of military capital too is much reduced, the question is: what are the 'exchange rates' by which one compares the value of today's frigates or missile regiments or multi-role combat aircraft with those of a generation past (always assuming that counterparts existed at all a generation past)? In short, the defence effort is certainly directed to somewhat different purposes now than hitherto. Military capabilities are different also and forces are deployed in different places. But to project such consequences of structural and technological change wholly in negative terms is quite absurd.

Notwithstanding this argument, the tendency to relate the undeniable loss of power and erosion of influence directly and exclusively to change in defence posture is understandable. But it should be equally clear that the fact that Britain no longer cuts the figure in international politics which she once did owes much more to other factors. In particular new denominations in the currency of 'influence' have entered circulation because of changes in the relative utility of military and economic (or commodity) power. And these changes have produced a relative decline in Britain's status. In absolute terms, however, her de-

Table 7.4: *United Kingdom Armed Forces 1955-74* (By service, at
1 April each year, thousands; excluding locally enlisted personnel)

Year	Royal Navy	Army	Royal Air Force	Total
1955	128.4	437.0	258.2	823.6
1956	122.1	408.0	242.6	772.7
1957	116.0	375.2	227.9	719.1
1958	106.6	328.4	191.0	626.0
1959	101.6	303.9	173.2	578.7
1960	97.8	264.3	163.5	525.6
1961	95.3	231.3	158.2	484.8
1962	94.3	202.9	148.9	446.1
1963	95.8	190.6	143.8	430.2
1964	97.6	189.4	136.1	423.1
1965	98.6	193.7	135.3	427.6
1966	97.8	193.6	127.0	418.4
1967	97.0	196.2	124.1	417.3
1968	95.1	189.4	120.5	405.0
1969	90.2	178.5	114.2	382.9
1970	86.1	173.9	113.0	373.0
1971	82.5	173.4	112.1	368.0
1972	82.4	178.3	110.8	371.5
1973	81.2	179.9	105.9	367.0
1974	78.3	171.7	99.3	349.3

Source: T. Stone, *Historical Abstract of British Military Manpower Statistics
1900-75,* Aberdeen Studies in Defence Economics (ASIDES), No. 7, Oct.
1976, Table 2:6, Part I.

fence effort has neither contracted nor diminished but has simply been
'reshaped'.

Stability in Defence Spending

Defence expenditure statistics make the point in striking fashion. It
goes without saying that in current price terms spending has risen,
more or less uninterruptedly, year in, year out. In fact in 1974 outlays
in the United Kingdom were more than two and a half times as high as
in 1955. But almost all the 'growth' was attributable to general price
inflation. When adjusted for this, to give a measure (albeit somewhat
imperfect) of the value in exchange of the real resources allotted to
defence, the data tell a different story. But it is *not* a story of reduction
and decline.

In Table 7.5, estimates of defence expenditure for 1955-74 at constant prices and exchange rates are set out alongside the current prices

figures. Index numbers (1960 = 100) accompany both series, for ease of interpretation. The significant thing about the data on spending in real terms is the remarkable stability. There are year-to-year fluctuations and short-run trends; but a range of 16.5 percentage points accommodates all the values. Closer inspection reveals that the average level for each successive five-year period from 1960 is in fact fractionally above that for the preceding one. Of the pronounced, persistent, downward drift which expressions like 'diminution of the defence effort' or 'shrinking defence budgets' connote, there is no evidence at all.

Table 7.5: *Defence Expenditure 1955-1974* (at current and constant prices and as percentage of GDP; SIPRI definitions: calendar year basis)

Year	Defence Expenditure (current prices)		Defence Expenditure (1970 prices and exchange rates)		Defence Expenditure (as % of GDP)
	£m	Index No 1960 = 100	$m	Index No 1960 = 100	
1955	1,567	94.6	6,379	108.2	8.2
1956	1,615	97.5	6,215	105.5	7.8
1957	1,574	95.0	5,859	99.4	7.2
1958	1,591	96.0	5,726	97.2	7.0
1959	1,589	95.9	5,719	97.0	6.6
1960	1,657	100.0	5,893	100.0	6.5
1961	1,709	103.1	5,886	99.9	6.3
1962	1,814	109.5	5,997	100.9	6.4
1963	1,870	112.8	6,057	102.8	6.2
1964	2,000	120.7	6,274	106.5	6.1
1965	2,091	126.2	6,256	106.2	5.9
1966	2,153	129.9	6,201	105.2	5.7
1967	2,276	137.4	6,394	108.5	5.7
1968	2,332	140.7	6,257	106.2	5.4
1969	2,303	139.0	5,864	99.5	5.0
1970	2,444	147.5	5,850	99.3	4.9
1971	2,815	169.8	6,159	104.5	5.1
1972	3,258	196.6	6,654	112.9	5.3
1973	3,505	211.5	6,554	111.2	5.4 (est.)
1974	4,148	250.3	6,686	113.4	5.4 (est.)

Source: The Stockholm International Peace Research Institute (SIPRI), *Yearbook of World Armaments and Disarmament 1975* (Stockholm: Almqvist and Wiksell, 1975).

A moment's reflection on this expenditure data, seen against the background of the manpower reductions and the widely held perception of generally reduced circumstances, is illuminating. It confirms the 'reshaping' hypothesis and also elucidates it. All the arresting, concrete, quantitative indicators – strengths, units, hardware and infrastructure – show a clear downward trend. Yet expenditure in real terms stayed more or less the same. Resources must therefore have gone heavily into qualitative improvement. The global distribution of the armed forces altered radically too, the later years of the period seeing almost total withdrawal from outside Europe. But to sustain the more closely circumscribed deployments cost at least as much. Clearly some major trade-off had been made. In particular the east of Suez run-down was a price paid that NATO obligations might be fully honoured; the regiments departed in order that they could stay.

Sharing Domestic Product

The data may also be examined against the background of the overall performance of the economy. The period 1955-74 saw modest economic progress. Growth was not rapid and sustained, nor was it on the scale which most other industrialised countries – including the European ones – achieved. But there was some, so that allotment to defence of a near-constant absolute amount of output meant that its share of gross domestic product (GDP) edged downwards over time (see Table 7.5, right-hand column). Until the early 1970s the defence/GDP proportion fell very steadily in fact, even when the short-run expenditure trend was upward as in 1962-4. From 1970 it rose a little, then levelled out and – following the expenditure 'cuts' of 1974-6 – began to fall again.

The decline in 'the proportion' is a significant characteristic of the period and records a special sense in which a 'diminution of the defence effort' did take place. But there is an alternative interpretation of the trend which is equally valid and instructive. Whether or not it was the declared intention of governments, the effect of their allocative choices was to stabilise defence provision in absolute resource-use terms allowing the benefits of growth to go to civil uses, i.e. private investment, private consumption and public sector civil programmes. As it happens, all the indications suggest that the outcome was deliberate rather than fortuitous. In the late 1950s Conservative priorities certainly favoured personal consumption. In the early 1960s the disposition was to allow defence to 'ride' the growth rate; but actual budgets were never permitted to go that high.[17] Labour took office in 1964 and imposed a budget ceiling: an unambiguous expression of the policy. The Conservatives' assertion of a higher place for defence among national priorities in 1970 led – as Table 7.5 reveals – to a reversal of the 'falling proportion' trend. By 1973, however, they were revising their plans, a job completed by their opponents in the 1974 Defence Review whose outcome (for all practical purposes) was another budget ceiling.

If the defence effort made no claims on the additional resources made available by growth, in which directions were they used? How, first, was GDP shared between private consumption and investment on the one hand, public programmes on the other? In 1954-5 public expenditure (including transfers) accounted for 38.8 per cent of GDP.[18] As has been said, the Conservatives were committed to checking public-sector demands in order to allow more for private uses. And this they did. The public share of GDP fell in the later 1950s. Thereafter, however, it rose slowly but steadily until the policies of another Conservative Government imposed a (temporary) pause. Which categories of public expenditure 'gained' in this process is evident from the detailed data on public programmes in Table 7.6. Defence accounted for a diminishing share of the total, as earlier argument has implied. Social security benefits and education, lying second and third in the pecking order to 1958, increased their shares to rise above defence. Taking the period covered by the table as a whole, provision for health and various environmental services also took increasing shares along with spending on housing, roads, industry and trade. (The latter categories, however, were less significant in the early 1970s than hitherto. Conservative policy favoured support for industry via the tax system rather than direct spending and attached less importance to funds for public housing.)

This overall appreciation of defence's place in national priorities from 1955 leads to two main conclusions. First, in approaching their resource allocation problem free from the special demands of post-war adjustment and the abnormalities of the 'Korean' episode, governments markedly altered the pattern of public provision and the balance between the private and public sectors. After an initial preference for personal consumption and industrial investment, the growth dividend accrued primarily to social welfare. Second, the commitment of real resources to 'security' was relatively stable. However the defence effort did undergo significant reshaping; there was qualitative improvement and a shift of spatial emphasis. Coinciding as it did with decline in the United Kingdom's relative power and an erosion of her influence, this process has been perceived as absolute diminution and contraction. This is misleading. For real defence spending was higher in 1974 than 1955; one would be hard pressed to argue that the United Kingdom mustered

Table 7.6: *Composition of Public Expenditure* (at current market prices: selected years)

	1958 £m	1958 %	1963 £m	1963 %	1968 £m	1968 %	1972 £m	1972 %
Military defence	1,543	18.6	1,892	16.2	2,443	12.8	3,097	11.4
Social security benefits	1,345	16.2	1,988	17.0	3,340	17.5	5,119	18.9
Education	785	9.4	1,282	11.0	2,182	11.4	3,508	12.9
National Health Service	728	8.8	1,035	8.9	1,688	8.8	2,644	9.7
Industry and trade, including employment services	543	6.5	791	6.8	2,016	10.5	2,322	8.5
Roads, transport and communications	531	6.4	832	7.1	1,497	7.8	1,950	7.2
Housing	419	5.0	592	5.1	1,129	5.9	1,449	5.3
Environmental services	286	3.4	475	4.1	837	4.4	1,321	4.9
All others	1,082	13.1	1,493	12.8	2,099	10.9	3,314	12.3
Debt interest	1,046	12.6	1,286	11.0	1,907	10.0	2,420	8.9
Total public expenditure	8,308	100.0	11,666	100.0	19,138	100.0	27,144	100.0
Public expenditure as % of gross domestic product	36.0		37.8		43.8		43.3	

Source: Derived from data in R. Klein et al., *Social Policy and Public Expenditure 1974* (London, Centre for Studies in Social Policy, 1974).

less military might than hitherto and certainly neither her security
policy aspirations nor her defence obligations were conspicuously less
ambitious or demanding.

All this is elucidation of the allocation of resources to defence during
the period. What of the allocation of resources within defence? What of
the actual course of the reshaping of the defence effort which
occurred?

The Reshaping of the Defence Effort Since 1955

The prescriptions for future policy and posture inherent in the logic of
the 1952 Global Strategy Paper had little discernible effect on actual
planning in the years immediately after its appearance. Although lukewarm about 'integration', the United Kingdom was sensible of NATO's
needs, including her obligation to contribute to its conventional forces.
Abandonment of post-Imperial global presences was neither practicable
nor palatable.

In fact important new undertakings were made in 1954-5 of a kind
barely compatible with the emphasis implicit in the policy paper.
Under the threat of Dulles's reappraisal the unprecedented commitment
to peacetime stationing of forces in Western Europe was assumed.
Earlier in 1954, the United Kingdom had joined in establishing a South-
East Asia Treaty Organization (SEATO) and in the following year the
Baghdad Pact was signed, leading to formation of the Central Treaty
Organization (CENTO). These affiliations reaffirmed the global role
and, among other things, gave a new rationale to the staging-posts *en
route* to India (and beyond). The idea that in discharging these responsibilities nuclear arms would have special weight was quite implausible.
Even so, there could be no question of not acquiring the 'great deterrent'. Such a contribution to the West's overall posture was required of
a country claiming world power status. 'The bomb' might also confer
some independence of American protection.

Confused Conservative Priorities 1955-64

Thus there was a nuclear 'priority' in 1955 and the government embarked on development and production of both the new thermonuclear
weapons and ballistic rockets to supplement manned bombers for delivery. There was a 'European 'priority' in which the contractual obligation of the Paris Agreements was reinforced by the curious thinking
that 'broken-backed' warfare would follow initial indecisive nuclear
blows. And there was the extra-European 'priority' whose credibility
Eden sought to maintain by mounting the ill-fated Suez operation.

There was not, however, a clear sense of priorities. Nor was there great clarity about nuclear doctrine (for strategic or theatre weapons), about the concept of operations for defence in north-west Europe or about the nature and durability of the global role. Hence policymakers lacked a firm sense of direction; and for the ten years after 1955 plotting the track of policy means logging a succession of tacks and jibes and course corrections, some of them very coarse corrections. Not all can be registered in a brief account. But some impression must be conveyed of the record of erratic movement. Three themes demand attention: nuclear policy and general posture, European theatre forces and commitments outside Europe.[19]

At bottom the confusions over nuclear policy and general posture arose from the doctrinal muddle and from indecisiveness over how far nuclear forces might substitute for conventional formations. After the early reluctance to face the latter question, Duncan Sandys addressed it directly in his *Outline of Future Policy* in 1957. Acquisition of 'a deterrent' lay at the core of all his plans. He asserted that (land-based) ballistic missiles would first supplement then supersede the V-bombers as the strategic nuclear delivery system. Assuming that others too would emphasise such capabilities, he proposed axing provision for air defence and reducing the British Army of the Rhine (BAOR). Revision of ideas about the future of forces outside Europe, prompted by the Suez débâcle, also pointed to lower force levels. Conscription could therefore be abolished. Sandys never lacked the courage of his convictions; so policy duly headed off in these directions. But in the event neither the revision of extra-European roles and missions nor the reduction of BAOR could be carried through as contemplated. Moreover technical and cost problems bedevilled the missile programme and the doctrinal assumptions underlying the planned nuclear posture came to look increasingly inadequate. The launcher procurement experience was a nightmare, Blue Streak failed and Skybolt proved unobtainable before a deal was finally done to acquire the Polaris system (at Nassau in 1962). The confusions over doctrine were astounding. Had Blue Streak been a success it would have been a sad anachronism. Recognising the desiderata for an effective retaliatory system, the Americans were at this time thinking of solid fuel and the Russians of storable liquids and mobility. Skybolt was a mistake on any reckoning. By the time the United Kingdom evinced serious interest in the programme Polaris was probably available. There should have been no doubt which was the better buy. Wohlstetter's celebrated elucidation of the first strike/second strike distinction, and of the delivery

vehicle requirements for stable deterrence which this implied, was
already in the open literature.[20]

Thinking about European theatre forces responded no less erratically
to the currents generated by both nuclear controversy and events in
Europe. In accordance with Sandys' design, large reductions in the
Rhine Army were scheduled in 1957 and 1958, Eden's commitment
notwithstanding. But renewed tension over Berlin halted the process
well before a planned run-down target of 45,000 ground troops had
been attained. Nor did anxiety recede sufficiently thereafter to revive
the force level issue. This might have happened when the crisis-laden
atmosphere of 1961-2 at last subsided. By then, however, the debate on
revision of NATO doctrine was under way. The time was not propitious
for resurrection of ideas based on minimal conventional capacities. Indeed the Nassau communiqué of 12 December 1962 recording the
agreement on Polaris declared that Kennedy and Macmillan were also in
agreement on the need for a 'non-nuclear sword' to complement the
'nuclear shield'. 'For this purpose', the announcement said, 'they agreed
on the importance of increasing the effectiveness of their forces on a
world-wide basis.'[21]

The United Kingdom's commitments outside Europe similarly
refused to define themselves according to a convenient prescription. The
guerrilla war in Malaya and Borneo could not be ignored. Dependent
territories grappling with internal security problems generated by either
militant nationalist movements or the plurality of their societies could
not be abandoned. Because the Far East laid claim to continuing attention the line of communication was crucial; after Suez, therefore,
the base at Aden and facilities in Africa and Arabia were developed.
Likewise the eastern Mediterranean — both NATO's southern flank and
CENTO's western one — remained important; hence a continuing
presence in Cyprus was required and was duly safeguarded by retention
of 'sovereign base areas' after the island gained independence in 1957.
Reconsideration of the manner in which commitments would be fulfilled was possible, however. Indeed, given the decision to end conscription, it was necessary. The chosen formula was simple. The
'increasing strength and efficiency of Colonial forces and the growing
capacity to send reinforcements rapidly from Britain' were invoked as
rationales for reduction in the size of garrisons. To enable reinforcements to be despatched promptly a 'Central Reserve' — later dubbed
the Strategic Reserve — would be maintained in Britain. It would have
'the means of rapid mobility' (i.e. appropriate transport aircraft) close
at hand. Strategic mobility was the catch-phrase; a run-down of forces

east of Suez was the consequence.[22]

The 'reshaping' of the defence effort to 1964 was, on this evidence, a piecemeal and pragmatic business. A nuclear capability was acquired, but not as planned and not for the role within the overall national posture first assumed. European theatre forces emerged as the main factor in military calculations, but only when expectations that nuclear status might be traded for an 'offshore European' stance had proved ill-founded. Commitments outside Europe were downgraded, as measured by the size of stationed forces; but no abrogation of strategic interest was implied and ambiguity hung over the precise place of the attenuated global role in national defence priorities.

Be that as it may, the process was regarded as complete. The Conservatives' defence programme for 1964-5 and after envisaged retention of all existing capabilities, including completion of several re-equipment plans. No change was contemplated in commitments to the three main alliances (NATO, CENTO, SEATO),under bilateral treaties (e.g. the Anglo-Malayan and Anglo-Libyan) or those arising from less formal Commonwealth and colonial obligations. The associated budgetary projections rose steadily in line with the anticipated growth of GDP.

Labour's Defence Reviews 1964-70 and 1974

The process was not, however, at an end. When a Labour Government took office in the autumn of 1964 it simply entered a second decade. To the new administration the scale of the defence effort envisaged by Conservative plans was unacceptable. Pledges to restore the emphasis on social programmes stood to be honoured, without increased taxation. Reduction of the proportion of national resources allotted to defence was thus obligatory. The obvious device to give effect to such an aim was soon adopted: a budget ceiling. Being forced in this way to contemplate exactly what in their predecessors' plans they would and would not retain, Labour's Ministers were inescapably driven to address the *pattern* of security provision.

In the first instance a radical redefinition of commitments was rejected. The re-equipment outlays which loomed large in spending forecasts offered the simplest, perhaps the only, way of bringing future budgets into line. Accordingly, the fifth Polaris boat was cancelled. Provision for the first of a new class of attack carriers was also struck from the naval programme. Three key aircraft projects were abandoned in favour of cheaper alternatives. Some degradation of

military capabilities was the inevitable, and undeniable, consequence
of these decisions. They were not, however, considered incompatible
with declaratory endorsement of retention of a nuclear capability, a
comprehensive European role and fulfilment of all obligations east of
Suez (subject to certain limitations). The first Healey 'defence
review' — which ran to March 1966 — did not, in other words, confront the tough questions of choice among these principal priorities.

It was in the second and subsequent phases of reappraisal — for
which the phrase 'continuing defence review' was coined — that these
matters moved to the forefront of attention. Having focused in earlier
analyses on capabilities and equipment, in 1966-7 Healey brought
manpower and overseas spending under scrutiny; and hence the size
and global deployment of the army. Issues of 'role and commitment'
could thus no longer be evaded. Ministers faced directly the necessity
for choice. They chose a run-down of force levels east of Suez plus
some reductions in strengths elsewhere, leaving the order of battle of
1(BR) Corps in Germany unchanged. Not that complete detachment
from extra-European interests found immediate favour. The first
formulation of the new posture in the *Supplementary Statement on
Defence Policy, 1967* reflected some reservations. It contained firm
undertakings on base closures (e.g. Aden) and on withdrawals (e.g.
from Singapore and Malaysia by the mid-1970s). But there was also a
vague reference to maintaining a special capability for operations outside Europe and a studiously imprecise redefinition of the SEATO
and Anglo-Malaysian undertakings. By the following year, however,
after a post-devaluation reassessment, the die was cast decisively. The
earlier run-down plan was accelerated and extended to include withdrawal from the Gulf. The special capability notion succumbed to
some official's 'weasel wording' to emerge in the Prime Minister's
statement of 16 January 1968 as 'a general capability based in
Europe (including the United Kingdom) which can be deployed
overseas as, in our judgement, circumstances demand'. There was even
an explicit declaration of the abandonment of a truly global role. In
this same speech Harold Wilson remarked that the defence effort
would in future be concentrated in Europe — including European
waters — and the North Atlantic.[23]

The promotion to primacy of NATO tasks was unequivocal. The
incidental changes and adjustments which accompanied or followed
this decisive setting of geographical priorities complemented the
central policy choice. The Strategic Reserve became the United Kingdom Mobile Force (UKMF) — for NATO contingencies. Amphibious

warfare forces acquired an Alliance rationale. Air transport squadrons
likewise assumed a European role: to provide the 'lift' for the UKMF
and other specialist reinforcement units. That is to say, new missions
for old forces were defined. Similarly, reduced service requirements for
equipment were implicit in the adoption of more circumscribed deployments. Thus some procurement plans were 'stretched' — e.g. the
naval construction programme, because of revised assumptions about
the size of the future fleet.

In addition, if less conspicuously, further hard choices were made —
following the 1964-6 decisions — about the shape of the future equipment inventory in general. They reflected judgements about how keenly
and in what company qualitative improvement would be pursued in
new weapons acquisition policy; and about whether all of the more expensive and demanding of existing capabilities should be retained. The
decision to buy the American F-111K was revoked in favour of a European project, for example. An earlier phase-out of the existing carrier
force was scheduled too. The inference was that the United Kingdom
would not in future feel bound to compete comprehensively and independently at the highest levels of arms technology or in operating some
of the most complex and costly weapons systems. This was an important additional aspect of the assessment of 'proper' provision for
security objectives in Labour's thinking, expressing a clear structure of
priorities in another defence dimension.

Even on nuclear matters the second half of the 1960s saw clarifica-
tion of posture and provision. At the strategic level, the Polaris programme was pursued — on a reduced basis — against internal opposition
in the labour movement. A doctrinal frame of reference for the force
evolved, albeit implicitly, with the aid of an ingenious bifurcation. On
the one hand the four boats were declared to be a contribution to
NATO's forces for deterrence. Presumably, therefore, the submarines
were deployed and missiles targeted consistently with the United
States' retaliatory strategy. On the other they were (and are) quite
evidently an independent national force and thus a status symbol, bargaining chips and *in extremis* a factor for any protagonist to enter in
his calculations. Such a formulation is a boon when budgetary provision
is at issue. For the first requirement any amount will do; and for the
second a little is enough. The problem therefore evaporates; nothing
need be done. Meanwhile comfort can be taken from the diminishing
financial burden of a wasting asset.[24]

Vexed questions concerning NATO's theatre nuclear posture were
resolved, though not for all time, by argument and consensus rather

than ingenuity. Transatlantic tension over various declensions of
'flexibility in response' had characterised the early 1960s. In 1967 this
was alleviated — the more easily after the *contretemps* with France —
by the Alliance's formal adoption of a tactical doctrine based on graduated response or flexible escalation (as set out by the NATO Military
Committee in its document MC 14/3). For practical purposes and
within limits the 'new strategy' provided a portmanteau rationale for
whatever force structures members' inclinations and circumstances
allowed them to contribute.[25]

To sum up: the various phases of Healey's 'continuing defence
review' were genuinely definitive. Furthermore a consistent and
coherent approach to matters of priorities is discernible in the 'reshaping' which occurred or, more correctly, was foreshadowed (for
change both 'on the ground' and in the budget was spread over 1965-6
to 1973-4). The elements in the approach were (1) the strategic nuclear
force in being was worth retaining, for functional and symbolic
reasons, at its annually declining costs; (2) being the capabilities most
relevant to core security interests, European theatre ground and air
forces and naval forces for the North Atlantic (including UK-based
units) rated a higher priority-in-value than all other components of the
national order of battle; (3) forces for extra-European roles and
missions, with some exceptions like garrisons in remaining large depen-
dencies (e.g. Hong Kong) or in politically vulnerable smaller ones (e.g.
Gibraltar), attracted the lowest priority of all.

The changes in the global deployment of the United Kingdom's
armed forces between 1965-6 and 1973-4 (financial years) reflect these
priorities. Table 7.7 shows that, whereas in 1965-6 more than one member of the services in four was stationed (or at sea) outside Europe, by
1973-4 that proportion — of a smaller total strength — was down to
one in ten. Over the same period, although the actual number of service
personnel stationed in Western Europe hardly changed, in 1973-4 they
represented nearly one-fifth of total strength compared with one-
seventh in 1965-6.

But it is the changing composition of the defence budget which
affords the most succinct statement of shifting security priorities and
thus the most instructive statistical complement to this account. In
their way the data in Table 7.8 encapsulate the story of the reshaping
of the defence effort which Healey's review(s) effected. The figures are
derived from the so-called 'functional costing' of defence expenditure
introduced in the mid-1960s as an information tool for defence planning, programming and budgeting. Under the system the costs of the

Table 7.7: *Global Distribution of the UK Armed Forces 1965-6 and 1973-4* (Percentage of total strength)

Location		1965-6	1973-4
UK (i.e. home forces)		57.3	70.7
Europe		14.3	19.5
Mediterranean		5.5	4.0
Middle East		6.8	0.2
Far East		14.1	4.5
Elsewhere		2.0	1.1
Total	%	100	100
Actual strength	000s	450.	363

Notes: (1) Includes locally enlisted personnel and personnel at sea assigned as appropriate.
    (2) 'Middle East' covers Aden, Persian Gulf, Mauritius.
Source: T. Stone, *Historical Abstract of British Military Manpower Statistics 1900-75*, Table 2.13.

resources used in defence are attributed to purposes, some directly to 'mission' programmes, others to 'support'. The changing weight of the different 'mission' programmes — which Table 7.8's percentage column exposes clearly — is the essential quantitative evidence of 'reshaping'.[26]

Table 7.8: *Defence Expenditure 1965-6 and 1973-4* (Functional analysis of defence estimates)

Major Programme	1965-6		1973-4	
	Amount £m	% of total	Amount £m	% of total
Nuclear strategic forces	128	6.0	39	1.2
Navy GP combat forces	294	13.9	419	12.4
European theatre ground forces	156	7.4	497	14.8
Other army combat forces	196	9.2	63	1.9
Air force GP combat forces	280	13.2	496	14.7
Air mobility	98	4.6	116	3.4
Sub-total 'Mission' programmes	1,152	54.3	1,630	48.4
Sub-total 'Support' programmes	968	45.7	1,735	51.6
Total	2,120	100.0	3,365	100.0

Note: GP denotes 'General Purpose'.
Source: *Statements on the Defence Estimates 1965-73: Functional Analysis tabulations*. Figures have been reallocated to take account of some attribution changes over the years.

That this synoptic view of the changes in the defence effort emanating from Labour's decisions can be read across a nine-year time-scale
illustrates two points. First, defence decisions are not, and usually
cannot be, given effect immediately. Today's posture reflects past
choices. Today's priorities prescribe tomorrow's programme. This is a
fact of policy-making life, born of the need to renegotiate agreements,
the management problems of manpower expansion or contraction, the
long lead-time of weapons systems and so on. At best two years are
needed, in normal circumstances, for an administration favouring a new
'mix' of capabilities to exert any leverage on the programme. This leads
to the second point. Labour's priorities are still clearly discernible in
the Estimates for 1973-4, the third defence budget framed by the
Conservative Government which entered office in June 1970 (see Table
7.8). This says something about the nature of the effect of the change
of government on defence: there was little or none on 'structure' or
'balance'. Conservative Ministers attached importance to the same
things as their predecessors. To be sure, the east of Suez run-down
which Healey had envisaged was halted and the presence in Singapore
and Malaysia prolonged under a hastily concocted Five Power Defence
Agreement. But this apart, the Conservatives' adjustments to the
pattern of provision were almost wholly cosmetic and insubstantial.
What they did do was to raise the level of expenditure on both manpower (under new service pay arrangements introduced in 1970-1) and
equipment (by increasing the rate of procurement on some existing
projects and initiating several new ones). In a phrase, they allotted
more resources to defence, but did not materially affect the allocation
within defence and, thereby, the transformation process we have been
considering. Conservative choices impinged on size, not shape, and on
equipment, not deployment. And even here their impact was only
transitory.

It was short-lived because, by 1973, economic circumstances impelled a re-examination of all spending plans. Concern for the internal
and external stability of the economy demanded it. Barber shaved the
budget for 1974-5 and put the rest of the future programme under
scrutiny. In the event, however, the task of systematic revision of plans
for the late 1970s and beyond again fell to Labour. On taking office in
the spring of 1974 they began an 'extensive and thorough review of
our system of defence' to frame new budgetary projections for
1975-84, an exercise which – like Healey's in the mid-1960s – turned
in due course into another 'continuing' reappraisal.

Neither the full background to the 1974 Defence Review nor the detailed proposals which it yielded need be recounted here. Suffice it to say that the 'new' programme and budget, presented in March 1975 (and since amended but not superseded), simply took the reshaping process one stage further. The framework of priorities which underlay it was virtually identical to that formulated a decade earlier. For instance, in 1975 it was decided to prolong the active life of the Polaris force but not replace it; to make no provision for new commando carriers; to 'stretch' other procurement programmes; and to seek 'European' solutions to future equipment problems wherever possible. It was decided to withdraw all remaining ground and air forces from Singapore/Malaysia, Indian Ocean bases and (later) Malta; to reduce the Hong Kong garrison; and to curtail naval deployments east of Gibraltar. In addition, substantial reductions were envisaged — and have been made — in the specialist reinforcement forces maintained for operations on NATO's flanks. Force levels on the Central Front, however, were not affected. Indeed the combat effectiveness of a restructured 1(BR) Corps was to increase. Nor was provision for a reasonable naval presence in the North Atlantic undermined. Significantly, neither a new cruiser programme nor fleet submarine building plans were modified. The dominant themes are clear. They are those noted in analysis of Labour's earlier appraisals: (1) retention of the Polaris force on a 'low budget' basis; (2) maintenance of force levels in the NATO area, especially in the heartland of the Allied Forces Central Europe (AFCENT) command and on the sea line of communication in the North Atlantic; (3) geographical contraction elsewhere, and now not only into but within the NATO boundaries. There are also instances of judgements on 'proper provision' which similarly evoke familiar antecedents. These include, first, the *de facto* 'opting out' of one or two costly and demanding missions, e.g. amphibious warfare; and, second, the emphasis on co-operation with allies at every opportunity to spread security's burdens.[27]

The Wake of Policy

The overall conclusions to emerge from this analysis are simple, even trite. The reshaping of the defence effort after 1964 was a continuous process (and is, indeed, still under way). It was effected via a succession of 'extensive and thorough' reviews in which choices were made according to broadly consistent criteria, implying a coherent set of underlying security priorities.

Recent experience contrasts most sharply in this respect with the confusions of the decade 1955-64. Then governments seemed to lack a clear sense of direction. Whether it is the pressure of events, doctrinal errors, the machinations of single service ministries or the idiosyncracies of certain Ministers which explain the glaring difference is a matter for conjecture. Maybe it is none of these. Perhaps in the 1950s setting priorities — or searching for 'a role' — was just inherently most difficult. Or perhaps it should have been simple but decision-makers were hostage to the 'hard residuums of national habits and deep-set attitudes towards international affairs' of Kenneth Waltz's biting comment.[28]

On the other hand to stress the obvious 'party political' difference between the periods may not be altogether facile. Conservative administrations have, in a general way, paid more attention since the Second World War to the allocation of resources to defence. (Consider the evidence of the 1950s, 1962-4 and 1970-3.) In contrast, Labour governments have usually been clear about that aspect. The 'Korean' period apart, their inclination has been to hold defence spending constant (or reduce it) to have resources available for other things. Under their management, therefore, the allocation within defence has been the focal issue. 'Where do security priorities really lie?' is a more pressing question when one is simultaneously asking, 'How little is enough?' And under that pressure perhaps the need to find a satisfactory answer more keenly concentrates the mind.

Certainly this is a conclusion which squares with another arresting feature of post-war defence experience: the fact that, when the scope and necessity for choice impressed themselves on governments most sharply, the broad configuration of national security interests seemed more or less the same to everyone. It is a striking thing that, after a quarter of a century of wrestling with defence's place in national priorities and the appropriate structure of defence priorities themselves, a long look along the wake of policy reveals that the progression actually followed conforms almost exactly to that apparently foreseen, and certainly prepared for, by Bevin back in 1949.

Notes

1. L. Robbins, *The Economic Problem in Peace and War* (London, Macmillan, 1957), p. 48.
2. Ibid., p. 49.
3. The data cited in this paragraph are from R.S. Sayers, *Financial Policy 1939-45* (London, HMSO and Longmans, 1956), Appendix I and Appendix III. The organisation of the war effort has been fully described and

analysed in the several volumes of the Civil Series of the Official History of the Second World War (edited by Sir Keith Hancock) of which Sayers's book is one. W.K. Hancock and M.M. Gowing, *The British War Economy* is the key introductory work; the series also includes a useful *Statistical Digest of the War.*

4. For accounts of the demand management dilemmas of the immediate post-war years see J.C.R. Dow, *The Management of the British Economy 1945-60* (Cambridge, Cambridge University Press, 1964), especially Ch. II.

5. Neither here nor in the third paragraph of this chapter are the words '*policy ... posture ... and provision*' strung together in this fashion merely for alliterative effect. Rather the contrary: I think differentiation among these notions is crucial to worthwhile defence policy analysis. It is incom-patibilities among the three which most commentators have in mind when they identify 'inconsistencies' or 'contradictions' or 'disjunctions' in de-fence 'policy'. For a formal differentiation see my contribution to J.J. Holst and U. Nerlich (eds.), *Beyond Nuclear Deterrence: New Aims, New Arms* (New York, Crane Russak, 1976).

6. On the trusteeship concept see G. Harries-Jenkins, 'The Collapse of the Imperial Role' in the Proceedings of a Conference on The Evolution of British Defence Policy 1945-70 held at Winchester, 29 April – 1 May 1975, under the auspices of the University of Southampton (Department of Extra-Mural Studies).

7. For an account of the arguments over the pace of 'demobilisation' see C.J. Bartlett, *The Long Retreat* (London, Macmillan, 1972), especially pp. 45-51.

8. See L.J. Halle, *The Cold War as History* (London, Chatto and Windus, 1970), Chapter XX, especially pp. 204-8.

9. R.N. Rosecrance, *Defense of the Realm* (New York, Columbia University Press, 1968), p. 31.

10. House of Commons Debates, 15 February 1951, col. 653.

11. House of Commons Debates, 23 April 1951, cols. 34-43. See also Dow, op. cit., p. 56f. and Rosecrance, op. cit., pp. 151-5.

12. Quoted by W.P. Snyder, *The Politics of British Defence Policy 1945-62* (Columbus, Ohio, Ohio State University Press, 1964), pp. 195-6.

13. A.J. Pierre, *Nuclear Politics* (London, Oxford University Press, 1972), p. 87.

14. Ibid., p. 89.

15. Rosecrance, op. cit., pp. 178-80.

16. The following paragraphs contain a summary of some ideas of mine which first appeared in print in an article entitled 'Constraints and Choices in the transformation of Britain's defence effort since 1945' published in the *British Journal of International Studies*, 2 (1976), pp. 5-26.

17. See *Statement on the Defence Estimates 1962*, Cmnd 1639, para. 12.

18. See R. Klein *et al.*, *Social Policy and Public Expenditure 1974* (London, Centre for Studies in Social Policy, 1974), Table 1. The whole of the intro-ductory section of this pamphlet is germane to the argument of the present paragraph.

19. The approach followed here is selective and impressionistic. For an auth-oritative account of nuclear policy matters see Andrew Pierre's book (cited at note 13). John Groom's *British Thinking about Nuclear Weapons* (London, Frances Pinter, 1974) and his contribution to the present volume are also relevant, of course. On 'extra-European' policy and posture see P. Darby, *British Defence Policy East of Suez 1947-68* (London, Oxford University Press, 1973) and his chapter in this book. There is no compar-

ably comprehensive study on the 'European forces' theme. But Stephen
Kirby has written a useful sketch, 'Britain's Defence Policy and NATO' in
M. Leifer (ed.), *Constraints and Adjustments in British Foreign Policy*
(London, Allen and Unwin, 1972), in addition to his essay in this collection. On defence policy in general in the period the best narrative account
is still that of C.J. Bartlett, op. cit. (at note 7), especially Chs. 4, 5 and 6;
and some of the best analysis is to be found in R. Rosecrance, op. cit.,
especially Chs. 7, 8 and 9.

20. The *Outline of Future Policy* is Cmnd 124. On the Wohlstetter study see
E.S. Quade (ed.), *Analysis for Military Decisions* (Chicago, Rand McNally
and Amsterdam: North Holland, 1964), Ch. 3 and Ch. 7 (by Wohlstetter),
especially pp. 122-7.

21. I am indebted to Colin Gordon for this reference.

22. The quoted phrases are from Cmnd 124. See also N. Brown, *Strategic
Mobility* (London, Chatto and Windus, 1963).

23. The official documents referred to or quoted in this paragraph are *Supplementary Statement on Defence Policy, 1967,* Cmnd 3357 (see especially
Ch. III) and *Public Expenditure 1968-69 and 1969-70,* Cmnd 3515 (text
of the Prime Minister's Statement of 16 January 1968). For a fuller
account of the 'continuing defence review' see D. Greenwood, *Budgeting
for Defence* (London, Royal United Services Institute for Defence Studies,
1972), Ch. 5. The flavour of the Whitehall debate on 'east of Suez' is
illustrated by a fascinating chapter in P. Gordon Walker, *The Cabinet*
(London, Collins/Fontana, 1972 revised edition).

24. Until the moment of truth when it is necessary to decide whether one
wants anything at all. For the United Kingdom that comes in 1978-80.

25. Needless to say, controversy continues over the role of theatre nuclear
weapons and the 'flexible response' strategy as a whole. See, for example,
L.W. Martin, 'Theatre Nuclear Weapons and Europe', *Survival*, XVI, 6,
November/December 1974, pp. 268-76; M.J. Brenner, 'Tactical Nuclear
Strategy and European Defence: A Critical Reappraisal', *International
Affairs*, 51, 1, January 1975, pp. 23-42; and J. Schlesinger, 'The Theatre
Nuclear Force Structure in Europe', *Survival*, XVII, 5, September/October
1975, pp. 235-41. (Also J.J. Holst and U. Nerlich (eds.), op. cit., at note
5.)

26. For a more detailed explanation and description of both the functional
costing system and programme changes 1966-72 see my *Budgeting for
Defence*, op. cit., pp. 10-12 and Ch. 4.

27. The 1974 Defence Review is reported in *Statement on the Defence Estimates 1975*, Cmnd 5976. For exposition of the exercise and comment see
Second Report from the Expenditure Committee, Session 1974-5, *The
Defence Review Proposals*, House of Commons Paper (HC) 259 (1974-5)
and two articles in *Survival*, XVII, 5, September/October 1975 under the
heading 'Setting British Defence Priorities'. (The first of these, by Roy
Mason, is a particularly interesting commentary by the Minister who conducted the exercise. The second attempts a systematic comparison of the
1964-8 and 1974 reviews and I have drawn on it heavily in this section.)

28. K.N. Waltz, *Foreign Policy and Democratic Politics* (Boston, Little, Brown,
1967), p. 7 and pp. 161-2.

Michael Dillon

The main purpose of this chapter is to provide a review of some of the
changes which have taken place in the defence decision-making process
in Britain. An attempt will be made to provide an intelligible account of
what features most characterised these changes. This account will
emphasise the persistence of certain dilemmas and outline the role that
rationalist rhetoric played in coping with them. It is not intended to
specify any progression in these changes from one unsatisfactory state
of affairs to another which might be regarded as more satisfactory, or
less unsatisfactory, depending upon one's enthusiasm for the reforms
involved. It follows, therefore, that the chapter will not examine any
further prescriptions for change or additional elaboration at the
national or alliance level of the remaining mismatches that may exist
between objectives and the organisation and distribution of resources.
It is generally acknowledged that these preoccupations have been the
favourite pursuits of students of defence and that defence structures
have been subjected to a long period of widespread organisational and
procedural change in the wake of approximately seventeen defence
reviews since 1945 and of other organisational investigations. Reflection
therefore is perhaps more appropriate at this juncture than prescription.

   Policy-making exhibits a multiplicity of potentially conflicting and
perhaps ultimately irreconcilable values.[1] We expect any policy process
and its associated organisational infrastructure to be responsive to
demands and perceived needs, and to be flexible and adaptive to the
exigencies of particular cases or particular situations. We expect simultaneously that it will be co-ordinated and consistent so that it will be
free from internal contradictions and reasonably predictable. Moreover,
organisational structures associated with public policy-making are, in
effect, agencies entrusted with a licence to overview and manage
matters of special public concern. They are therefore expected to display a degree of initiative and leadership in anticipating policy
problems, defining their character, generating answers and implementing
agreed solutions. Policy-making and its associated administrative behaviour are, in addition, expected to be deliberate and informed; cog-

nisant of and where possible guided by specialists and the professional disciplinary standards to which they adhere. In the public domain, probity, candour and accountability are further obligations, whose requirements have to be met by policy, its formulators and its implementors.

Finally, and not least, the policy process is expected to be effective and perhaps even 'efficient'. Prescribed activities should be implemented and agreed objectives attained. Performance of these tasks should be achieved in a timely manner, at a conservative cost and, as far as might be calculable, they should be done efficiently. That is to say, those courses of action should be pursued, where possible, which are not merely effective but which can be demonstrated to have a particular degree of effectiveness relative to the costs involved. Efficiency is an economic approach to the general notion of rationality, whereby a score for rational performance is derived from a consideration of input/output ratios (of resources to objectives) for some course of action, calculated on the basis of some common denominator. That common denominator is an accurate form of measurement which can honestly represent an agreed value or objective. Such a device is indispensable for efficiency calculations because it acts as a form of decisional currency, elucidating, evaluating and ultimately determining questions of efficient choice. The notion of 'efficiency' when it has any specific meaning at all, therefore, only extends as far as the jurisdiction of the common denominator used. It is primarily a function not of organisational structures and managerial processes but of reliable measurements and unambiguous, fixed intent.[2]

Defence policy and defence policy-making have been subject to these conflicting demands and obligations over the past thirty years perhaps more than any other area of government activity. Like any other area of governmental policy-making, too, they have not resolved the dilemmas involved in these values or provided an easy environment for efficiency calculations, but merely arrived at some variable and more or less satisfactory accommodation of the dilemmas to a changing strategic environment, to institutional dynamics and variable public expectations. Neither have accommodations in these three areas been simultaneously achieved. They cannot be, given the different and largely independent time-scales that appear to operate strategically, institutionally, and in the public domain.

It is accepted that the defence policy process, like any other, is incremental, sometimes confused and often confusing.[3] And that, as the aphorism has it, the policy-maker's difficulty is not to decide where to

go, but where to go from here. However, defence policy was among the
first policy issue areas to be converted to, or acquiesce in, a rationalist
rhetoric and idealism associated with that managerialist approach to
policy-making which seems to be required by the multiplicity of goals,
responsibilities and requirements which devolve on government in a
collectivist state.[4] Historically, providing for the state's security has
been one of the few undisputed functions of government. The changed
strategic environment of the United Kingdom, its persistent economic
decline, the retreat from Empire and the development of collectivist
politics were some of the principal reasons why rationalism became a
dominant theme in the post-war decades. It provided a rationale for
articulating policy-making and a reformist ethic for changing the
practice of it. Moreover, changes in defence organisation and decision-
making seemed from an early stage to be closely attuned to the developing administrative and policy concerns of those years; for example,
efficiency, rationality, managerial expertise and accountable management.[5] In general terms these expressed the desire for some ideal harmonisation and coherent integration of goals, resources and organisational structures in forms which would satisfy both policy and efficiency.

There is no one best way of organising any institution or set of institutions and similarly there is no one best way of arriving at a decision
or policy.[6] Yet the reforms in defence have been distinguished by the
centralisation of its policy-making structures and the reorganisation of
its administrative agencies and practices to enable them both to attain
more nearly this rationalist ideal.[7]

Rationalism therefore is characterised by the following attributes.[8] Goal-
directed behaviour becomes the paradigm of rational action. Goals may
then determine action, provide a reference without which the efficiency
of it cannot be measured, and enable those who are responsible for
action to be held accountable. A persistent theme in any rationalist
policy process therefore, and one which has been evident in defence, is
the requirement to specify objectives. Second, rationalism rejects tradition, custom or habit. It aspires to some objective understanding
devoid of opinion or preconceptions. Such understanding would be
encapsulated in explicit rules or principles. It provides a second theme
characteristic of the defence policy process, the desire for objectivity,
for a non-partisan overview of the 'defence problem', and for analytical
and authority structures which would provide and apply this knowledge. Third, from the rationalist perspective the policy process would
be exclusively concerned with problem-solving, with identifying and

applying the processes by which optimal or sub-optimal solutions to policy problems could be calculated. A third theme therefore of the defence policy process has been a concern with techniques, organisational or budgetary. Although the introduction of such techniques may have been responses to specific difficulties, the rhetoric associated with them persistently advanced them as indispensable general procedures to cure the existing systematically disordered processes, rather than as specific cures for specific ills.

Apart from the parallel that exists between the military requirements for precision with regard to objectives, economy with regard to means, and clarity with regard to authority which derive from the exigencies of combat, a number of additional features have provided a fertile environment for rationalism in the defence field. The first of these was the advent of nuclear weapons and the adoption of a deterrent posture with regard to the major security threat represented by the Soviet Union and its allies. The nuclear environment was an unknown one, past practice and past experience of the preparation for and the conduct of war appeared to be, in varying degrees, irrelevant to the novel security issues which emerged. The sting in the adage that planners always prepared to fight the last war seemed to be especially sharp. Where past practice and experience did retain relevance, as for example in the colonial holding operations through which imperial responsibilities were steadily given up, these security issues were ultimately transitory, and less salient to the central defence problem, the security of the United Kingdom and Western Europe. Moreover, the adoption of a deterrent posture required forces in-being to be trained and equipped to fight in such a way and to such an extent that the costs involved for any aggressor would be seen to be too great.

Nuclear weapons themselves represented an additional novel feature of the post-war environment with which defence decision-makers had to deal. The technological parameters of weapon systems and hence the cost of those systems changed, and continued to change with disturbing speed. The pace of change again appeared to leave practice and experience behind. Something had to fill the gap to manage the problems involved, new techniques, new structures or both.

Deterrence and change required historically high levels of peacetime military expenditure. Although the expenditure of public resources since 1945 appeared to be generally sympathetic to this defence need, expenditure was popular and unconstrained by notions of a balanced budget, in practice it was more sympathetic to a multiplicity of other needs.[9] The defence sector in short had many more competitors than

before in making claims on public expenditure. In making those claims
a reputation for profligacy, waste, duplication or general managerial inefficiency, however that might be identified, was less than advantageous.
To be seen to have one's house in order was a necessary requirement,
especially when competing with other politically popular and more immediately justifiable social claims.

Finally, there is the general perception that the mismanagement of
defence has unique and possibly irretrievable consequences. In a sense
defence policy-makers cannot afford to produce the wrong answers.
But as there are no right answers, and as the answers that defence
policy-makers come up with will only be tested when the purpose for
which they are generated (peace) will already have been lost, they are
under a much greater obligation to provide defensible, co-ordinated,
coherent and consistent policy postures. Moreover, the success of their
endeavours in sustaining a peaceful environment seems necessarily to
erode the value that is placed on their activity relative to other social
causes, especially in a declining economy.

The progressive centralisation of defence and the erosion of the
pluralism of service autonomy, the abortive attempt at institutional-
ising policy analysis in the Programme Evaluation Group (PEG) and the
introduction of functional budgeting have been three major areas of
reform which best illustrate the rationalist themes outlined above. They
expressed the desire for an overview of defence issues unprejudiced by
service rivalry and preferences. They were concerned to generate objective analysis of defence policy problems and alternative courses of
action unencumbered by institutional inertia and the force of en-
trenched programmes. And they were advanced as systematic attempts
to re-order the policy process, clarify its outputs and improve its performance.[10] In more general terms, they represented a predisposition
to resort to organisational reform, procedural change and the espousal
of managerial principles as responses to recurring and persistent difficulties and dilemmas. It was a pattern of action repeated across the
spectrum of governmental responsibilities.

The persistence of such problems and dilemmas at the level of high
policy has always been accepted. Their recurrence is associated with
matching long-term planning with short-term requirements and with
deriving operational goals from, and coherently relating them to, necessarily diffused and ambiguous general policy statements and values.[11]
These issues have found particular expression in defence in the difficulties associated with matching resources and responsibilities; with
matching force structures and equipment to existing and predicted

tactical and strategic environments; with mixing policy analysis and organisational routine (the PEG experience):[12] and with using budgets both as planning and management tools as well as a means of precise fiscal accountability and control. However what is less readily accepted is the persistence of dilemmas at lower levels of operational and organisational concern. But even at these levels standard themes recur. It is worth examining at some length an example of this in an area which has been central to defence decision-making, the managerial processes and organisational structures associated with technological development and weapon system procurement.

In this area three characteristics were in evidence. The first of these was the persistence of administrative dilemmas and the second was a progressive shift from one pattern of preoccupations to a marginally but discretely changed one. The third feature was the enthusiasm of reformers for a particular organisational development or managerial innovation as a way of resolving intractable difficulties. In this context the difficulties were of two sorts, substantive and organisational. Cost over-runs and time slippages in weapon system programmes were the outstanding substantive difficulties. Finding, within a complex administrative context, an acceptable balance between the virtues and disadvantages of *differentiation* (of functions and specialisms) and *integration* (of these functions and specialisms in the service of a more specific task) was the outstanding organisational problem.[13] The reformers in this instance were, primarily, the Select Committee on Science and Technology and the industrial witnesses who gave evidence to it, and later the Rayner Report which led to the establishment of the Procurement Executive.[14] The progressive and selective introduction of project management in defence procurement agencies illuminated the dilemmas, provided the object of reformist enthusiasm, and together with the espousal of the wider managerial philosophy associated with accountable management identified the shift in orientation. For analytical convenience the shift in preoccupations may rather loosely be identified as a change, on balance, from a control orientation to a promotional orientation in the management of development and production programmes.

The notion of a control orientation is premised upon the assumption that failure has to be guarded against by building incremental steps and constraints into the decisional and evaluational process. Incremental steps operate as firebreaks at appropriate stages in the development process. They provide formal and regular opportunities for external review and assessment of a programme's progress and of its relevance in other broader organisational, financial and strategic planning contexts. In particular a programme's progress is measured against cost, time and technical parameters which function as constraints to which administrative action must conform. Close control is further exercised through highly constrained access to the organisation's resources (money, men, facilities and consent) by limiting administrative authority and financial discretion.

On balance, the notion of a promotional orientation is rather more concerned to accord a greater prominence and visibility to individual programmes. This is done by identifying specific agencies to be exclusively concerned with sponsoring their progress, and the agencies are correspondingly allowed greater degrees of administrative and financial discretion. In this way a wider licence is granted on an alternative assumption to that obtaining in the control orientation, that success has to be achieved by mobilising and deploying organisational resources so that parameters which here function as targets and mile-stones, rather than constraints, may be attained.

If, then, within the control orientation initiative is limited by constraints and inhibited by assessments, within the promotional orientation there is a greater awareness that definitions of discretion are also licences to act and that an assessment procedure can also operate as a process of progressive commitment. The differences, therefore, are not merely structural as between project managers and functional managers, but are also significantly stylistic.

For most of the 1960s, with few exceptions — notably that, for example, of the Polaris Executive — a control orientation predominated.[15] Two categories of constraints gave effect to this control orientation. There were the procedural constraints derived from the Gibb-Zuckerman Report[16] and, with some elaboration, from the Downey Report.[17] There were also the discretionary constraints which were inherent in the traditional organisation of the departments concerned, where administrative hierarchies followed functionally specific and technologically specialised lines and financial discretion was relatively limited.

The procedural constraints constituted the incremental system of control by which the progress of and commitment to development programmes was carefully monitored. This process was initiated by an operational requirement or staff target. Ideally, it then progressed through essentially four stages from a feasibility study, through a project study to full development and ultimately production. Two senior committees operated directly as overseers of the process — the Operational Requirements Committee and the Weapons Development Committee. Major programmes were also subject to endorsement by the Chiefs of Staff and ultimately by the Defence and Overseas Policy Committee. The Gibb-Zuckerman procedures had four objectives; to improve development cost estimating; to control cost escalation; to reduce the number of programme cancellations; and finally to reduce the redundancy of demands for development programmes.

By 1966, however, the Downey Report had determined that the basis of control, the identification and evaluation of areas of technological uncertainty and difficulty in any development project, was not as adequate as it could have been. Accordingly it recommended a two-stage project definition phase. The first stage was based on the previous project study phase and was designed to 'firm-up' the staff target. The second and more elaborate stage was designed to consolidate, elaborate and define a sophisticated and detailed development cost plan.[18]

In sum, the firebreaks imposed by the stages of the process, the reviews of progress within particular stages as for example in 'trend meetings', and the deliberations of the Operational Requirements and Weapons Development Committees constituted what was described as a very tight system of control.[19] Taken together, the Gibb-Zuckerman and Downey procedures imposed a severe discipline and were said to have produced a marked decline in cancellations.[20] The constraints imposed meant that delays to progress were, in some degree, deliberate — a function of the requirement to review the state of a programme concerned. By far the longest delays occurred at the threshold of full development and this constituted the most significant firebreak. A year's delay here was regarded as a 'medium' time to wait for a verdict to be arrived at.[21]

The discretionary constraints which operated, however, were not instrumentally designed to foster the control of advanced technological defence-development projects. Rather they were a product of the two prevailing features of existing administrative structures. First of these was the structuring of organisations in terms of departments which represented, primarily, staff functions (like contracts) and established technological specialisms, and not projects. The second was the relatively limited degree of financial discretion which existed.

By 1969 reactions to this overall system of control expressed a wider dissatisfaction with its performance. There were a number of aspects to the criticisms which were voiced but the most common theme was that the pace of decision was too slow and the procedures too inhibiting. All three parties to the investigations of the Select Committee on Science

and Technology which investigated 'Defence Research', and whose
report was published in that year, displayed a large measure of agreement on this point. One of the members of the Committee, for example, complained that,

> Somehow or other the Secretary of State managed in his answer to
> give the impression that this proliferation of committees was nec-
> essary to ensure we had proper monitoring of the system; because
> we did not have this structure beforehand we were running into
> waste and slipping off the scale. Is this really so? Could you not have
> a look at this from the point of view of cutting down the number
> of committees without in any way sacrificing the improved moni-
> toring you have secured?[22]

The Confederation of British Industry submitted that 'the inter-
woven committee structure involved in new weapon development does
not lend itself to rapid and effective action';[23] and that its emphasis on
controlling costs and technical performances made it ineffectual in the
context of 'the wider implications of military procurement.' Finally,
Sir Robert Cockburn (Director of the Royal Aircraft Establishment)
concluded that the procedures had become 'almost entirely restrictive
in their application'.[24]

The consensus of opinion which emerged — with some exceptions —
was that financial discretion was far too limited and that the division of
administrative responsibilities defied 'all the rules of a sensible management structure'.[25] A system of project managers for major programmes
was generally recommended as the major requirement to resolve these
difficulties. The most pressing need which was identified was to extend
current practice and remove the 'frustrations' of those already in re-
ceipt of project responsibility. In the terms of the recommendation of
the Select Committee Report:

> To achieve maximum benefit from the method, it is essential that
> the project director should be given total responsibility for the con-
> trol of the technical, timing and financial aspects of the project
> within the overall plan. No system of organization can work effic-
> iently without delegation of these responsibilities and the necessary
> authority to carry the venture through to completion.[26]

In this regard the report was contributing very little analytically to
what defence managers already knew, and were trying to do, about the

problems with which they were faced.[27] What it did represent, though, was a reflection of and a stage in the shift towards a promotional, as opposed to a control orientation, which was ultimately to receive official endorsement in the Rayner Report.[28] Since at least 1966 the major organisational difficulties associated with rapid technological development had been identified within the defence procurement establishment. The progressive but highly selective introduction of project managers, which had been taking place throughout the decade, indicated this awareness as well as the lack of confidence in the total 'projectising' of procurement as a definitive solution.

Technological development appears to display an inherent dynamic which regularly transcends the boundaries of the categories created for organising work. Administrative work flow, and the authority and career patterns derived from it, has generally been established in three categories; technical specialisms; staff functions; and phases of activity. This sufficed for managing work programmes associated with tasks which exhibited at least the following three features:

(a) those that were confined essentially to one technical specialism:
(b) those in which the interfaces and interrelationships between specialisms were reasonably manageable, within the existing framework, and relatively well defined:
(c) or thirdly, those in which individual projects did not assume such major technical, financial and political proportions that they supersede the established infrastructures necessary to service both them and other projects.

But these factors are not the prevailing features of advanced technological programmes or the determining characteristics of major weapon systems procurement. Such programmes require the concurrent development and integration of a number of complex equipment sub-systems, which themselves may represent major technical advances. Obsolescence of skills is a function of rapid technological development, the acquisition and fostering of new ones may be crucially dependent on one major project. Projects of such significance require a discreet 'institutional home' to marshall the 'captive' resources they need and give them an administrative visibility appropriate to their status. A more holistic (or 'system') view of weapon development has been generated as a consequence, and was well represented by the following observation from the Select Committee on Science and Technology:

The sub-systems and units which make up modern military systems
are no longer regarded as providing additional or independent functions. Even with basically developed sub-systems and units a major
task exists in the successful development of an effective overall
system.[29]

The problems of co-ordination and integration which were then presented demanded the particular attention and the new forms of administrative authority, financial discretion and managerial expertise associated with project management. To the extent that it has been introduced, therefore, project management represents the eclipse of established technological disciplines and staff functions by the individual
projects which they in large part sustain. The resultant organisational
complex, in which project structures overlay the existing administrative
structures and in which functional and project lines of responsibility
coexist, has been termed matrix organisation.[30] Within such complexes
the patterns of authority, definitions of competence and questions of
accountability are particularly involved. Project managers may not rule
by fiat (if managers ever do), or rely on prompt instinctive acquiescence
to formal authorisations. In any event, consistently congruent and co-
operative administrative behaviour cannot be pre-programmed and
formal powers have to be operationalised in the course of implementing
project responsibilities. Project style, ideally reflecting the philosophy
of accountable management, is entrepreneurial and committed.[31] In
addition, for industrial agencies, the project office provides the socket
into which they plug to simplify the conduct of their transactions with
the Ministry of Defence procurement agencies.

But there are no factors inherent within the general characteristics of
the philosophy of accountable management that necessarily make it a
more effective overall control agent. All is dependent on the specific
nature and environment of a task, the authority and discretion delegated, and the expertise and experience of the personnel involved. Sir
Solly Zuckerman pointed out in 1968 that, for example, in determining
what degree of authority to grant project directors:

> Full financial control is one thing. Access to all the resources he
> wants is another. We have got to differentiate between those two. I
> want my project manager to have full financial control of the
> resources which are allocated to him, but I think one has got to be
> careful in some cases. I can think of one or two project managers . . .
> I shall take illustrations from the other side of the Atlantic — who

have been given, as it were, not only full financial responsibility but also an assumed access to unlimited resources, who have pushed their projects up into the stratosphere.[32]

Concentrating responsibility and delegating corresponding degrees of authority and discretion also grants a measure of promotional licence. Therefore, the requirement to ensure that this promotional licence is compatible with other organisational considerations persists, and is not satisfied or materially reduced by the espousal of a particular managerial philosophy or principle.

A process of responding to and managing these questions of compatibility was reflected in the selective introduction of project management in the 1960s. As the government's response to the report of the Select Committee on Science and Technology argued, the issue was 'to find the right compromise between line management and project management' for individual tasks.[33] Ultimately a project manager was 'entrusted with control within a predetermined plan. Changes outside the limits of this plan can be authorised only at a level of management capable of balancing the proposed change against other competing claims.'[34] Three factors were central here: uncertainty reduction; conflicting competences; and career structures.

By 1968-9 attribution of project authority in two areas of major uncertainty, finance and to some extent task refinement, was still quite tentative and limited. This feature was generally reflected in the Secretary of State's greater enthusiasm for project organisation as an instrument of production management rather than of research and development control.[35] Departments, then, had delegated financial authority which enabled them to undertake and carry through a project costing up to £250,000 without reference to the Treasury.[36] Such limited financial discretion on programmes where the research and development component was a source of considerable uncertainty was defended on the basis that 'the amounts of money involved and the unpredictability is so much greater . . . that you cannot give, and Parliament would never allow us to give, a single individual this right of control.'[37] Few defence projects have been completed on-cost, and cost inflation appears to be directly related to the research and development element. In practice, therefore, there was a predisposition to reduce uncertainty about the cost-estimates and financial implications of a project before individual authority and responsibility was licensed. 'Continuous monitoring of development from outside' and 'limits on the degree of authority you can give to the man in control where you are dealing with unpredictable areas of development' were favoured.[38]

Task refinement in detail takes place during the research and development stage also, and the number of project authorities engaged here varied from department to department. Only in selected instances in the Army Department, for example, was the management of a project during the development stage put under the control of a project manager.[39] In addition the authority of project managers over the investigation and specification of the technical parameters of a weapon system was compromised by their necessarily limited technical competence. Both the Navy Department and, at the time, the Ministry of Technology recognised the utility, as the task became reasonably well defined, of according project managers design authority. In this way a moratorium on design changes (or at least rigid control of them) could be imposed so that the objective could be kept fixed and attainable.[40]

The conflicting competences of project managers and functional managers or technical specialists in general represents one of the most characteristic features of matrix organisation and a source of some of the constraints on a project manager's executive authority. Take, for example, the following observations on the situation that existed in the management of aircraft projects in 1968:

> at the moment . . . we give the project director complete executive responsibility within the Ministry for air frame production. However, we do not give him executive responsibility over specialist areas, which may mean engines, radar and other types of equipment, because as a rule you cannot find a man who can span the whole of this field of specialisation. He has a co-ordinating responsibility for the specialist system.[41]

These constraints are derived not only from the limitations of individual project managers but, more significantly, are related to the requirement to retain the advantages of functional and technical establishments. Such establishments are not merely means to the ends defined by individual projects but their welfare may be a value in itself. They are in effect an important organisational resource providing an accumulation of experience, a catalogue of standards, and a career and training structure to generate skilled personnel in a given area. Interchange and storage of ideas and solutions are facilitated by these features in a way in which they may not be in 'one-off' projects.[42] This organisational infrastructure is necessary, in addition, to provide the capacity to support a number of projects running concurrently. The continuing significance of technology establishments received affirmation in a recent Statement on the Defence Estimates.[43] Research and Development Establishments, in the first stage of a process of rationalisation announced in 1973,[44] have been grouped into 'Systems' Establishments (sea, land, air and underwater), complemented and supported by a number of 'Technology' Establishments. It has, that is, been considered

> neither practicable nor economic to make the individual Systems Establishment self-sufficient in all the technologies required, particularly where these technologies are common to all or several environments or relate to a variety of likely users. They will therefore be supported by Technology Establishments which concentrate on specific technologies and the appropriate sub-systems (such as communications and engineering equipment or propulsion units).[45]

Most career structures, and therefore the development of expertise that they represent, have been fixed in non-project patterns. This not only limited the degree of experience of personnel with any one task, but was a primary source of the absence of continuity in the management of projects. On the other hand, continuity of experience in one project narrows the training of personnel and increases the difficulties of moving them. These general difficulties, again, had been identified in 1966:

> While career planning often makes it difficult to retain staff on project management for long periods, we take the view that the primary purpose of staff employment is the execution of a Department's work as expeditiously and efficiently as possible. We therefore repeat the recommendation . . . that steps should be taken to extend the length of tours of duty of Service officers in key posts, and to ensure that staff within a Supply Department posted into branches engaged on project work remain for longer periods.[46]

The development of project management as a discrete specialised category of managerial expertise led the management consultants, who had worked in conjunction with the Downey investigations, to recommend the establishment of a 'professional class' of project managers. The Report, however, rejected this proposal and preferred instead to recommend a more limited measure supporting an increase in the opportunities for specialised training, and encouraging a 'professional approach' to project management rather than the development of a 'professional class'.[47]

These issues were also raised in evidence before the Select Committee on Science and Technology, in which the promotional aspect of project management was reflected in the concern expressed about how project directors get their 'ideas across in the face of skepticism if not opposition from senior people' whose authority they had to a degree preempted; and in the emphasis that was placed on the personal qualities project management required.[48] The Committee's Report, however, contained no specific recommendations about any of these issues. The matter of full career opportunities for project management specialists was ultimately dealt with in the Rayner Report, which identified the shift in official policy from a balance of concern reflecting a control orientation to one expressing a promotional orientation.

The White Paper on *Government Organisation for Defence Procurement and Civil Aerospace* employed Fulton's notion of accountable management as a way of organising many of the various reforms that were instituted.[49] Consequently the new Procurement Executive was described as 'designed in such a way as to foster the creation of accountable units of management down to project manager level'.[50] In practice this has meant a basic structure consisting of a Chief Executive and four Systems Controllers with accounting authority;[51] the identification of the 'development of project management'in a meaningful way', as the second major problem of the new organisation;[52] and an emphasis on ensuring that 'a full career is offered to procurement specialists'.[53] These features specifically identify the shift to a promotional orientation.

However, this move represents only a marginal shift. First, the apparently greater financial discretion which has been accorded by identifying Systems Controllers as Accounting Officers appears to have been partially a response also to the need to break up the accounting responsibility for £1,000 million into more manageable proportions.[54] Second, there is no evidence to suggest that the existing procedural control devices have been measurably relaxed. Third, in some ways they have been increased, by the introduction of a mandatory review by the central committees for projects whose costs go up by 20 per cent or more, and by the attempt to introduce a system of twice yearly and possibly quarterly 'across the board' review of outstanding projects.[55]

Moreover, there is similarly no evidence available yet to determine whether the potential clash of competences between functional authorities and project authorities (the Rayner Report specifically identified dual functional and project responsibilities for specialists) has been consistently resolved in favour of the latter, as the general impulse of the reorganisation suggests that it should be. There is little evidence, either, to suggest that the dilemmas identified here have been passed over by current procurement preoccupations, or that they have lost any of their basic significance.

In more general terms, while defence decision-making has been characterised by these dilemmas in the past twenty-five years, it has also illustrated the persistence of some other themes. These themes have principally been concerned with rationalisation and standardisation of equipment and equipment procedures. Two impulses seem to have been directly responsible for these. The first has been that more general rationalist impulse which rejects the untidy proliferation of equipments and the associated procedures for the formulation of equipment requirements. The second impulse has been a more pragmatic one. In the context of Britain's economic decline and the inflation of equipment costs, its armed services could no longer afford the profligacy involved in specially tailored equipment for particular service requirements, and their associated traditional service procedures derived from historical service autonomy. Rationalisation and standardisation within the United Kingdom has therefore progressed measurably. However, persistent decline, persistent inflation and a return to European preoccupations have progressively shifted the focus of interests in these themes from a national to an international level.

Standardisation and rationalisation have, therefore, been equally persistent themes in the NATO context, but progress there has been markedly less satisfactory.[56] More recently, however, at least within the United Kingdom, the same pressures which forced considerable national standardisation have been acknowledged at the international level too.

Reasons of military effectiveness, reasons of cost and the requirement to retain industrial technical expertise in strategic areas have meant that collaboration in weapon system procurement for major weapon systems has become an alternative which increasingly receives automatic consideration. At the alliance level the recent introduction of the Independent European Programme Group (which includes France amongst its members) to consider the harmonisation of equipment replacement cycles and areas for future collaboration represents a re-affirmation of this common concern.[57] This should not suggest, however, that progress has been or is likely to be systematic. Very real political and industrial obstacles remain in the way of co-operation within NATO, and especially between its European partners. Defence decision-makers within Europe, however, are having to accept that there is no alternative but to attempt to tackle such issues, if weapon system costs are to be borne, and if the remaining technical capacity to continue to be able to produce major items of equipment is to be retained. No European state is self-sufficient in defence equipment. The United Kingdom, for example, has abandoned any national procurement policies for attack — aircraft-carriers, long-range bombers and air superiority fighters. In varying degrees collaboration is therefore a necessary requirement, but it can take a variety of forms.

Rationalisation of equipment and equipment procedures may come about through increasing specialisation of roles and sharing of combat tasks. Some of the difficulties here include France's unwillingness to engage in NATO military planning, the fears within the Alliance of United States technical hegemony and possibly too, within Europe, mutual suspicions between Germany, France and the United Kingdom. Standardisation may come about through collaborative joint procurement policies, joint purchasing policies or, failing these, through the introduction of programmes to ensure the interoperability of different equipment. One of the principal difficulties here is finding an acceptable and comprehensive procedure for co-ordinating and replacing all the individual and *ad hoc* collaborative arrangements that have developed in the past twenty years, and so provide the formal systematic machinery necessary for intergovernmental defence equipment collaboration.

Rationalisation and standardisation within the Alliance and within Europe are already prominent themes and they are likely to remain so. Now that the United Kingdom has relinquished its world role and has largely accomplished the associated reorganisation of its military structures these themes will perhaps become more totally preoccupying. A fundamental tension exists here too, however, between the 'European connections and the Atlantic connection. The European impulse towards collaboration and co-operation exhibited most recently in the Spinelli proposals for the (defence-related) European aerospace sector[58] are not necessarily congruent with Alliance impulses towards rationalisation and standardisation if these proceed on the basis of United States equipment and planning. Indeed the two, both rhetorically and substantively, are competitive and opposed. The balance struck in France, Germany and the United Kingdom between European impulses and Alliance impulses and the interpretations each makes of their own self-interest in these matters will continue to be reflected in the procedures adopted to manage co-operation and materially affect the progress of it.

The rationalist rhetoric of the 1960s and its associated organisational and managerialist proclivities now fuel the arguments about and stimulates the proposals for greater standardisation within NATO. At the policy level within the United Kingdom the enthusiasm with which these impulses were embraced a decade ago has abated. Rationalist urges have to some extent been satisfied by reform, but they have also been reduced by long hard confrontation with the well-grounded stubbornness of bureaucratic structures, the practical wisdom of bureaucratic animals and the resistance of policy problems to resolution by formal analytical and intellectual techniques alone.

Interestingly the dilemmas which characterise decision-making and the legitimacy of the difficulties they present are much more clearly exhibited at the international level. Although national actors may genuflect to the desirability of rationalist solutions in principle, the problem of implementing them through specific common courses of action in weapons programmes, logistic and supply arrangements is widely acknowledged and much debated. The intransigence of national structures and the acknowledged legitimacy of national postures is accepted in a way that the intransigence of bureaucratic structures within their domestic environments is not.

The basis of policy-making and administration is the acceptance by the actors concerned of common understandings about what was, what is, and what ought to be, and a willingness to act accordingly. Withdrawal from Empire, reduction of forces and an assumed irreducible commitment to NATO have been the principal elements of the understandings which characterised and shaped post-war defence policy in the United Kingdom. Political and administrative authority provided some direction for that policy in detail. Authority alone, however, does not decide policy matters and its absence at the international level only exacerbates the inherent difficulties of policy-making. NATO is now the only referent for the United Kingdom's strategic defence posture. But common alliance interest is not a sufficient spur or guide to future action. Political and administrative initiative is required more than before to thrash out the essential policy understandings to specify and accept common courses of action and to assure their implementation.

Notes

1.   See, for example, an early discussion on this theme by Charles E. Gilbert,

'The Framework of Administrative Responsibility', *The Journal of Politics*, Vol. 21, August 1959.

2. See the discussions in the following: A.Wildavsky, 'The Political Economy of Efficiency: Cost-Benefit Analysis, Systems Analysis and Program Budgeting', in F.J. Lyden and E.G. Miller (eds.), *Planning, Programming, Budgeting: A Systems Approach to Management* (Chicago, Markham Publishing Company, first edition, 1968); E. Rheuman, *Organization Theory for Long Range Planning* (London, John Wiley, 1973); and B.R. Wilson (ed.), *Rationality* (Oxford, Basil Blackwell, 1970).

3. Two classical discussions of incremental decision-making are, D. Braybrooke and C.E. Lindblom, *A Strategy of Decision* (New York, Macmillan, 1963); and A. Wildavsky, *The Politics of the Budgetary Process* (Boston, Little, Brown, 1969).

4. For further elaboration see G.M. Dillon, 'Policy and Dramaturgy: A Critique of Current Conceptions of Policy Making', *Policy and Politics*, Vol. 5, 1976.

5. For a review of these concerns and associated reforms see J. Garrett, *The Management of Government* (Harmondsworth, Penguin Books, 1972); and F. Stacey, *British Government, 1966-75: Years of Reform* (London, Oxford University Press, 1975).

6. The pioneering work which was done to establish these sensible propositions in the relevant literature on organisations and decisions is to be found in J. Woodward, *Industrial Organization, Theory and Practice* (London, Oxford University Press, 1965); T. Burns and G. Stalker, *The Management of Innovation* (London, Tavistock, 1961); and A.K. Rice, *The Enterprise and its Environment: A Systems Theory of Management Organization* (London, Tavistock, 1963).

7. For an account of these reforms see principally, M. Howard, *The Central Organization of Defence* (London, Royal United Services Institution, 1970); D. Greenwood, *Budgeting for Defence* (London, Royal United Services Institution, 1972); R. Burt, *Defence Budgeting: The British and American Cases* (London, International Institute for Strategic Studies, Adelphi Paper 112, 1975); R.M. Hastie-Smith, *The Tin Wedding. A Study of the Evolution of the Ministry of Defence 1964-74* (London, Seaford House Papers, 1974); K. Hartley, 'Programme Budgeting and the Economics of Defence,' *Public Administration*, Vol. 52, 1974; and G. Kennedy, *The Economics of Defence* (London, Faber and Faber Ltd., 1975).

8. See M. Oakeshott, *Rationalism in Politics and Other Essays* (London, Methuen, University Paperbacks, 1967).

9. The best account of the budgetary process and its association with policy is to be found in H.H. Heclo and A. Wildavsky, *The Private Government of Public Money* (London, Macmillan, 1974).

10. Interestingly enough, defence by committee with considerable degrees of service autonomy in the United Kingdom in the 1950s was admired by some students of defence in the United States. See, for example, J.C. Ries, *The Management of Defense* (Baltimore, The Johns Hopkins Press, 1964).

11. With regard to the general relationship between defence and foreign affairs in policy matters, see W. Wallace, *The Foreign Policy Process in Britain* (London, The Royal Institute of International Affairs, 1975).

12. See in particular, Howard, op. cit., and more generally Heclo and Wildavsky, op. cit.

13. This may be further regarded as that classical administrative dilemma of generating an acceptable balance (i.e. defensible balance within the system of prevailing preoccupations) between centralisation and decentralisation.

14.   *Second Report from The Select Committee on Science and Technology.*
      Defence Research, H.C. 213 (London, HMSO, 1969); and *Government*
      Organization for Defence Procurement and Civil Aerospace, Cmnd. 4641
      (London, HMSO, 1971).
15.   See J. Simpson, 'The POLARIS Executive: A Case Study of a Unified
      Hierarchy', *Public Administration,* Vol. 48, 1970.
16.   *Report of The Management Committee on the Management and Control of*
      Research and Development (London, HMSO, 1961).
17.   *Ministry of Technology, Report of the Steering Group on Development*
      Cost Estimating (London, HMSO, 1969).
18.   These procedural steps represented to some degree an 'ideal' because there
      was a measure of flexibility in the system — all projects did not necessarily
      advance through all stages sequentially, *H.C. 213,* p. 59. For two very
      useful discussions of weapons technology and the organisation of procure-
      ment see *Defence Planning and Weapons Technology* (Southampton, Uni-
      versity of Southampton Collected Papers, 1969); and *Weapons Procure-*
      ment, Defence Management and International Collaboration (London,
      Royal United Services Institute, October 1972).
19.   See for example, Sir Robert Cockburn's Evidence, *H.C. 213,* pp. 27-8;
      'trend' meetings were instituted in 1965, *H.C. 213,* p. xvi.
20.   Sir William Cook, *H.C. 213,* p. 371.
21.   *H.C. 213,* p. 31.
22.   *H.C. 213,* p. 442. For a catalogue of more specific difficulties which were
      identified in the proceedings of the Select Committee, and especially by
      the industrial witnesses, see D.E. Greenwood, 'Defence R and D: Industry's
      Role', in *Defence Planning and Weapons Technology.*
23.   *H.C. 213,* p. 405.
24.   *H.C. 213,* p. 28.
25.   *H.C. 213,* p. lv.
26.   *H.C. 213,* p. lv.
27.   See the government's reply to the Select Committee's report, *Defence*
      Research and Development, Cmnd. 4236, 1969. The Downey Report, for
      example, had identified many basic problems, except that by 1971 it was
      generally accepted that 15 to 25 per cent of the ultimate cost of a weapon
      system needed to be committed to development so as to reduce uncer-
      tainty to relatively manageable proportions, and provide a reasonably reli-
      able basis for cost estimating. See *Cmnd. 4641,* p. 22 (Downey had argued
      for a figure up to 15 per cent).
28.   *Cmnd. 4641.*
29.   *H.C. 213,* p. liv.
30.   See D.R. Kingdon, *Matrix Organization* (London, Tavistock, 1973).
31.   See Kingdon, op. cit., and see also L.R. Sayles and M.K. Chandler, *Mana-*
      ging Large Systems (New York, Harper and Row, 1971). See also the
      comment of a witness to the Select Committee on Science and Technology
      to the effect that 'the whole thing turns not on whether you have a good
      tool, but whether you have a man who has the power, who has the respon-
      sibility and intelligence and initiative to do something.' *H.C. 213,* p. 199.
32.   *H.C. 213,* p. 358.
33.   *Cmnd. 4236,* p. 13.
34.   Ibid.
35.   'Where project management works well, and you can afford to give a man
      total control, is where you are dealing with the production of an intensely
      complicated product and no great R and D is concerned.' *H.C. 213,* p. 438.
36.   H.C. 213, p. xviii; later this limit was raised to £1 million. See *Cmnd. 4236,*

p. 7.
37. Mr Healey, *H.C. 213*, p. 439.
38. Mr Healey, *H.C. 213*, pp. 438-9. A control orientation, in other words. For the wider discretion favoured by the Select Committee on Science and Technology, see *H.C. 213*, p. 1.
39. *H.C. 213*, 'Annex B. Research and Development in the Army Department', p. 52.
40. See especially *H.C. 213*, p. 421, and also p. 61.
41. *H.C. 213*, p. 84.
42. See Sayles and Chandler, op. cit. pp. 186-8. Both Downey and Rayner described development cost-estimating as a slow process of accumulating experience; *Report of the Steering Group on Development Cost Estimating*, p. 30; and *H.C. 516-II*, p. 328. The Downey Report also recognised the need to build up a project experience 'memory-bank' by recording and documenting project work in an accessible and retrievable manner.
43. *Cmnd. 5976*, 1975.
44. In the *Statement on the Defence Estimates*, Cmnd. 5231.
45. *Cmnd. 5976*, p. 83.
46. *Report of the Steering Group on Development Cost Estimating*, p. 9.
47. Ibid., pp. 9-10.
48. *H.C. 213*, pp. 422-4.
49. *The Civil Service: Volume 1 – Report of the Committee, 1966-68*, Cmnd. 3638 (London, HMSO, 1968).
50. *H.C. 516-II*, p. 318.
51. *Cmnd. 4641*.
52. *H.C. 516-II*, p. 334.
53. *H.C. 516-II*, p. 318.
54. *H.C. 516-II*, p. 336.
55. *Cmnd. 4641*, p. 29.
56. See, for example, C. Harlow, *Defence Technology and the Western Alliance, No. 2* (London, International Institute for Strategic Studies, 1967); R.R. James, *Defence Technology and the Western Alliance*, No. 3 (London, International Institute for Strategic Studies, 1967); and R. Facer, *The Alliance and Europe; Part III Weapons Procurement in Europe – Capabilities and Choices* (London, International Institute for Strategic Studies, Adelphi Paper 108, 1975).
57. See the *Second Report from the Expenditure Committee Session 1975-76, Defence, H.C. 155* (London, HMSO, 1976); and the government's reply, *Defence Expenditure*, Cmnd. 6489 (London, HMSO, 1976).
58. See the *Action Programme for the European aeronautical sector (Commission Communication and Proposals to the Council forwarded on 3 October 1975)* (Bulletin of the European Communities Supplement 11/75).

9 CIVIL-MILITARY RELATIONS

John Sabine

Contemporary events may be cited as sufficient justification for a concern with civil/military relations. Professor Finer[1] has noted that there were 104 military *coups* between 1962 and 1975, and Ruth First has complained of the growth industry in Academe to which these events have given rise.[2] As a phrase, civil/military relations refers predominantly if not quite exclusively to relations between government and the armed forces. Governments have relations with many professional institutions, however, and sceptics may object that a disproportionate degree of interest is being taken in one case among many. The number of publications available on the relations between government and dentists, or government and dustmen is few indeed, and whilst it may be admitted that the number of *coups d'état* mounted by members of either of those professions is even fewer, the critics suggest that the explanation for military take-over is the disarmingly simple one that soldiers have the guns and dentists and dustmen have not. This is to suggest that the obligation of the political scientist is to explain not why the military sometimes seize power but why government by soldiers is not a universal phenomenon.

Social theorists such as Maine and Spencer[3] have suggested that in earlier and simpler societies than our own the warrior class have, as possessors of the skills and qualities most required to protect society against internal disorder and external attack, been accorded a privileged status and military and political leadership has been co-extensive. In times of war or national crisis, modern states have often reverted to the practice of vesting ultimate control in those with military skills. The observations of Maine and Spencer, however, emphasise that deference to the warrior class is instinctive in primitive societies where practice of the military virtues is demanded by the elemental struggle for survival even when war and social disruption are not threatened. The establishment of civil control was incidental to the specialisation of labour that marked the transition of society from nomadic or agricultural communities to those of a settled and semi-industrial kind. Even in the most complex of these, a military internship was regarded as the typical if not the pre-requisite preliminary to a career in public affairs. A high proportion of the membership of the eighteenth- and nineteenth-century

House of Commons had direct, if limited, experience of military life, and this was true also of the diplomatic corps and chancellories of the more aristocratically ruled Continental countries.

The widespread, if not universal, phenomenon of military rule (both in time and place) may thus be owed at least as much to social esteem and an intuitive understanding of the miseries and hazards of insecurity as to the military's possession of the instruments of coercion. Most of those who have been labouring in the 'growth industry' to which Ruth First refers have been seeking to explain the incidence of military rule and her strictures, among others, have reinforced the scepticism accorded to general theories relating to political events. Less study has been made of the cases of civil control, though these might be as productive of explanation for its breakdown. Britain provides the most long-standing example of a state which has maintained civil control of its armed forces, and although we must acknowledge that in studying civil-military relations we are inclined to consider only overt pressure or insurrection, it seems reasonable to suppose that covert control by the military could not sustain itself as covert over such a long period.[4] It would either be intermittent and adventitious or it would manifest itself in institutional changes or the development of acknowledged and constraining conventions on the discretion of those in power.

The British armed forces have not lacked any of the five attributes — hierarchy, *esprit de corps*, an independent communications system, strict discipline and near monopoly of weapons which give to the military such unique opportunities to impose their will on civil government. What they have lacked, to a degree that has made them invincibly subordinate, is what Finer terms the disposition to intervene in civil affairs. Finer has specified a miscellany of circumstances and conditions that may engender such a disposition. In what follows, four types of circumstances are regarded as especially relevant to the British case: equivocal orders (the incipient stage of civil breakdown), redefinition of the sphere of military autonomy, association of the military with a sectional interest, and a sense of alienation on the part of the military *vis-à-vis* the nation as a whole.

Whilst it is proper to regard sceptically the claims made by successful military conspirators that their conspiracies were necessary in the national interest and their assumption of power designed to save the nation from its politicians and the anarchy they were creating there have, none the less, been cases where this claim was justified (for example, this has been the general, if not unanimous view taken of Ayub Khan's *coup* in Pakistan in October 1958).

Britain's own military dictatorship in the seventeenth century was certainly attended by an army of radical spirit and commanders of great ambition. None the less, fundamentally the army sought to fill a power vacuum created by the upheavals of the Civil War and the vacillations of the politicians, and it is significant that the Restoration was effected by part of the army's leadership and those regiments which remained paid and disciplined. British experience of civil breakdown is happily most limited[5] and we rely on a narrow basis of native empirical evidence and much of a comparative kind in suggesting that a factor most injurious to military morale and most conducive to dissidence is lack of clear and decisive orders. Equivocal instructions and lack of candour were major aspects of the alleged mutiny of officers at the Curragh in 1914.

On that occasion the government wished to use army units to reinforce the security of certain stores depots in Northern Ireland, since it had been rumoured that these might otherwise be raided by the Ulster Volunteer Force. However, not all members of the Cabinet regarded this as the sole objective of the movement of troops from the Curragh to Northern Ireland. The orders that were given by Colonel Seeley, then Secretary of State at the War Office, were, it is generally agreed, largely verbal ones transmitted by an intermediary, General Paget, who was far from dispassionate regarding their content and temperamentally unsuited to the task of passing them on.

When made known to the officers most closely affected, many of whom were Anglo-Irishmen of a Loyalist stamp, the orders were accompanied by a discursive commentary on hypothetical developments arising out of the immediate circumstances which suggested officers domiciled in Northern Ireland could decide for themselves whether or not to attend for duty in the coming weeks. Such orders, and the manner of their presentation, ignored most of the rules for the transmission of instructions to the military and, it might be said, any common-sense notions as well.

The Ulster Workers' Council Strike of 1974 presented another example of equivocal orders, though one so far less reliably documented.[6] The suggestion that the army was left without clear directives from the government as to what action it should take in regard to the erection of street barricades and the intimidation of non-strikers is dependent on newspaper comment and hearsay evidence. Some of the leaders of the strike have since attributed its success to the pusillanimity of the Northern Ireland Office in the first few days. We may sense that a policy of masterly inactivity appears the prudent course to those faced with widespread civil disobedience, especially when only

limited forces are at their disposal. By the time the government had
gained in resolution, however, the strike had gathered support and
momentum, and any chance of mastering events rather than being their
victim was lost. It is, of course, more than likely that the government's
lack of decisiveness was increased by the service leaders' apprehension
that there were not within the services themselves technicians possessed
of the skills needed to maintain essential services, nor sufficient troops
to protect the public service installations against UWC sabotage.

'Aid to the civil' operations, so frequently and successfully conducted in colonial possessions, have the greatest potential for causing
dissension between government and the armed forces when attempted
in the metropolitan territory. It is, perhaps, fortunate that notwithstanding its legal status, Northern Ireland is commonly regarded as
being outside rather than within the United Kingdom. In such circumstances as Northern Ireland has provided in recent years, it is difficult
for either government or the army to apply the rule of 'minimum force'
with agreement or consistency, most obviously because army weapons
are not suited to that precise degree of control in the application of
force that is desirable in ending civil commotion, and private soldiers
are given little instruction in the very complicated rules relating to
summary arrest or entry on private premises. For officers, especially the
most senior of them, the dilemmas are somewhat different. There are
to be resisted the pressures for 'success' in the type of conflict which
yields no tangible victories. By contrast, because sentencing is reserved
to the courts and punishment to the prisons the police do not have the
same emotional commitment to the reduction of the enemy as the
military quite properly do. How is morale to be maintained in such
debilitating conditions[7] and how is training to be reinforced against the
day when the army may be needed to fulfil its classic role of defence
against *external* threats? Officers and men have families, friends, individual association with civilian groups, religious and political convictions.
How far, if at all, in the genuinely metropolitan territory, can the strain
on loyalties imposed by operations 'in aid of the civil power' be discounted? Above all, how far can the army's political masters be
trusted? The sacrosanctness of civilian control is always attested, but
the day-to-day directives are often oblique and equivocal.[8] Tactical
successes are readily added to the credit of the civil administration, but
it is suspected that the military would as enthusiastically be made the
scapegoat in the event of ultimate failure or adverse public reaction.[9]

Difficulties of this sort would have affected any attempt to provide a
'military' solution at the time of the Rhodesian UDI. There were then

unconfirmed reports in the press that the armed services would be less
than whole-hearted in mounting operations against the Smith regime.
There were, in any case, severe logistical difficulties in the way of in-
vading Rhodesia.

Any attempt to coerce Rhodesia by military means would have been
highly contentious politically and accompanied by acrimonious public
debate of the kind that attended the Suez operation in 1956.[10] There is
a view, which servicemen are likely to share, that any use of the forces
to secure objectives which occasion deep and manifest divisions of
principle among the public at large is imprudent and ought to be
avoided.[11]

The military form both a separate profession and an autonomous
society. In either guise they can be said to be one among many interests
pressing upon government demands for enhanced rewards, status or
protection. Yet the military are a special case whether regarded as a
profession, a caste or a pressure group by virtue of their relationship
with the state.

Though occasionally in history the military (such as the Condottierri
Bands or the Swiss Companies) have existed independently, in modern
times they are a profession not merely serving, but created and monopolised by, the state. It is not feasible for them either to claim or to
exercise the self-regulation or autonomy of lawyers or doctors. The
concept of military professionalism only recently gained acceptance
and is still attended by dispute. The close connection, not to say confusion, of military and political leadership inhibited the development of
professionalism and Britain was among the last of the European states
to recognise the functional specialism of the military and to offer a
genuine career to those entering the commissioned ranks. Nevertheless,
there are characteristics of professionalism evident in the British military, some of which are of long standing and others which have been
reinforced by seminal tendencies common to twentieth-century development such as the continuous application of science and technology.
First, and most obviously, the military have sought to regulate entry
according to criteria developed by themselves and this has involved, by
implication at least, the regulation of matters such as discipline, promotion and internal organisation. Second, and to an increasing extent,
governments have had to rely on the military for judgements as to the
practicality and cost of military action and this is reflected in the
manner in which service training emphasises the desirability of initiative
and capacity for independent judgement on the part of even junior
officers, and includes an increasing amount of liberal and social studies

as part of service training.

Unlike many other professions, however, self-regulation is not provided for by articles of association independently agreed or negotiated
by the memberships with governments, nor are the regulating bodies
elective or co-optative. In these matters, the military is not so much a
profession as a bureaucracy. In formal terms, at least, it is wholly
regulated by its employer, and its members receive salaries and wages,
not fees, for the services they perform. Of necessity, the services do
exercise a great deal of freedom over standards of entry and conditions
of service, since neither Parliament nor the civil service is fitted to
determine such matters. However, there are aspects of corporatism in
this exercise. The Attlee government's insistence that *all* those to be
commissioned should serve a short preliminary term in the ranks was
never liked and early abandoned. Although the RAF utilised large
numbers of non-commissioned air crew during and immediately after
the Second World War, it was clearly happier when technical developments justified a return to the Trenchard style, whereby all air crew are
commissioned. It is hard to believe that a host of minor, and rather
anomalous regulations, such as that of the Royal Navy, which forbids
the wearing of moustaches, would persist in any organisation which did
not have a strong sense of corporate identity. Even so, governments
have much greater opportunity to alter or abrogate the professional
standing of the military than they have in regard to lawyers or doctors.

The development of corporative organisation and attitudes among
occupational groups may be actively promoted and not merely toler-
ated by governments as a means of gaining access to specialist advice
and securing the co-operation of the interests involved.[12] The irony of
the tandem development of the welfare state and pluralism has frequently been commented upon. Yet here again the military is a special
case. It is notable among social groups for the high degree of cohesiveness and unity that it exhibits, yet unlike other social or interest groups
it is denied any opportunity to lobby in its own interests or campaign
in elections or in the press. With some rare exceptions,[13] the military
are forbidden trades unions or professional association memberships
even of the 'company union' type permitted to the Police Federation in
Britain. The only representative spokesmen of the military are official
spokesmen who occupy the equivocal position of being the very people
to whom the sectional demands of the military are likely to be
addressed. In this respect, silence is not an attribute of the Royal Navy
alone.

The absence of lobbying and the lack of designated representatives may ensure the continued appointment of titular heads of (each) service even if the Chiefs of Staff Committee should be abolished, for the officers having the title appear to enjoy some licensed freedom to make statements implicitly critical of policy, especially where it is thought to bear adversely on the future prospects of the services. Governments are disinclined to ignore or ride roughshod over the professional or sectional interests of the military. A tendency to do so continuously might engender that 'disposition to intervene' about which Finer has written; but, altogether apart from this, governments will commonly wish to maintain efficient military forces and high morale is a salient feature of efficiency.

As noted below, the regimental system renders the army the least unified of the three services, and some benefit accrues to civil government from this fractionalism in terms of power relations. However, the inability to recruit sufficient infantry to the less popular regiments, together with the need to reduce the order of battle in the interests of retrenchment has led, since the Second World War, to a series of regimental amalgamations deeply disturbing to many officers and men.

The disbanding of former regiments (many of them with a long and illustrious history) clearly marked the redefinition — and reduction — of the army's autonomy. A few reformers did not conceal their hope of substituting for the old regimental pride a loyalty to the army in general, but it is significant that the amalgamations, necessitated by the Sandys reforms of the late fifties and the defence cuts of the mid-sixties, proceeded slowly and were attended by some cameo changes of plan, most notably the survival of the Gloucesters and the eleventh-hour reprieve of the Argyll and Sutherland Highlanders as a one-company regiment. Though the amalgamation process did involve the intrusion of central and civilian agencies into what had formerly been regarded as domestic concerns, and in the long run betokened a reduction in the particularities of army messes, colonels of regiments were closely involved in deciding the actual style and manner of amalgamation. Moreover, the destiny of the officer cadet leaving Sandhurst is still dependent on the impression he makes on the officers of the regiment he aspires to join rather than by his place in the Academy's order of merit or by the personnel branches at the Department of Defence. The creation of a genuine corps of infantry is still light years away.[14]

The wider reorganisation of the administrative machinery of defence was similarly one of making haste slowly,[15] despite the strong personalities of those (such as Montgomery, Sandys and Mountbatten) who

were known to favour it and the trenchant and convincing nature of
the reports (by Sir Claude Gibb and Sir Solly Zuckermann on procurement and General Lord Ismay and Lieutenant-General Sir Ian Jacob on
administration) which recommended it.[16]

The two key changes in the central organisation of defence which
engendered suspicion among servicemen were, first, the appointment in
1958 of a Chief of Defence Staff, who was *ex officio* Chairman of the
Chiefs of Staff Committee and who might both arbitrate between the
heads of the three services and (in the event of their continued disagreement) proffer his own independent advice to the Minister of
Defence, and, second, the amalgamation in 1963 of the separate service
ministries into one super-department under the control of the newly
styled Secretary of State for Defence.

Michael Howard's study makes clear that these changes were
implemented gradually and their effectiveness depended at least as
much on personalities as on formal enactments. Indeed he suggests that
when the trouble-shooting and abrasive Duncan Sandys was moved
from Defence to Aviation in 1959 'matters tended, in spite of the
efforts of his successor, Mr Harold Watkinson, to return to the status
quo.'[17] He suggests that the potentialities of the post of Chief of Defence Staff were not to be exploited until 'the tactful and self-effacing
Marshal of the Royal Air Force, Sir William Dickson' was replaced by
the First Sea Lord, Admiral the Earl Mountbatten of Burma, 'a man
who had exercised supreme command fifteen years earlier and who did
not conceal his dislike for the reversion to separate service responsibilities which had taken place since the Second World War'.

The individual services were thoroughly appreciative of the diminution of their autonomy that the disappearance of 'their own' ministries
portended. Howard remarks, 'It is difficult to overemphasize the importance of this change'.[18] Some of its importance is best illustrated by
Kingston McCloughry's earlier observation that 'The different ways in
which the Admiralty, War Office and Air Ministry conduct their affairs
often reflect the respective characters of the three services.'[19] Under
the new dispensation announced by the White Paper of 1963, civil
servants who joined the Department of Defence were to be rotated to
prevent the development of any single-service loyalties, the former
Service Ministers were replaced by mere parliamentary under-secretaries,
and their permanent under-secretaries by deputy under-secretaries.

Yet, considerable though these changes were, they did not go as far
as some reformers (among them Earl Mountbatten) had wished in reducing the independence of the individual services. It took time to

implement them, and that time might have been greater but for the appointment of Denis Healey as Secretary of State for Defence in 1964. Not only was Healey unusual among incumbents of the post in having spent a long apprenticeship as an Opposition spokesman on strategic and service matters, he also held the defence portfolio for a long time (1964-70) by contrast with the period 1954-60 when it was held in turn by seven different Conservative politicians, only one of whom could be said to have had a particular interest in defence matters. Frequent change of Minister was certainly one of the factors which slowed the pace of organisational change in the 1950s, much as the relatively lengthy incumbency of Denis Healey quickened it thereafter. Even so, the Programmes Evaluation Group set up in 1967 to present for the Secretary of State a critique of the advice he was receiving from more elevated sources was very short-lived. The Chiefs of Staff and those subordinate to them disliked the innovation for the same reasons as civil servants opposed similar expedients designed to create 'dynamic tension' between themselves and gilded amateurs in other departments in the 1960s.[20]

Sentimental attachment to the pre-1963 arrangements even provided for a mild reversion to them under Mr Heath's government of 1970-4 by the appointment of Ministers for each of the separate services.[21]

Examination of the manner in which both regimental amalgamation and amalgamation of service departments took place suggests the not very profound conclusion that the government's formal power to redefine the boundaries of the armed forces autonomy must be used with tact and moderation, and exercised at the most propitious moment for it. The dangers of not using the power with circumspection are, perhaps, best illustrated by Canadian service amalgamation, a more drastic reform imposed rather high-handedly, which resulted in a lowering of morale and a spate of resignations on the part of some valued officers.[22]

In Britain, in times past, commissioning of officers[23] from the patrician element of society and recruitment of soldiers from virtually outside the ranks of society inhibited the development of the military as a vested interest. The extent to which the Royal Navy was more tolerant of bourgeois origins in its officers and had to 'press' skilled and sober merchant seamen to its service was unimportant, except in so far as it created rivalry and distance between the two institutions.

Outside Britain, the disposition to intervene in civil affairs has sometimes been elicited by the close emotional ties existing between the military and sectional class or ethnic groups within the wider society. The military revolts of the Middle East countries in the 1950s are, in part, explicable in terms of the class origins of the officer groups which carried them out.[24] In less homogeneous societies than that of Britain, the disproportionate recruitment of the military among particular ethnic, religious or regional groups has provided a potentiality for revolt.

Some might argue that the Curragh incident was explicable in these terms; yet it is clear that though many officers of the day had Irish connections and the vast majority disapproved of the Liberal Government's plans to grant Ireland Home Rule, only a few, the egregious Sir Henry Wilson among them, believed they ought to do other than follow the orders of the government of the day.[25] Similarly, the services acquiesced in a long series of evacuations of colonies and garrisons after the Second World War, despite the sentimental attachment that developed in regard to some of long standing. The point is especially remarkable in regard to India, where an expatriate community, of which the military formed an important part, had existed for generations. The French armed forces, when faced with a similar prospect in Algeria, acted quite differently. There was no semi-skilled *pieds-noirs* or *petit bourgeois colons* for the services to coerce in India as part of the process of relinquishing power there, and the expatriate community was not only absurdly small in relation to the total population of India, but small in absolute terms as well.

As mentioned above, there is no evidence that service opposition precluded efforts to put down the rebellion of Ian Smith and his supporters by force of arms. Reports on the extent to which army and RAF officers had family connections among the white Rhodesians appear exaggerated and Sir Harold Wilson's memoirs do not even mention the point. What *is* said there is that the probable electoral consequences of applying a military solution to the problem of UDI ruled it out from the very beginning. 'It is true, of course, that had we decided to intervene by force of arms he [Mr. Heath] would have led a united party and almost certainly won majority support in the country. But this was never on.'[26]

The most reliable technique used to establish civil supremacy over the military in a polity is to ensure social identity between the civil and military élites. Yet it is by no means certain that this technique can be readily applied in a complex, plural, urban and socially mobile one. The social origins of those granted commissions in post-war years have become as varied as those in the middle and upper ranks of other sections of society. If there has been some lag in the extent to which social exclusiveness has diminished in commissioned ranks of the armed forces by comparison with other sections of society, it is a slight one and most evident in the army. The explanation lies not in any bias on the part of those granting commissions, but rather in the propensity of ex-officers' sons to follow in their fathers' footsteps in an age when well-educated young men generally are less than eager to become soldiers. One factor that needs further examination is the decrease in the number of MPs, especially Conservative MPs, who have an ex-service background or military connections.

There are other axes, and ones more pertinent, along which divergences between the civil and military élite might be measured. Most salient in recent years, with the ever-increasing application of science in warfare, is that of professional education and training. One suspects that the military in Britain are more numerate than their masters and certainly their formal training and education is more sustained and continuous.

Less obvious, but clearly demanding enquiry in a society characterising itself as permissive and materialistic, are divergences of attitude, values and temperament. A disposition to intervene may be engendered, not by association with dissident or external elements but by an internal distemper, an alienation to civil society. The theoretical possibility of this is considerable, given that military establishments consciously aspire to the status of what sociologists term a 'total institution'. In practice, the possibility is less evident because the concept discounts, if it does not ignore, the complex heterogeneity of the membership of the contemporary military — a heterogeneity founded not only on function, but also on term and type of membership, on age and peer grouping,[27] and on the incidence of marriage, children and 'second career' aspiration which necessarily disturbs the degree of commitment of members to the institution.

In examining this question, there is the crucial difficulty of identifying which values and life-styles are typical, prevalent, or merely promoted. Manners, social and moral, are dynamic and judgements regarding their saliency can only be valid in the short term, if at all. Such judgements are subjective and any dissonance between our own values and those of society at large are likely to be perceived with diffidence rather than Angst. Such a dissonance will be the more tolerable if, despite it, we command a relatively privileged status or fair material reward. Officers as individuals, if not servicemen as a class, have generally enjoyed that in Britain even if the autonomy exercised by the armed services has been limited and the degree of public regard for them as

institutions has not been very high.[28] A distinction exists in public
attitudes to the institutions on the one hand and their members on the
other: commissioned service has been regarded as a worthy and
rewarding career and the rention by many ex-officers of their rank as
a style of address is indicative of this regard.[29] Until at least the 1880s
service in the ranks was regarded as best only to a prison sentence
among many sections of the working class. 'Going for a sojer' was the
resort of the orphan and the pauper, and these were joined only by the
footloose townsmen or the adventurous rustic. Even today, recruitment patterns to the ranks of the army are noticeably skewed in favour
of certain towns and regions and the lower-skilled sections of the
working class.[30] Although job adverts that promise preference to the
long-service NCO are still frequently published, attitudes to non-
commissioned servicemen are more closely related to attitudes to the
services as institutions. These wax and wane in hostility or affection
according to circumstance,[31] but are fundamentally ones of indifference.[32]

   The belief that the traditional attitude of the British to their armed
forces, or more particularly their army, has been one of hostility must
be accepted with some reservations. Indifference tempered by a dislike
of high defence budgets is a more accurate summary of attitudes in the
last hundred years or so. This is scarcely surprising, given Britain's geographical position and her long immunity from successful invasion.
Only a coalition of internal subversives with the attacking force could
provide the hope of success, and since the Armada the only invasions
actually made have been those led by claimants to the throne who
expected to secure a substantial if not predominant part of their
force from within the country. Until the First World War the Royal
Navy was judged to be sufficient in strength to make the question of a
seaborne invasion wholly academic and even in the Second World War
the practicality of such an operation was highly dubious, despite the
possibility of a loss of air superiority and an airborne supplement to the
amphibious forces.[33]

   An army which is regarded as merely a second (and rather unnec-
essary) line of defence was bound to lack prestige by comparison with
the armies of Continental countries, such as Prussia, whose land
frontiers were under constant threat of attack by hostile neighbours.
Such an army could not offer the certain chance of action and glory to
those who might join it. The persistent difficulty of recruiting sufficient men to the army both reflected and reinforced this lack of prestige. Most major reforms of the army have had the ending of this diffi-

culty as their major objective — almost all have proved unsuccessful in this regard. Men joined the army to escape prison, poverty or social ostracism or from an ill-founded belief that the army provided chances of adventure or plunder. The poor quality and low mentality of recruits engendered harsh discipline and a menial order of work and training which did nothing to enhance the army's reputation or encourage enlistment on the part of the few good quality recruits it obtained. Since the army had little importance for national defence and counted principally as a means of suppressing civil riot at home and garrisoning the colonies, it was regarded as a marginal institution by politicians who were content to leave much of its domestic regulation and senior posts as perquisites of the monarch.[34] The major concern of British politicians and civil servants — and this has become much more traditional than the alleged popular dislike of the army — has been to save money on the armed forces. The relatively poor pay and low standard of equipping which has been so endemic a feature of British military and naval history may owe something to the cynical calculation that these characteristics would inhibit the growth of any praetorian spirit. More important, however, was the notion that informed the late seventeenth-century legislation regarding the army and the attitudes of government for generations after, that the army (and the Royal Navy to only a smaller degree) were not only marginal but also temporary institutions. Indeed, until 1860 there was no Royal Navy, only 'ships in Her Majesty's Commission'. The army was a contract army which provided neither career nor security for its members, and was frequently augmented (even supplanted) in the eighteenth century by mercenary regiments hired for the occasion or the payment of subsidies to allies to fight Britain's battles for her.

Given this background, it is perhaps a little odd that governments never sought to offer British regiments for hire to other powers, but if the army couldn't be made to pay for itself it was made as cheap to its employer as possible by a series of expedients which did much to impair its efficiency and damage its standing in the eyes of the public. The practice of forcibly billeting troops in ordinary homes and common alehouses which persisted right up until 1786 was a far more potent factor than the rule of Cromwell's Major-Generals in engendering popular dislike of the military.[35] Billeting was a type of hidden taxation, collected from the common people by a rapacious and arbitrary class of agents. Nor did the upper classes go free. The costs of the conferment of a colonelcy[36] and raising a regiment for the King could rarely be defrayed out of the public funds provided for that purpose and would only be made tolerable by the sale of commissions and contracts, not to mention the more squalid subterfuges of 'dead-pays' and 'the drop',[37] which degraded conditions of service still further.

Whiggish reluctance to maintain and pay for a standing army was added to Whiggish resentment of entangling alliances and the burgeoning demands of the emergent nation-state. The sense of military service as both a duty and a right, as the hallmark of citizenship that became so considerable an element in the thinking of Continental Europe during the Napoleonic period and thereafter, largely passed Britain by.[38] If it had a contemporary reflection in Britain, then it was in the Spithead Mutiny and the bitter wrangling about 'impressment' of the Younger Pitt's administration. Militia service was confined by statute and proclamation to the home territory and when, during the First World War, conscription was belatedly and reluctantly instituted, it was for the duration of the war only. The 'nation in arms' notions of Jean-Jaques Jauré and his British counterpart, Robert Blatchford, never caught on. A succession of appeals to the Anglo-Saxon notion of the 'fyrd' and the educative possibilities of National Service have been made during this century, but they have fallen on deaf ears.[39] Volunteer or contract forces are the norm in Britain and both civilians and soldiers are easily persuaded that this is a beneficent arrangement.

Thus the proposal to phase out National Service was the least contentious of the recommendations of the White Paper of 1957, even though the army was then highly dependent on conscript manpower. As a system, National Service was extravagant in its use of service manpower because of the large training establishments that had to be maintained. It was also believed to undermine the morale and reduce the recruitment of regulars. In so far as service chiefs resisted the abolition of conscription they did so on the sole ground that an insufficiency of volunteers would come forward to provide the services, especially the army, with the manpower needed to fulfil existing commitments.[40] Thus even those supporting conscription regarded it as no better than a necessary evil, and most officers clearly discounted or were unaware of the career and promotion advantages that were a consequence of the large establishments of the National Service period.[41]

The White Paper argued that the expansion of airlift capability and the introduction of tactical nuclear weapons would make good the reduction in army manpower that was entailed in the abolition of conscription. The Chiefs of Staff regarded this argument as altogether over-sanguine. The Hull Committee of 1956 had reported that the best that could be hoped for under an all-volunteer system was an army of

165,000 men, but that the minimum required to meet future commitments was one of 200,000. Antony Head, then Secretary of State for War, and subsequently Minister of Defence, toyed with the idea of selective service, but this was politically unacceptable. Head was at one with the army leadership in believing that an army with an establishment of 165,000 was quite inadequate for the tasks that it would have to undertake,[42] but his power to help determine the issue of army manpower lapsed when Harold Macmillan appointed Duncan Sandys in his place after Eden's resignation in 1957.

When the government announced the end of National Service, it qualified the decision in two ways; first, by delaying its full implementation until 1960, and, second, by undertaking to reintroduce conscription if, because of poor regular recruitment the number of volunteers for the army was less than 165,000 by that time. The army Chief Staff considered resigning over the issue, but the other Chiefs of Staff were not prepared to join him.[43]

An intriguing aspect of this debate between the service leaders and politicians is that the former never appear to have suggested a reduction of commitments as a means of solution.[44] How far they were inhibited from doing so because such a suggestion would have been political rather than strategic is difficult to say. Both Phillip Darby and C.J. Bartlett, in their studies of defence policy, mention reports of the Chiefs of Staff Committee that made assessments and predictions over the whole field of international affairs. Even so, it would seem that the agenda for discussion of policy is set by the politicians, and that typically the service leaders are asked for comment and observations on proposals, ideas and scenarios that originate with others than themselves. There was a measure of conflict between the recreation of all-regular forces and the continuance of British Imperial power and forward diplomacy. The judgements of the service leaders regarding Britain's diplomatic role and aims were left unstated, but there was no doubt that the ethos and character of all regular forces were of a kind most congruent with the Chiefs of Staffs' own values and preferences.

A long-service army is one that is likely to induce a feeling of exclusiveness and alienation among its soldiers and promote corporatism and praetorian values among its officers. Britain has been spared the latter development because of the strong identity of interest, if not identity of personnel, between officers of the army and the members of the ruling class.

There was some possibility of praetorian rule developing under the Conqueror, for the Normans in the immediate post-Conquest period

were few in number and mostly soldiers by occupation. It was fortunate
for later generations that the conventional form of reward for the
King's supporters was then land and plunder rather than governmental
office. The military adventurers who arrived with William were thus
soon transformed into territorial magnates contesting the exactions of
central government rather than a bureaucratic class refining them.

The arcane rituals associated with purchase and the appointments of
colonels of regiments developed to maintain this identity of interest.
Typically, colonelcies were conferred on territorial magnates who
could be relied upon first to make some material sacrifice for the sake
of the prestige conferred by the colonelcy and, second, to ensure
attachment of their country or region, and especially its socially important elements, to the Crown. Indeed the nomination of colonels of
regiments, much as the appointment of JPs (and the two offices were
frequently combined in the same person), was a way of ensuring the
cohesion and loyalty of 'the political nation'. The practical aspects of
the purchase system, until at least the early nineteenth century, were
thoroughly consistent with this arrangement. The pecuniary consideration ensured that, for the most part, only those socially acceptable presented themselves for commissions. At the same time there was a
measure of flexibility. The Artillery and the Engineers never adopted
purchase, nor did the Indian Army, whose officers had a markedly
more bourgeois stamp, but in whose area so large a part of Britain's
military operations took place. Even the most socially exclusive regiments appointed long-service NCOs as Riding Masters, and the seniority
principle was operated in time of war and in the field to allow talented
but impecunious officers to rise to senior posts.

This system broke down in the last quarter of the nineteenth century not because of political controversy (the middle class, though
anxious to gain access to preferments in the public service, had never
been interested in the army), but because an insufficient number of
men from the traditional source wished to be officers. The abolition of
purchase was followed by changes in the arrangements of the public
schools in an effort to augment the supply of suitable candidates.[45]
Despite these changes, the period immediately prior to the First World
War is especially interesting because there did develop, for the first time
since the seventeenth century, a difference in social conditioning and
political interest between those running the army and those who were
leading the country. By that time the Liberal Party had discarded its
Whig pretensions and no longer saw any benefit in maintaining a connection between landed property and political power. Its Imperialist

wing was penetrated by representatives of the country's major commercial interests, whilst its radical wing was influenced by the ideas of the trades unions and the minor professions. The divergence of political interest between the political élite and the military leadership was reinforced by differences of education and social conditioning. Professional education in the services remained casual and old-fashioned in style whilst the Cabinet was dominated by people with university and legal training.[46] Moreover, the so-called 'Army Class' of the public schools selected out the least articulate of a generation for commissioned service. It is possible, of course, to make too much of these factors. The character of the events of these years — army reform following the Boer War, the international arms race, Ireland, and the bloody disasters of the First World War — would likely have caused conflict between civil and military authorities in any case.

Whilst tradition and identity of interest between civil and military leadership might be taken as the most important factors ensuring civil supremacy, formal constitutional controls cannot be ignored. Indeed these were established in a very conscious fashion in the late seventeenth century so that it is, technically speaking, incorrect to speak of a standing army existing in Britain at all between 1660 and 1955. The most celebrated of constitutional authorities have made much of Parliament's legal and financial powers *vis-à-vis* the army and the rigorous limits placed by law on the use of the military in the United Kingdom territory.[47] The annual need that governments had to seek renewal of these legal and financial powers by re-enactment of the Mutiny Act arose partly from the belief that the need for an army was itself likely to be transitory; though experience soon undermined this innocent assumption, the Mutiny Act (incorporated in the Army (Annual) Act of 1881) remained a constitutional control of formal importance until 1955.

The armed forces are pre-eminently Crown rather than state institutions. The strong personal connection between the services and the reigning monarch already mentioned is sedulously maintained, and all volunteers — officers and men — are attested members. A whole panoply of ritual and symbolism is employed to sustain the importance of the personal oath of allegiance. Badges in use in the Royal Navy and the Royal Air Force are surmounted by the cipher, all mess-halls hang a portrait of the monarch, all principal ordinances are Queen's Regulations. None of this is mere anachronism. Though there is unlikely to be much day-to-day consciousness of the oath of allegiance among servicemen, it nevertheless enables them to make a plausible distinction between the Crown and the government of the day, easing the sufferance of legal orders and providing a basis for scruple in regard to any possible unconstitutional action.[48]

Yet the contemporary deference of the armed forces to civil authority may be owed more to administrative constraints and informal procedures than to constitutional enactments. Pepys established the Board of Admiralty as the supreme arbiter of naval administration after 1660[49] but administrative direction of the army in the eighteenth and nineteenth centuries was divided among a plethora of conflicting authorities. The tardiness with which this state of affairs was mended suggests that in the minds of its authors an inefficiently run army was a lesser threat to civil supremacy than an efficient one. The confused administrative system served to ensure that there was no single individual – soldier or politician – who could readily, and without reference to others, command the movement or equipage of large bodies of troops. Administrative direction, though nowadays more efficient, remains a collegial matter. Service officers seconded to the Department of Defence work in tandem with civilian counterparts. Plans, orders and contracts are formulated and agreed in committee. This Whitehall atmosphere must have a formative influence on senior service officers, for few of those reaching the most important staff or command posts will not, at some stage in their career, have been surrounded by it. This is not to say that decisions made within the official structure are not susceptible to modification by external pressures. But these are subfusc and compatible with the ethos of the politicians' and officials' world. Informal contacts of all kinds that the services have with the backbenchers of Parliament and the boardrooms of industry can be useful in securing government attention to service interests. 'Men of war are, in general, deprived of the habit of the word' according to Marshal Marmont, but if British senior officers are conscious of the disadvantage they suffer in having to meet the politician on the latter's home ground, they are even more conscious of the impropriety and counter-productive nature of military appeals to the public over the heads of the politicians.[50] An early retirement is perhaps the most ultimate of the expedients of protest that senior officers are likely to permit themselves,[51] but they are not without resource or guile in employing the politician's own weapons against him.[52]

A willingness to accede to civilian direction and success in dealing harmoniously with politicians and officials is regarded as an important aspect of military professionalism by the professional military. Though holding themselves aloof and evincing some distaste for party political wrangling, servicemen do not now show that spirited animosity for 'the Frocks' that Paget possessed when he spoke of those 'swine of politicians'.[53] Any general who, by his words or actions, made the armed services the subject of public controversy would be widely ill-regarded by his peers.[54] Underlying these general, and perhaps superficial attitudes, is the fact that the armed services cannot, on many occasions, present a monolithic front to politicians. Their tri-service organisation, their complex internal structure, and the highly specific nature and varied incidental effects of most policy proposals rarely permit them to respond in unison.

On several occasions since the Second World War, this consideration has prevented effective use of the ultimate means of protest possessed by service leaders, that of resignation. Governments have exploited divisions between the services by presenting changes in defence policy in terms of cuts in establishments and programmes rather than in terms of strategic doctrine or diplomatic requirements. This tendency was, indeed, a natural consequence of the fact that most changes in British defence policy have been occasioned by economic considerations. Resignations, actual or contemplated, have thus never been in unison, and increasingly they have been seen, not so much as a means of defying the government's decision or appealing over the politicians' heads to the public but more as a means of asserting a sense of obligation to one's service and subordinates.

Lord Montgomery's memoirs[55] record several instances of civil-military dispute and of threatened resignations. Thus Montgomery argues that he secured Attlee's agreement to a system of staff chiefs in command in the army by threatening to resign. He also suggests that Attlee was privately informed that all three Chiefs of Staff would regard any evacuation of the Middle East as a matter for joint resignation. Montgomery, who believed in the need for National Service to a far greater extent than his counterparts in the other two services, in order to secure government agreement to an eighteen-month period of National Service led the military members of the Army Council to threaten their joint resignation. For a period in July 1948, Montgomery claimed that he and the other two Chiefs of Staff had agreed to approach Attlee with a demand that A.V. Alexander, then Minister of Defence, be replaced. At the eleventh hour this agreement broke down, Marshal of the Royal Air Force, Lord Tedder, arguing that such an approach, backed by the threat of resignation, would be unconstitutional.[56] In a similar fashion, the army Chief of Staff failed to pursue his plans to resign over the decision to end National Service in 1957.

Rosecrance suggests that the Chief of Air Staff would have resigned at this time if Fighter Command had been reduced to any greater extent than it was in 1957.[57] In 1966, Admiral of the Fleet Sir David Luce prematurely retired in protest at the decision to cancel the CVA 01 Carrier, upon the building of which the future of the Fleet Air Arm depended. The motive in this instance also seemed to be one of demonstrating that the navy's battle, though lost, had been stoutly fought, rather than any belated effort to oblige the government to change its policy.

The army, which is the service most capable of challenging the civil authority, is in Britain the least unified of the three services because of the persistence of the regiment as a major unit of organisation and focus of loyalty. Ironically, it was the series of forced amalgamations of regiments which, of all post-Second World War shifts of policy, most disconcerted the army in its dealings with politicians.

Soldiers themselves are largely content to rest their defence of the regiment on its effectiveness as a weapon of war.[58] Understandably, they forbear to mention that in time of peace, regimental soldiering absorbs energies that might otherwise be employed in more disturbing pursuits. 'The regimental system may isolate the military but it also tames them, fixing their eyes on minutiae, limiting their ambitions, teaching them a gentle parochial loyalty difficult to pervert to more dangerous ends.'[59] Bredin allows that 'it may look a bit snobbish' but the pecking order is of the essence of the regimental system, and the exclusive spirit that regiments generate among their members would gravely hamper when it did not actually forbid co-operation between units for any questionable end.

The style and manner of life of a good regiment or a happy ship is exclusive and strange to those outside it. It is reasonable to suppose that some of those who join and stay in the armed services do so precisely because they find there an atmosphere very different to and infinitely more palatable than any available to them in civilian organisations.[60] For such people the services are not just a job but another country, a counter-culture, an 'alternative society'. Within the armed services there is no unionism, no class system, no free enterprise, no party politics. In the civilian world outside the military virtues of courage, duty, loyalty and patriotism are at a discount, while the habits of acquisitiveness and self-advertisement are at a premium. The armed services are hierarchical, paternalistic and, in some senses at least, other-worldly. This is a stark contrast derived from a consideration of full-blooded stereotypes. Reality has no such simplicity. Detailed examination of the manifold occupations and grades of the services' work-force give a very indefinite understanding of what it is to be a military man.[61] Such social psychological data as is available cannot provide a clear temperamental profile of the typical serviceman and the findings of Adorno and others on the nature of the 'military mind' have to be regarded with caution in the light of subsequent research.[62]

None the less if, as some allege,[63] there is little prospect of active employment for the military outside the sphere of internal policing and counter-insurgency operations there is some potentiality of growing disaffection between civil and military communities. In regard to international affairs, the moral status and utility of force is doubted by civilians to a greater extent than the military. More important is the fact that Britain's military men have an understandable prejudice in favour of settling civil disputes by civil means. The use of the military in aid of the civil power gives rise to those confused circumstances in which equivocal orders are the only orders likely to be given.[64] Operations directed against one's own fellow-citizens, however recalcitrant they may be, strains the loyalties of rank and file and excites reflection among junior officers on the propriety of the task in hand. Senior officers will want some assurance that they are not being cast in a scapegoat role by being handed a task for which they have neither the resources nor the skills.[65] They are also likely to be concerned with the adverse effect protracted 'aid to the civil' commitments have on the armed forces' readiness to perform their more classic task of external defence.

'It can't happen here' was said earlier of so many of the events that Britain has experienced since the Second World War that we can derive only limited comfort from the long, uninterrupted record of military subordination to civil authority. Other catastrophes — mass unemployment, hyper-inflation, irredentist disaffection — are now spoken of as real rather than hypothetical possibilities. These rival incipient dangers do, however, suggest a continuance rather than an interruption of the tradition considered in this essay. British service leaders emphasise frequently the small size and limited resources of the forces they command, a tendency doubtless engendered by the habit of comparing them with those of their principal potential enemy and their major NATO partner. This consciousness would subtly weight the scales in favour of acquiescence with any legally constituted orders they found highly repugnant to themselves and might extend even to legally dubious orders of the same character.

The powers of government, once secured, often present more problems than opportunities for their possessors. Political responsibility is sometimes an embarrassment to those who have long sought it, and service chiefs are among those who have spent a career observing and suffering its exercise. Not the least of the military virtues is to be jealous of one's reputation and concerned with that of the company one keeps.

Notes

1. S.E. Finer,'The Mind of the Military', *New Society,* 7 August 1975, p. 297.
2. Ruth First, *The Barrel of A Gun* (Harmondsworth, Penguin African Library, 1972), p. 13.
3. Sir Henry Maine, *Ancient Law* (London, John Murray, 1861); Herbert Spencer, *Principles of Sociology* (London, William and Norgate, 1876), Vol. 1, Part 2, pp. 576-96. More recently Stanislaus Andreski has developed this theme in his book *Military Organisation and Society* (London, Routledge and Kegan Paul, 1968).
4. S.E. Finer, *The Man On Horseback* (London, Pall Mall Press, 1962), especially Chapter 10, discusses distinctions between overt and covert influence.
5. We might, however, study the events of May 1974 in Ulster as evidence, not of military insubordination, but military dismay with the indecisiveness of politicians when faced with crisis situations.
6. Robert Fisk, *Point of No Return* (London, Times Books and Andre Deutsch, 1976).
7. H.C. Debs. 866, cols. 425-36.
8. Case law is not a very specific guide to action in regard to a soldier's legal obligation to obey superior orders. Consider especially the judgement provided in R.V. Smith (1900) Cape of Good Hope S.C. 561 and Professor de Smith's comments on the hazards attending application of the rule. S.A. de Smith, *Constitutional and Administrative Law* (Harmondsworth, Penguin, 1971), pp. 205-6.
9. Such might be said to have happened in the enquiries that followed the Amritsar Massacre of 1919. Ian Colvin, *The Life of General Dyer* (London, Blackwell, 1929). The official account is provided in the Report (Hunter) of the Disorders Inquiry Committee of 1920.
10. Thus Sir Harold Wilson admits as much in his memoirs, even to the extent of saying that the use of force might have cost the Labour Party the loss of the general election of 1966. Harold Wilson, *The Labour Government 1964-1970* (London, Weidenfeld and Michael Joseph, 1971), p. 181.
11 The manner in which a divided public opinion may impair the efficacy of the use of military force is amply documented in a number of studies of the Suez operation. For example, Terence Robertson, *Crisis: The Inside Story of the Suez Conspiracy* (London, Hutchinson, 1965); A.J. Barker, *Suez: The Seven Day War* (London, Faber and Faber, 1964); Antony Nutting, *No End Of A Lesson: The Story of Suez* (London, Constable, 1967).
12. Consider, in particular, the promotion of producer-orientated regulatory bodies in agriculture in the inter-war period mentioned in J.W. Grove, *Government and Industry in Britain* (London, Longmans, 1962) and

P.J.O. Self and H.A. Storing, *The State and The Farmer* (London, Allen and Unwin, 1962).

13. In West Germany servicemen of certain categories are permitted to join the relevant public service trades unions. In Sweden the long-service cadres are organised independently for negotiating improvements in pay and conditions of work.

14. For comment on the idea of a corps of infantry see Alun Gwynne Jones, 'Training and Doctrine in The British Army Since 1945', in M. Howard (ed.), *The Theory and Practice of War* (London, Cassell, 1965).

15. Michael Howard, *The Central Organisation of Defence* .London, Royal United Service Institute, 1970).

16. Report of the Committee on the Management and Control of Research and Development (Gibb-Zuckermann), HMSO, 1960. The Ismay-Jacob Report was an internal one made to the Prime Minister.

17. Howard, op. cit., p. 10. Lord Carrington was to say of Mr Watkinson's position in 1959: 'He was still really only a Chairman – although a Chairman with more power – of three separate and almost sovereign states.' From a lecture, 'British Defence Policy', *Royal United Service Institution Journal*, Vol. 115, December 1970, p. 4.

18. Howard, op. cit., p. 23.

19. E.J. Kingston-McCloughry, *Defence* (London, Stevens, 1960), p. 117.

20. One account of this administrative fashion and the controversies to which it gave rise is provided in S. Brittan, *Steering The Economy* (London, Secker and Warburg, 1969).

21. Carrington, op. cit., p. 4.

22. Michael E. Sherman, 'A Single Service for Canada', Adelphi Paper No. 39 (London, Institute of Strategic Studies, 1967).

23. The term 'officer corps' is deliberately avoided here because of the regimental basis of organisation in the British Army.

24. Cf., for example, Eliezer Be'eri, *Army Officers in Arab Politics and Society* (London, Praeger, 1970) and J.C. Hurewitz, *Middle East Politics: The Military Dimension* (New York, Praeger, 1969).

25. An account of the Curragh incident which is highly sympathetic to Wilson is provided by Basil Collier, *Brasshat* (London, Secker and Warburg, 1961). None the less, Collier suggests the same judgement about the average officer's attitude as the one expressed here (see especially p. 150).

26. Wilson, op. cit., p. 181.

27. Cf. Robin Luckham, *The Nigerian Military* (Cambridge, Cambridge University Press, 1971) for a discussion of the manner in which age and peer grouping may undermine the cohesiveness of the military.

28. There is a suspicion that, perhaps because its recent establishment post-dates the close connection between the military and the landed gentry, the Royal Air Force commands less social prestige than the other two services. Thus John Vaizey specifically excludes the Royal Air Force from his list of institutions that the public schools identify with. 'The Public Schools' in *The Establishment*, Hugh Thomas (ed.) (London, Ace Books, 1962), p. 32.

29. Both Anthony Eden and Clement Attlee were thought eccentric in discarding this privilege, and it is thought that they did so in response to the exceptionally strong pacifist feeling of the time. Many other politicians have been eager to avail themselves of the social cachet that military title confers even when only temporary commissioned service has qualified them for it.

30. J.C.M. Baynes, *The Soldier in Modern Society* (London, Eyre Methuen, 1972).

31. As so ably parodied by Kipling.
32. Cf. chapter by Capitanchik.
33. Cf. Friedrich Karl von Plehwe, 'Operation Sea Lion 1940', *Royal United Service Institute Journal,* Vol. 118, March 1973, p. 47.
34. George II, for example, issued a Royal Warrant which determined the facings, numbering, badges and emblems of the army of his day. Many contemporary regimental colours are owed to this personal inspiration.
35. There is some evidence that the peasantry and labouring classes of seventeenth-century England actually found some comfort in the rule of the Major-Generals, whose exactions were made mainly at the expense of the smaller gentry, whose position in local administration they undermined.
36. Our much vaunted tradition of voluntary public service owes its origins (and persistence?) to the bureaucratically inspired habit of exploiting the human weakness for status symbols and *noblesse oblige.*
37. 'Dead-pays' were originally a legal means whereby pensions were paid to men no longer on active service; for most of the Elizabethan period and thereafter, however, the term referred to the system by which those managing companies or regiments pocketed the pay of the dead or absent whose names remained on the muster roll. 'The drop' was the payment made by civilian contractors or suppliers to those charged with feeding or equipping the troops – the stores or equipment thus supplied being of short measure or inferior quality.
38. The privilege of bearing arms was likely to be thought the greater in those countries where there had formerly been a general edict against their carriage or possession.
39. Cf. in particular, *Lord Robertson's Message to the Nation* (John Murray, London, 1913), Correlli Barnet, 'The British Armed Forces in Transition', *Royal United Service Institution Journal,* Vol. 115, June 1970, pp. 13-21, Charles Douglas-Home, *Britain's Reserve Forces* (London; Royal United Service Institution, 1970). Montgomery, as CIGS, is also said to have extolled the moral and educative value of National Service. It is not altogether easy to discern a 'tradition' of National Service, however, since at an early stage in Anglo-Saxon history service in the fyrd could be avoided by payment of a tax which was ultimately used to hire mercenaries – often foreign ones.
40. In this, they proved more prescient than their political masters, as it proved necessary to introduce the Emergency Army Act of 1961, which retained the last batch of National Servicemen in the forces for a further six months beyond the proper term to meet the needs of the Berlin Crisis.
41. Phillip Darby, *British Defence Policy East of Suez* (London, Oxford University Press, 1973), pp. 103-8 and 115-16.
42. H.C. Debs. 592, Col. 99.
43. Lawrence Martin, 'The Market for Strategic Ideas in Britain: The Sandys Era', *American Political Science Review,* Vol. 56, March 1962, p. 28.
44. Alun Gwynne Jones argues that the politicians anticipated such a reduction as an incidental result of decolonisation. Michael Howard (ed.), *The Theory and Practice of War* (London, Cassell, 1965), p. 325. Phillip Darby suggests this was a post-war rationalisation, op. cit., p. 119.
45. C.B. Otley, 'The Educational Background of British Army Officers', *Sociology,* Vol. 7, May 1973, pp. 191-209; Ian Worthington, 'Antecedent Education and Officer Recruitment: The Origin and Early Development of the Public School-Army Relationship'. Paper delivered to British Inter-University Seminar on Military and Society, University of Hull, 1973.
46. Gwyn Harries-Jenkins, 'The Military Image'. Paper delivered to British

Inter-University Seminar on Military and Society, University of Hull, 1973.

47. Most obviously Blackstone, Dicey and Maitland.

48. Thus Major-General Anderson, Chief of Staff in Rhodesia, was summarily retired by Ian Smith because of his opposition to the projected UDI. Anderson said, 'I have taken an oath to the Queen and to me that means one is an upholder of constitutional government.' The Governor-General's ADC, a native Rhodesian officer, repudiated UDI on the same grounds.

49. As recently as 1963 W.P. Snyder characterised the Admiralty as 'the most effective of the three service headquarters'. W.P. Snyder, *The Politics of British Defence* (London, Benn, 1963), p. 124.

50. Thus General Sir John Cowley's adverse remarks on the policy outlined in the 1959 White Paper to the RUSI occasioned angry exchanges in the Commons despite the fact that the lecture had been cleared. In his memoirs, Montgomery mentioned several occasions when he was taken to task for statements judged indiscreet by politicians.

51. Consider Admiral of The Fleet Sir David Luce's resignation in 1967, at a time when plans for a new aircraft carrier were rescinded.

52. Lord Hankey (a former Marine) and Field-Marshal Sir Henry Wilson were both people who appear to have possessed political skills greater than those of most of the politicians they had to deal with. Although Leslie Hore-Belisha had considerable success enforcing his reforms on the army in the late thirties, it is the judgement of his biographer that Hore-Belisha's own political career was shortened as a result of the hostility and intrigues of the generals opposed to him. R.J. Minney, *The Hore-Belisha Papers* (London, 1960). It has been asserted that the choice of Mr Roy Mason to succeed Mr Merlyn Rees as Secretary of State for Northern Ireland was made in the knowledge that Mr Mason would be particularly acceptable to the army commanders in Northern Ireland.

53. Anthony Farrar-Hockley, *Goughie* (London, Hart-Davis, MacGibbon, 1975).

54. General Sir Walter Walker appears to be regarded with some coolness by many of his former colleagues on this account. Consider also James Lunt, 'Fighting On Two Fronts', *Royal United Service Institution Journal*, Vol. 118, September 1973, p. 82.

55. Montgomery of Alamein, *Memoirs* (London, Collins, 1958).

56. Montgomery, ibid., pp. 443-4.

57. Richard Rosecrance, *Defense of the Realm* (London, Columbia University Press, 1968), p. 240.

58. The argument is set out by Major-General H.E.N. Bredin, 'Problems of Infantry Reorganisation', *Royal United Service Institution Journal*, Vol. 114, March 1969, pp. 19-22, and implicitly by J.C.M. Baynes, *Morale* (London, Cassell, 1967).

59. Michael Howard, 'Soldiers In Politics', *Encounter*, Vol. 19, September 1962, p. 81.

60. Consider the observations of Philip Mason, 'They All Shall Equal Be . . . ', *Royal United Service Institute Journal*, Vol. 120, June 1975, p. 40.

61. A random selection of items which throw considerable light on this issue but provide no definite conclusion are RADIX, 'How Military is the RAF', *Royal United Service Institution Journal*, Vol. 103, November 1958, pp. 542-8; Wing-Commander R.A. Mason, 'Are the Armed Services Out of Touch with Social Change Within the Community?', unpublished paper presented to conference on 'The Armed Services and the Community', Cumberland Lodge, December 1975; a fictional treatment: Warren Tute, *HMS Leviathan* (London, Panther, 1975); Antony Verrier, *An Army for*

the Sixties (London, Secker and Warburg, 1966); and Ranulph Fiennes, Where Soldiers Fear to Tread (London, Hodder and Stoughton, 1975).

62.   Cf. Donald T. Campbell and Thelma H. McCormack, 'Military Experiences and Attitudes Towards Authority', American Journal of Sociology, 62, March 1959, pp. 482-90; Roger Brown, Social Psychology (New York, Press/Collier Macmillan, 1965), pp. 477-548; and H.W. Tromp, 'The Assessment of The Military Mind: A Critical Comment on Methodology', in M.R. van Gils, The Perceived Role of The Military (Rotterdam University Press, 1971), pp. 359-77.

63.   Frank Kitson, Low Intensity Operations (London, Faber and Faber, 1971), especially its introduction. See also Jacques Van Doorn, 'The Crisis of Legitimacy In Military Institutions', Armed Forces and Society, No. 1, Autumn 1974.

64.   The confusion attending occupation of the Lenadoon flats which marked the end of the short-lived IRA truce serves to illustrate the point.

65.   The circumstances of the Ulster Workers' Council strike of May 1974 highlighted the difficulties. Had force been used in an effort to reverse the Rhodesian UDI, it might have been discovered that resources were not adequate to achieve the objective sought. Cf. Ian Smart, 'British Violence', The Listener, 3 August 1972.

10 PUBLIC OPINION AND POPULAR ATTITUDES TOWARDS DEFENCE*

David Capitanchik

On any reckoning the United Kingdom's defence effort has undergone profound transformation in the thirty years since the end of the Second World War. Service strengths have fallen sharply. The pattern of global deployment has changed beyond all recognition. The national order of battle comprises fewer warships, field force formations and squadrons of combat aircraft than at any time for generations past. All this has been reflected in a gradual decline in the share of national resources allocated to defence and in a diminution of the nation's power and influence.

Yet none of this has stirred much popular feeling. Regarding national security affairs the British public has been remarkably quiescent. Little importance appears to have been attached to 'life and death' issues of the most fundamental kind. And, in general, the public has appeared indifferent towards matters concerning the size, shape, equipment and deployment of the nation's forces; and passively supportive of government policies and doctrines. However, it does not follow that popular attitudes have had no influence on policy-making and planning for defence. On the contrary, there is no doubt that they have. But they have impinged subtly, obliquely, indirectly, within the central process of 'setting national priorities'.

There is a hint of irony here. No major 'anti-military' lobby has successfully mobilised wide popular support. Nor have pacifist, radical or left-wing elements critical of defence provision had evident impact on opinion. Even in the deepest economic troubles of the last few years, some polls suggest, fewer than one-quarter of the population thought the budgets for defence too high.[1] But groups pressing rival claims on

*This is an updated and extensively revised version of a paper written four years ago under the auspices of the Universities-Services Study Group (Scotland) and published in *Defence, the Services and Public Opinion in Britain and Germany*, Report of the University-Services Study Group (Scotland) (Edinburgh: HMSO for HQ Scotland (Army), 1973). I am grateful to my colleague David Greenwood – co-author of the original paper – for his advice and assistance in the revision of the material and for his comments on a draft of the chapter as it now appears.

255

national resources *have* been successful, obliging successive governments
to assign decreasing shares of total public spending to military purposes
and increase provision for the satisfaction of virtually all other societal
needs. Thus implicit public support for the actual allocations to defence
has to be seen in the light of a steady downward trend in such allot-
ments; and, in this sense, such support is clearly not at odds with
ascription of a lower priority in value to 'security' compared with other
societal goals.[2]

The aim of this chapter is to elucidate these various phenomena. In
so doing the answers to these questions emerge. The first is: why did
the public acquiesce in reductions in the armed forces, contraction of
the global reach of Britain's military power and dimunition of her
status? The second is: how, in the absence of insistent security imperatives but with acute concern about threats to accustomed living standards, the environment and suchlike, have governments found it
possible to assign defence, year in year out, sums equal to 5-7 per cent
of national resources with so little public debate and controversy? That
both questions can be illuminated by the same analysis is faintly paradoxical. But that is in the nature of the case.

The structure of the argument is straightforward. To clear the
ground for the main discussion it is necessary to explain how attitudes
in general are formed and the relationship between attitudes and
opinions. This leads to consideration of those who do participate in discussion of security issues in the United Kingdom, the contexts in
which debate takes place, and how such activity impinges on the
public-at-large. Parliament and 'the political community' in general
feature in this review, along with certain interest groups and 'specialist
publics'. The role of the media is considered also. The justification for
focusing attention on these institutions is that, in Britain, most political
debate is conducted on a hierarchical basis. In defence, as elsewhere, the
attitudes held and views expressed by the public tend to reflect those
which are articulated within the political community, promoted by
interest groups and disseminated via the media. Furthermore, the
attention the public gives to military matters corresponds to the
amount devoted to them in these circles.

The Formation of Attitudes and Opinion

It is no mere semantic quibble to distinguish between the words 'attitude' and 'opinion'. Indeed, it is important that the terms are not used
interchangeably. The essence of the distinction is the latent character of
attitudes and the active nature of opinions. Attitude connotes disposi-

tion, inclination. An opinion is something more precise and more explicit; you don't have one, usually, unless someone asks you for it. The relationship between the two has been expressed very succinctly as follows: 'An opinion may be defined as an expression of attitude in words. An attitude may be said to be a person's disposition or tendency to act or react in a particular manner.'[3]

These are the definitions which will be used in this analysis.

What about the phrase public opinion? How much validity does the concept have? Should one not always recognise that there are many publics holding many opinions? Clearly, the latter is the realistic notion. But just as obviously there is some sense in which, on given issues, what the public 'in general' or 'on average' thinks does have some meaning. It has been suggested that public opinion on any matter, in this broad sense, is 'the hypothetical result of an imaginary plebiscite thereon.[4] This seems a useful specification: it is what public opinion means in most of this discussion.

However, some opinions carry much more weight than others. In any commentary on political affairs in which the role of 'public opinion' is under consideration, the term is often used in a second, more restrictive sense: to mean 'those opinions held by private persons which governments find it prudent to heed.'[5] There is obviously an important idea here, too. In most issue areas a working distinction *can* be drawn between the mass public — for whom defence, pollution, animal welfare or Lord's Day observance are not matters of everyday concern — and those who make it their business to inform themselves about such things, usually because they have some vested or altruistic interest in the matter and often because they wish to bring pressure to bear on policy. Moreover governments customarily at least take note of what they say. That is why this discussion must take particular account of 'attentive publics' or 'sources of informed opinion'; that is, of interest groups and pressure groups.

Any attempt to understand how and why people come to have the attitudes they do towards defence issues must begin with some consideration of the process which leads to the formation of attitudes in general. This is a complex area in which there is no complete professional consensus. But it is commonly accepted that attitude formation is a lifelong process. It begins in the so-called 'formative years' within the family and continues through schooldays and working life as new experiences are enjoyed (or suffered), new relationships formed and the unfolding of events perceived. It is also agreed that few attitudes acquired by individuals are strongly idiosyncratic. Most are shared by

many others in society. Indeed, the sharing of common attitudes towards such things as morality, law and religion is seen by many as a pre-
requisite of a stable society; for the broad agreement they produce
buffers and limits areas of conflict which otherwise would shred the
social fabric. What is important in this context is that most people in
countries like Britain hold certain political values and attitudes in
common, particularly towards such things as the legitimacy of government and the way in which major political decisions should be made.
The framework of national politics is thus a system whose members,
consciously or unconsciously, share a high degree of allegiance and
accept numerous social sanctions.

The collection of shared values, beliefs and emotions about political
principles and institutions make up what social scientists have called the
political culture.[6] This is transmitted from generation to generation by
that same learning process within which attitudes in general are formed,
i.e. via the various institutions with which an individual is involved
(family, school, church and occupational group). At first sight the idea
that even attitudes to the political aspects of their society begin to take
shape with individuals in childhood is surprising. But several studies
have suggested that the process known as political socialisation does
begin within the family. This is where attitudes towards authority, towards others and towards an outside 'community and nation' are first
acquired. The evidence indicates that 'political life, like sexual life,
starts much earlier than we had thought.'[7] Needless to say, attitudes are
modified as the individual proceeds through life, by immediate and
personal experience on the one hand, and by the observation and perception of key events like war and depression on the other. However,
without adopting too strongly Freudian a line, it is clear that early experiences create basic dispositions which influence political attitudes
and opinions well into (and perhaps throughout) a person's adult life.

The utility of the political culture concept for understanding
political behaviour has been the subject of controversy and criticism
among political scientists.[8] Yet it provides some useful insights for
present purposes. As Dowse and Hughes have noted,

> From the historical study of the evolution of the institutions and
> values which compose the political culture and from studying the
> political socialisation process through which individuals are inducted
> into the culture, it can be seen how institutions impinge on the
> members of the society.[9]

This is significant because the political culture into which people are socialised in Britain has important characteristics. In the absence of a written constitution, the political system depends upon a relatively enduring consensus based on acceptance of the right of governments to govern. Even those who disagree with a law or policy usually comply because they acknowledge government's authority to decide for the entire society. This allows a large degree of independent action to political leadership. A corollary is that authority can be exercised over, and need not always defer to, the popular will. No constitutional propriety is at issue. (One of the most striking examples of this was Parliament's decision to abolish capital punishment when all available evidence showed that mass public opinion favoured its retention.)

Even so, the willingness of the governed to allow freedom of action to their rulers is not absolute. Rather the contrary: it depends in large measure on the willingness of the governors to act only within limits set by their sense of what the public will stand. But the freedom is none the less significant. There is a big difference between a government which feels it must do what the mass public wants, and one which feels it can do what *it* wants, so long as it does not provoke outright dissent.

Clearly this is acutely to the point. For the defence and overseas policy area — 'high politics' *par excellence* — is the one in which, within this cultural tradition, government's own writ has run most unconstrainedly. Acquiescence has been an attitude instilled. Whether this public 'disposition to defer' is currently as strong as hitherto is in some doubt, however. For foreign policy and security may now be entering the 'low politics' arena, as the culture itself evolves. At least one writer discerns 'the politicization of defence issues' in the contemporary scene.[10] The argument runs as follows: the dilemma of rising demands and insufficient resources is bringing defence needs into sharper competition with domestic spending programmes, *forcing* 'cuts' on governments (regardless of politico-strategic repercussions) in a manner previously unknown. The freedom of action governments have hitherto enjoyed on defence matters may therefore, in future, be more tightly circumscribed.

However, this argument does not wholly undermine the point at issue here. The degree of independent action allowed to the political leadership in the British system has never been unlimited or absolute. To a considerable extent, policy is made with an eye to the next general election. More important, the massive scope of government responsibility in the social and economic life of the nation, and its overriding responsibility for the allocation of scarce resources, means that it must constantly consider the opportunity cost of every aspect of public expenditure. It must weigh every item against what other purpose might have to be forgone. In these circumstances what the public will stand comes to include willingness to support long-term and costly military programmes when the threat appears remote, but there is acute awareness of inadequacies in housing, health and education. (People might be deluding themselves about the threat to their security; but unemployment, inadequate housing and poor health and education services generate demands no government can, or should, ignore.)

Influences on Attitudes

In varying degrees, then, government's margin for manoeuvre is invariably limited. It seems to be true, however, that during the last three decades defence and overseas policy has remained an area in which public attitudes have been most powerfully conditioned by the accepted authority of government. For all but the most attentive publics the general disposition of the people has been to go along with the official line on security affairs. It follows that the most influential sectors of British society in shaping attitudes towards defence have been (a) government itself and (b) those individuals — Members of Parliament, leading officials and members of the military establishment — who, because of their close association with governments, share to some degree the authority and legitimacy to which in these matters the public still defers. (In what follows this central source of influence will be described as the political community, although this term has wider connotations as conventionally used in the literature of political sociology).

This political community is not only of overriding importance in the formation of attitudes to defence, it has also been the main agency in evoking popular expressions of opinion on security matters. In the absence of controversy in the political arena, there has been little expression of public opinion. Discussion of defence affairs has taken place in other contexts. But, like most political debate in Britain, it has been conducted on a hierarchical basis. Argument on defence and overseas policy is confined among a limited élite in Whitehall and Westminster, Fleet Street and St James's, and in some academic institutions. When the general public pays attention to defence or foreign affairs, concern is confined among better-informed people in the workplace, the union and the local political party. The argument is shaped by so-called 'opinion-leaders' — some of them people who are interested in the issues as such, some of them people who simply purvey a party line to the rank and file. But the key point is this: all such discussion tends to be a reflection and extension of the most influential public debate — that carried on by Ministers, Members of Parliament and others within the corridors of power and influence.[11]

Despite its predominance, however, the political community is not the only agency at work in shaping attitudes and evoking opinion. Other groups, formally outside Parliament and government, function permanently or intermittently and with varying degrees of intensity and effort: interest groups and specialist publics. Such groups seek to affect attitudes and mould opinion by various means, direct and explicit or indirect and implicit. Some campaign openly for support, others content themselves with unobtrusive lobbying. Occasionally there has emerged to prominence a body like the Campaign for Nuclear Disarmament, operating at various levels and adopting a variety of routes and techniques to promote its cause. But two things must be borne in mind when appraising the significance of these other participants where national security is involved. The first is that, while helping to give content to opinions by generating information, their influence has been modest when compared to that of the political community. Nothing bears this out more strikingly than the way in which pressure groups have made the political community the main target for their efforts. The second is the resistance the public have presented whenever such groups have tried to propagandise directly about defence. Military matters are acknowledged to be an appropriate subject for party political debate, as part of parties' efforts to mobilise opinion and win support. But the concern of other groups in society with defence has not been readily accepted.[12]

It is commonplace these days to attribute to *the mass media* of communication — television, radio, the popular press — considerable influence in both creating public opinion and shaping attitudes. Yet, the time and effort devoted to studying the effects of the media on their audiences (e.g. on the level of crime or the pattern of voting) has not yielded firm conclusions. Research results have been ambiguous. With the possible exception of isolated 'laboratory experiments', no clear link has been established between what people view or read and their attitudes or behaviour. People certainly derive much of their information about the world from the media in general and television in particular. But there is broad agreement among researchers that how this information is perceived and interpreted is largely determined by the social circumstances of the audience. For instance, Conservative and Labour voters who exhibit all the classical characteristics of their respective types tend to react quite differently to the same phenomena. Similarly an individual citizen's reactions to the scenes of (say) British Army activity in Northern Ireland appearing nightly on his TV screen depend essentially on his views of the 'Northern Ireland problem' in the round and the role the army has been called upon to play there. The origins of such views are complex and deeply rooted. They may be activated and given content but they are unlikely to be changed by information imparted during a short space of time in the middle of his evening's viewing.[13]

None of this is to deny that the mass media have been (and are) important in enhancing general awareness of what is going on. Moreover their activities induce expressions of opinion which might not otherwise have been voiced. One notices how TV discussion programmes are themselves quite frequently a subject for discussion, for example. But it is only in this sense that the 'opinion-makers' tag can be assigned to them with confidence. Whatever part the media play in evoking opinions, there is little evidence that in the short run they determine attitudes. Their main significance stems from their role in providing information about events and a channel of communication between the political community and society-at-large.

To sum up: over the past thirty years public attitudes to defence as such have been favourable or indifferent, rarely hostile; this is because government's authority dominates in these affairs. Accordingly, the most potent force in shaping attitudes and evoking expressions of opinion about defence has been the activity of the political community.

The Political Community

If the linkage between political debate and popular sentiment is as asserted here, the quiescent character of public attitudes to security provision and the infrequency of expressions of opinion suggests an absence of salient controversy about defence in and around the Parliamentary forum. Has this been so, and if so why?

Given the level of spending on defence since 1945 — rarely less than 5 per cent of gross national product (GNP) and typically higher than the funding for health and education — one might expect considerable Parliamentary attention to have been given to questions of military policy, posture and provision.[14] In fact, however, neither House has spent much of its formal business time on such concerns. Throughout the three decades the House of Commons' norm has been a couple of days each year on each of the Service Estimates and two or three other days debating current issues. Even when defence programmes were undergoing major transformation – in 1964-8, the years of Denis Healey's 'continuing defence review' – there were only eight major policy debates plus eight Supply debates on military Votes, occupying 130 hours in all. In other words, in those four years of intense activity in defence, the Commons spent the equivalent of only 10-12 reasonably full Parliamentary working days debating the government's proposals.[15] Prior to that, only the unilateral disarmament controversy of the 1960s produced unusual activity. Since then the only exceptional attention has been to the army's role in Northern Ireland, in the context of general debate on the security position there. Nor have defence debates been especially arresting or of conspicuously high quality. More often than not they have done more to highlight intra-party differences than to illuminate the structure of official policy. At no time have they aroused substantial public interest.[16]

In addition to debates, however, one of Parliament's most important features is Question Time, at which Ministers reply to questions on any matter touching on their Departmental responsibilities. It is an important activity in the Commons, allowing the attention of the House to be focused on current issues and providing an opportunity for eliciting information from Ministers. On many occasions MPs have used it to bring into the open matters which might otherwise have been kept from public knowledge and escaped their scrutiny. Yet relatively few MPs use this arrangement to raise questions on security affairs.[17] Moreover, such questions as are put often seek specific details with a narrow constituency interest. Because of this, and also because of Ministerial reluctance to be drawn when broader questions are raised, Question Time rarely contributes much to policy elucidation.

Despite growing demands for participation in policy-making, it is remarkable how much freedom and autonomy British governments have enjoyed in policy choices. Parliament has been involved *directly* in few major policy decisions on defence since the Second World War. It debated neither the crucial options concerning strategic nuclear capabilities nor the firm commitment to maintain ground and air forces in Germany, for example. (It was not even informed about, let alone given the opportunity to discuss, the initial action of the Attlee government in embarking upon development of atomic weapons and delivery vehicles!) Moreover, during the period of intensive change already mentioned (1964-8), the number of 'regular participants' in the defence debates which did take place was 55, from a House over 600 strong.[18] In the absence of thorough consideration of defence issues in Parliament, it is not surprising that the mass public appears to have been relatively subdued.

But this does not mean that Parliament's influence has been negligible. In framing their policies governments have recognised the need for Parliamentary support, albeit passive or acquiescent. They have tended not to propose courses of action which would endanger their legitimacy and authority. Furthermore, when some matter *has* generated controversy in Parliament wider discussion of it has been prompted; opinions have been evoked and attitudes might have shifted. This is what happened in relation to conscription, for example. A poll in January 1949 asked: 'Do you think that conscription should be continued or discontinued at present?' Only one-third of the respondents favoured ending it. Not until 1956, when support for National Service had already declined among political leaders, was public support for its retention seen to fall. This situation, of public attitudes and opinions responding mainly to the activities and pronouncements of political leaders, does not seem to have been unique to Britain. Indeed there is an interesting parallel in the development of public opinion in West Germany during the mid-1950s. Prior to the Bundestag's ratification of the Paris Treaties, opinion on rearmament was divided with a majority opposing military revival. But following the Federal Parliament's decision public opinion began to change. In May 1955, polls showed 42 per cent opposed to the establishment of the Bundeswehr and 37 per cent in favour; one month after the Bundestag's decision the proportions were reversed.[19]

Furthermore, the formal sessions of the House of Commons do not constitute the whole of Parliamentary activity. It is largely through 'informal' means — party structures and, particularly, back-bench committees — that government policy is influenced and the public (or sections of it) kept informed. For some time the influential Conservative back-bench '1922 Committee' has had a defence committee with sub-committees for each service (and even a space subcommittee) in addition to the official party committee on defence. The Parliamentary Labour Party has a Defence and Services' Subject Group. Nevertheless, governments (and Shadow Cabinets) have been able to keep defence policy matters very much to themselves. Back-benchers look to the party for their careers and, more often than not, take care to toe the line.[20] Their influence is usually indirect, arising from the steps that leaders take to avoid the embarrassment of dissension in the Parliamentary ranks. Party leaders and back-benchers depend on each other and share an interest in avoiding open confrontation.

Another informal channel is that arising because many, if not all, MPs act as 'advocates' for a variety of political pressures. However, as a general rule, MPs are selective in choosing those they wish to represent, either in parliamentary debate or in their contacts with Ministers. And few have adopted military causes. What an MP cannot choose to do, except at great risk to his political career, is ignore his own constituency party organisation. His entire existence in political life, and his seat in Parliament in particular, are in the last resort dependent upon his local constituency supporters. All MPs are vulnerable in this respect, as the case of some of the Conservative 'Suez rebels' showed (in 1956), not to mention the more recent cases of Mr Prentice, Sir Sidney Irvine and Mr Tomney. But constituency organisations have rarely dictated to their Members on defence issues. This has been partly because of their relatively low interest in defence. But it also reflects the fact that, in these matters, once a Member is elected he enjoys considerable freedom of manoeuvre for so long as he appears in general to be following the party line.

One of the main reasons why Parliament and Parliamentarians have performed only a limited role in influencing government policy and articulating public opinion on defence is because the ordinary MP is severely handicapped by a lack of information. Efforts have recently been made to increase the amount available to them through the memoranda and oral evidence submitted to committees, visits to service establishments, briefings and so on. In particular, during the last few years, the Defence and External Affairs Sub-Committee of the Select Committee on Expenditure has produced several informative commentaries on defence policy-making and planning. But defence is one of those areas where Members have been particularly handicapped, partly because of security restrictions and partly because of the normal reluctance of governments (and their officials) to reveal much of what they are doing. In these circumstances one might have expected Parliamentarians to seek out assiduously whatever facts and analyses on security questions have been available from unofficial sources. Yet they do not seem to have done so. It is necessary to rely on indirect evidence on this, of course. But it is surely significant that, for example, the 1975 members' list of the International Institute for Strategic Studies includes the names of only 15 MPs.[21] The Institute is undoubtedly a potentially invaluable source of information and contact, particularly for the back-bencher or MPs in opposition. But throughout its existence scarcely more than one MP in twenty, and currently only about one MP in forty, has sought membership.

To sum up: Parliament has given very little formal attention to defence, certainly far less than to more contentious social and economic issues. Nor have questions of national security been a major preoccupation of its informal business, or a leading interest of individual MPs. To a considerable extent this has been a reflection of government's authority in the field of defence and overseas policy and the freedom of action which that confers. But it also owes something to information difficulties on military matters. Even so, MPs have had some influence on policy, for all governments depend upon Parliamentary support. They have thus played an indirect part in shaping public attitudes by ensuring that the government's activities have been confined within those limits which have commanded support, or at least acquiescence, among the electorate.

Defence as an Election Issue

Discussion of the political community would be incomplete without reference to the occasions when Westminster and the grass-roots come into direct and immediate contact: general elections. In particular, although the issue is not in the mainstream of the argument of this essay, it is interesting to put the following question: is the assertion that the lack of popular animation on security affairs reflects an absence of salient political controversy about defence, borne out by the observation of parties' and candidates' approach to elections? Specifically, has defence been the 'low profile' theme on these occasions which the hypothesis requires? To this last, the answer is clearly that it has. With one notable exception, defence has *not* figured as an issue of any significance in any British election of the last thirty years, as the following paragraphs show.[22]

The 1945 election took place in the shadow of the Second World War. But politicians and people were looking to the future, a future into which Cold War anxieties did not as yet intrude. Thus an analysis of the election addresses of candidates throughout the country reveals defence to have been a minor theme. Although 59 per cent of Conservative addresses contained some reference to defence, only 12 per cent of Labour's did so. For the 1950 ballot the story is the same, despite the fact that in the intervening years a whole fresh crop of security problems had arisen in Europe and elsewhere. The Labour Party's manifesto made no mention of defence (or even of conscription). The Conservatives had a reference; but merely to say that it stood by conscription while believing that 'by wise arrangements its burdens might be sensibly reduced'. In candidates' addresses defence was featured by

28 per cent of Tories and 10 per cent of Liberals, but only two Labour nominees had anything to say!

In contrast the 1951 election took place against the background of the Korean War. This was the exceptional post-war election in that there was much greater emphasis on issues of war and peace. The need for adequate defence was cited now by many more Conservative candidates (72 per cent) and by more than half of Labour's. For Labour, however, rearmament was a controversial issue. Around it centrists, left-wingers and pacifists conducted bitter interlocking and cross-cutting arguments. Thus, for example, the Bevanite faction found itself under attack from the party's pacifists because its opposition was to the *level* of rearmament rather than to rearmament in general. Yet at the Labour Party Conference dissident views were all submerged in the general assertions of party loyalty and support for the government, particularly from the unions. The 'official' policy on rearmament — as set out in the election manifesto — was quietly accepted. Even so, 1951 stands out as the one occasion during the past thirty years when defence and foreign affairs were aired at length and with some vigour before the British electorate. (The campaign produced scandalous allegations of Tory warmongering; and a violent reaction. At one stage the *Daily Mirror* produced its infamous headline 'Whose Finger on the Trigger?' and was sued, after polling day, by Winston Churchill.)

By the time of the 1955 election, the Korean War was over and conflict in Indo-China had subsided (for the time being). The Paris Agreements of December 1954 had resolved many of the difficulties over collective security in Europe. In spite of the detonation of the first H-bombs and recurring crises in the Middle and Far East, the general mood was one of relaxation following the anxiety and austerity of the first post-war decade. Thus both the Conservative and Labour election manifestoes made peace, rather than defence, their first and major theme. The main defence issue was conscription, with both major parties promising to review the period of National Service. But there were also many references to 'the bomb'. The important difference between the Labour and Conservative parties was one of spirit rather than of substance, reflected in differences of emphasis and style among their candidates. It is very much an open issue whether Labour gained many votes from questioning conscription, despite evidence of its growing unpopularity.[23]

It was during the course of the 1959 election campaign that the H-bomb emerged as a significant defence theme and with it demands for the unilateral renunciation by Britain of all nuclear weapons. But the real controversy was within the Labour Party and did not emerge fully until a year after the election, when Frank Cousins replaced Bevan as the major spokesman of the militant left. At the time of the election the left had made only a limited impression on party policy. The official campaign emphasised muddles in defence policy rather than criticism of its underlying assumptions and fewer than a quarter of Labour candidates declared support for unilateral nuclear disarmament. In this election, as in the previous one, defence was a minor theme compared with the economy and welfare issues.

Voting in 1964 took place against a background of continuing divisions within the Labour Party not only over the nuclear deterrent but also on Britain's role in the Atlantic Alliance. But the election itself was again fought chiefly on domestic issues. Contemporary poll evidence suggests that in any case a majority of voters supported the Conservative desire to retain an 'independent' nuclear capability. Not that there was general interest in the subject. Only Sir Alec Douglas-Home insisted on keeping it to the fore. Mr Wilson referred to the subject only infrequently and then ambiguously, accusing the Prime Minister of 'dangerous illusions which must lead to the spread of nuclear weapons to yet more countries'. Conservatives countered Labour attacks by claiming that Britain was able to play a role in negotiating the 1963 Nuclear Test Ban Treaty only because she possessed nuclear weapons — the 'seat-at-the-conference-table' argument. Naturally enough, given the serious divisions which had emerged within the party in previous years, the Labour manifesto left defence in general to its very last section. Candidates stressed such issues as the need to build up conventional forces rather than nuclear arms and the need to combat waste and inefficiency in military procurement. (Several cited the evidence on cost escalation and mismanagement which had emerged in projects like Blue Streak and TSR 2, and in 'the Ferranti affair'.)

It is worth a brief digression to note that the 1959 general election was known as the first 'television election'; and that by 1964 extensive campaign coverage with programmes such as 'Election Forum' was established. In these elections, too, polling of voters' opinions and intentions became a campaign feature. 'Election Forum' included a crude testing of the prominence of issues by inviting viewers to raise matters for discussion on it: in 1964 only 4 per cent of viewers posed questions on defence. In a Gallup Poll, also in 1964, only 7 per cent saw defence as the single most important issue; in a NOP sample survey, however, 13 per cent put 'the nuclear deterrent' in a list of particularly important issues.

The next election, in March 1966, took place just after the results of the Labour Government's reappraisal of defence had started to appear. The Conservatives deplored the cuts in the Territorial Army and the decision not to acquire new attack carriers for the Royal Navy for the 1970s. Controversy arose also over the continuing deployment of UK forces east of Suez and, for a while, it looked as though this might play a major part in the campaign. In fact, however, because of the unorthodox views of some Conservatives (notably Enoch Powell) and dissaffection in the government's own ranks (a junior Minister resigned), this issue (among others) cut across party lines. In the end very little was made of defence at all. Significantly, the only defence-related lead story to appear in a national newspaper during the entire campaign was an article in the *Guardian,* about NATO, on 16 March 1966.

Not much attention was paid to defence in the June 1970 election either. It was generally known that the Conservatives had it in mind to halt, if elected and if possible, the planned cuts in service strengths and the run-down east of Suez. But party differences on policy were marginal and never salient. Economic and social policy dominated the campaign, as usual.

The election of February 1974 took place in an atmosphere of economic (and some thought imminent social) crisis: energy problems, a miners' strike, the three-day week and general industrial unrest originating in the trade unions' opposition to the Conservatives' Industrial Relations Act. Small wonder then, that only 11 per cent of election addresses mentioned foreign affairs while defence was referred to by a mere 13 per cent of Conservative and Labour candidates and 5 per cent of Liberals. Given the domestic preoccupations, these proportions might not be thought unduly low, although the election analysts have called them 'an eloquent commentary upon Britain's changed status in world politics'.[24] (The preoccupations were not only domestic but exclusively economic. The Northern Ireland 'troubles' — by now a major military commitment — were given reasonable coverage only in the Conservatives' manifesto. They rated a mere passing reference from the Liberals, albeit in the context of a discussion of electoral reform, and were not mentioned at all in Labour's document.)

The inconclusive outcome of the ballot in February 1974 having produced a minority Labour Government, a second election was held in the October of that year. The overriding preoccupation with the country's deteriorating economic situation again left little room for attention to foreign policy and the principal, virtually the sole, defence issue was the acceptable level of defence expenditure. The Labour

Party's manifesto in February had included an undertaking to effect savings of 'several hundred million pounds over a period of years' in pursuit of which an 'extensive and thorough' Defence Review was under' way. Elements in the party wanted a more specific commitment, to the cut of £1,000 million called for in a 1973 Party Conference resolution. But this lacked general support and in October the manifesto version stood as party policy. The Conservatives, of course, opposed the aim and the Review which was in progress. The issue did not, however, feature prominently in candidates' addresses: there were references by 20 per cent of Tory and 12 per cent of Labour nominees.

At elections parties focus on issues of public concern on which they believe their own position is distinctive. These are the issues given prominence in manifestoes and individual candidates' addresses. Moreover, despite a general scepticism about 'promises' and 'undertakings' parties themselves 'recognise that their manifesto, however little it is read by the electorate, will affect their campaign and, if they win, will be one basis for judgements on their performance in government'.[25] These declaratory statements are not, therefore, unimportant, making it valid to infer from those prepared for elections since 1945 that defence has *not* been a salient issue. Questions of national security have not been a focus of controversy, the parties regarding their differences in this area to be insufficiently large or fundamental to warrant emphasis. Thus it is not surprising that the attitudes to defence of the public at large have been characterised by indifference, apathy or 'protracted acquiescence'.[26]

One must recall, however, the thrust of the mainstream argument. This absence of major controversy and the fact that party differences have been minor does not mean that the political community's part in attitude formation has been insignificant. That the disposition of the general public has been passive and supportive, broadly reflecting the position within the political community, in fact testifies to the latter's importance. Moreover, the willingness of Parliament and the public to 'go along' with government policy requires that what the public will stand be judged correctly. The political community's role is crucial; in discovering, defining, communicating and testing what it is the public will or will not stand. That is what much of the formal and informal, collective and individual activity of Parliament is about, in relation to defence as elsewhere. Parliament is 'part of a network of intellectual activities by which an articulate public attempts to influence policy decisions through criticism and commentary.'[27] But in the British system initiative lies with the executive, so that the influence is exercised predominantly in setting bounds to acceptable official policies.

Interest Groups and Specialist Publics

We can, then, regard the political community as having been the central
element in British society in shaping attitudes towards and evoking
opinions about defence and overseas policy. But, as in other countries
in the West, there exist in the United Kingdom many other groups —
independent of government — which represent particular sectional
interests. The activities of such groups also enter into the long-term
process of attitude formation. Yet their main concern is to influence
government policy. Hence their effect on the general public is mainly
indirect, a by-product of attempts to participate in and influence
debates within the political community.

The major political parties of Great Britain consist of broad coali-
tions in which particular sectional interests tend to be played down for
the sake of producing a coherent policy with broad popular appeal. In
this environment one of the main activities of outside groups is the promotion of the interests they represent, if possible with those who make
policy directly but, failing that, with those who have access to the
policy-makers. The number of groups which have involved themselves
in defence matters has been fairly small, however. Moreover, over the
past three decades, most of those which have shown a *direct* concern
have played generally supportive roles.

The interest groups which have influenced defence policy most have
been those with little direct interest in defence. In recent years debates
about defence in the United Kingdom have revolved around questions
of resource allocation. Trade unions, child action and anti-poverty
groups (plus many others) have been pressing for greater expenditure on
health, education and social welfare. And whichever party has been in
power, resources have indeed been switched from defence to these
other public purposes. This state of affairs reflects and is in turn reflected in expressions of popular opinion towards defence, notably in the
last ten to fifteen years. Of late the public has shown and declared itself
in favour of diverting expenditure from military to civil uses. Opinion
polls show that when asked about alternatives in the allocation of
government expenditure respondents tend to favour cutting defence
outlays if the choice lies between economising on defence or on education and that defence savings are overwhelmingly preferred to raising
taxes.[28]

This general but important point aside, what kinds of interest groups
can either be shown or presumed to have had some influence in modi-

fying public attitudes towards defence in recent years? There are, first, groups which strive to influence government policy and for whom any associated effect on public attitudes or opinions is incidental. These belong, primarily, to the type of interest group which is 'self-oriented'; more often than not they represent an economic interest. One such group is the Society of British Aerospace Companies. Over the years this body has maintained exceptionally close contact with relevant government departments, and for good reasons. In the second half of the 1960s, for example, firms in the aircraft and electronics industries provided almost half of all defence equipment. At times military sales have accounted for as much as 75 per cent of the value of output of aircraft firms. Interests such as these have usually operated unobtrusively. Their public activities have been limited. However, they have clearly been in a position to influence public attitudes indirectly, through their contacts with MPs (in addition to Ministers and civil servants) and by displaying their products at air shows and similar activities. Every sales pitch is to some extent a public relations opportunity. To develop the aerospace example, since 1945 these interests have pressed, at one time or another, for new generations of strike aircraft and more airlift capacity for the RAF. Others have advocated greater expenditure on research and development, the procurement of more ships for the Royal Navy and much besides. They have stressed the 'non-military benefits' of defence expenditure, by reference to technological spin-off, potential export sales, and to the job opportunities in depressed areas which higher outlays could provide.[29]

Other self-oriented interest groups exist which can be presumed to have effects upon the long-term formation of general public attitudes towards defence in general and the armed forces in particular. These include the various 'veterans' organisations, such as the British Legion, the Association of Jewish Ex-Servicemen, and the British Limbless Ex-Servicemen's Association. Day to day, these are principally concerned with such matters as pensions and welfare cases. But, in various ways their influence is wider. For instance, by sustaining the annual Remembrance Day ceremonies the British Legion in particular not only honours the dead but also — to some extent at least — sustains, to the services' advantage, a sympathetic climate of opinion and a basic disposition supportive of defence.

Another category of interest groups consists of organisations which set out to promote support for a particular cause. The most notable group in this category, which attracted much attention in the United Kingdom in the early 1960s, has been the Campaign for Nuclear Disarmament (CND). A distinguishing feature of this type of group is that it represents no specific section of society. CND included among its leading members left-wing political activists, church leaders, Members of Parliament, trade unionists, students, pacifists, as well as those whose opposition was to the nature of nuclear weapons but who were not necessarily pacifists. Nor did the CND have a particular focus in the sense that the Ministry of Defence has been virtually the exclusive target of the Society of British Aerospace Companies, or that the social security departments are the main focus of the attention of the British Legion. The organisation directed its activities towards the general public, in an effort to create a broad popularly based movement; and to the Labour Party especially, in an effort to have its cause adopted by a major British political institution.

The extent of public support for CND fluctuated markedly in the later 1950s and 1960s. Opinion poll data indicated that at best its objectives commended themselves to one-third of the population; and at worst to just under one-fifth. The zenith seems to have been reached in May 1960. Yet a year later support for the movement was as low as at any time in the decade 1955-64. Regarding its methods evidence is more fragmentary. But one poll conducted in the autumn of 1961 recorded that 60 per cent of those interviewed disapproved of the type of activity undertaken by the Campaign, particularly by its militant 'Committee of 100'.[30]

The CND reached the height of its influence with the Labour Party at the time of the Party's 59th annual conference held at Scarborough in October 1960. At this gathering an official statement on *Foreign Policy and Defence* embodying the views of the leadership was defeated by just under 200,000 votes out of a total of 6,400,000. In place of this statement, which supported the idea that Britain should only disarm when all nations were ready to disarm, the conference adopted a unilateralist resolution sponsored by a major trade union. This urged British renunciation of her own nuclear capability and the refusal of the British Government to allow any nuclear weapons to be deployed in the United Kingdom. During the following year the party leadership, under Hugh Gaitskell, fought against this decision and at the 1961 conference it was indeed reversed.[31] But this experience had a lasting effect on the party: in its manifesto for the 1964 election, Labour announced that if returned to power it would abandon the UK's independent nuclear deterrent. In the event, when elected, the Labour Government chose not to do so, but many of its supporters continue to regard this as an inexcusable breach of faith.

How successful was the CND movement in Parliament? On 13 December 1960, the Opposition (Labour) introduced a motion in the House of Commons which, while criticising the government's defence policies, did not urge unilateral nuclear disarmament. Almost one hundred Labour MPs failed to vote on this motion. This was the apogee of the unilateralist effort in the Parliamentary Labour Party (although of the abstainers probably only 50-odd were hard-core unilateralists).[32] The episode also illustrates that it is the political community around Westminster which must be 'won over' by interest groups if they wish their cause to make effective headway. For several Members of Parliament, sponsored by trade unions which had supported the unilateralist motion at the 1960 conference, ignored their sponsors at this division and voted with the party leadership. In general CND attracted no more support in Parliament than in the country as a whole. But its record merits this attention, for it did prompt one of the more significant debates on an aspect of defence policy to take place in Britain since 1945. And one result of its early activities was to give a stimulus to study and thought on defence-related matters in academic institutions and elsewhere.

No other group of this type has achieved the prominence of CND or sustained its effort in a comparable way. But there have been a handful of less prominent organisations which over the years have had some impact on aspects of defence policy and management. The National Council for Civil Liberties (NCCL), for example, was instrumental in prompting revision of official practice in the recruitment and terms of engagement of boy soldiers.[33] Moreover, in the 1970s, a number of organisations have emerged to campaign for the cessation of the army's presence in Northern Ireland as an internal security force. Many former CND stalwarts have been active in these bodies and broadly similar methods have been adopted by them. However, neither of the two leading organisations — Troops Out and the British Withdrawal from Northern Ireland Campaign — have won the breadth and depth of support which CND achieved in the early 1960s. Nor are they likely to do so, if the core thesis of this paper is correct, unless (or until) they are able to deploy formidable forces of their own within the Parliamentary forum.

In addition to the interest groups mentioned thus far, there are a number of 'specialist publics' — some of comparatively recent origin — whose interest in defence and the armed forces has been more than just sporadic or occasional, and whose members have what often amounts to a professional interest in these subjects. It is not easy to assess their

effect on attitudes towards defence among the public at large. But
within and between them ideas and views are exchanged — among
policy-makers, serving officers, and a small but significant academic and
lay public — which can result in solid and articulate support for, or
opposition to, given lines of policy. In the defence field two institutions have been (and are) of particular importance: the International
Institute for Strategic Studies (IISS) and the Royal United Services
Institute for Defence Studies (RUSI). By no stretch of the imagination
do these compare with the American research organisations which
address national and international security questions (such as the RAND
Corporation or the Hudson Institute). But over the years they have
helped promote contacts among various sections of the attentive public
and 'official circles' by bringing together members of the services,
academics, civil servants, MPs, journalists and industrialists to discuss
security problems. In addition to those activities (and those of Royal
Institute of International Affairs — Chatham House), service officers
and Ministry of Defence officials participate in study conferences,
seminars and other discussions with the academic world from time to
time.[34]

Specialist publics and interest groups both influence and are influenced by the defence establishment and their activities, and together
they constitute that part of the general public concerned (directly or
indirectly) with defence affairs. They hold opinions about them and
seek to influence, either by propaganda or academic argument, those
who make policy and those whose support policy-makers require. Together with the services themselves they communicate their ideas and
opinions to the general public and also — perhaps most important —
generate the information necessary for 'informed debate'. Such activity
involves the media, to whose role and influence attention must now be
turned.

The Mass Media

It is fashionable to attribute considerable influence in shaping attitudes
and stimulating expressions of opinion to the mass media of communication: the press, radio, television, even films and paperbacks. Indeed,
they are often assumed to be such potent 'opinion-makers' that
numerous organisations think it worthwhile to spend considerable time
and money on either influencing their messages or in using them
directly (e.g. as a means of advertising products, propagating political
views or imparting information). The advertising revenue of the commercial TV companies and the number of hours devoted to party poli-

tical broadcasting, particularly at election times, are evidence of this.

Moreover, judging by their comments, many groups in society have felt threatened by the media; especially by the mass-circulation newspapers and, most of all, by television. It has often been argued that these media purvey material to mass audiences and readerships which not only questions but even undermines the values of society and thereby the very foundations of society itself.

The armed forces have clearly believed that the media are effective for recruiting purposes, especially since the ending of conscription; and that they are important for creating a favourable 'image' among the population at large. In each of the services, public relations organisations prepare news of national and local interest, feature articles and so on, about the armed forces and their activities. Every effort is made to insert in the media as much favourable material as possible, in addition to the large sums spent on recruitment advertising.

However, while it is true that people obtain the bulk of their information from the media in general and television in particular, there is little evidence to date to show how, if at all, the media shape attitudes. The authors of one major study of the impact of television on British political life have made the point that 'there is a vast gulf between what we *know* about the political impact of television and what television is often *supposed* to have done to Britain's political life.' They go on to say that 'because television itself is such a dramatic medium . . . many observers have been tempted to exaggerate its effects and to discount the staunch firmness of popular resistance to persuasive campaigns.'[35]

By their nature, the media have only a limited direct impact on their audiences. In any communication what matters is how the message is perceived and interpreted: this is determined mainly by the social circumstances of the recipient. Attitude formation is a complex process. Mass media messages are necessarily general and of broad popular appeal. In order to influence attitudes, they would need to be more specifically relevant to the interests and circumstances of particular audiences. The national audience is a heterogeneous collection of people of different ages, sex, religion, social class, political persuasion, occupational and geographical affiliation: it is many audiences. But the national media cannot select a particular audience. Hence any strongly partisan message is likely to be rejected by as many people as it appeals to. The point is made very well in Professor Brian Barry's remarks on political communication,

> it will obviously pay a [political] party . . . to channel different
> information about its policies to different sections of the electorate.
> This, of course, depends on being able to segregate the messages so
> that one intended for one set of recipients does not also get to a
> quite different set. The mass media of communication no doubt
> make this *more difficult* than it used to be when a politician could
> adapt his speech to the group he was addressing.[36]

The effectiveness of the media in influencing attitudes has thus been
less than is often assumed.

There is, however, general agreement among all media researchers
that there is room for more study of this complex and obviously important subject. What has been suggested here about the effects of the
media could be described as the current 'conventional wisdom' on the
subject among social scientists generally.

Two specific qualifications are worth making in the present context,
however. First, in Britain, local media are becoming more important.
There has been evidence of a decline in the circulation of national newspapers and new interest in local ones. Television programmes like the
BBC's 'Nationwide' and Thames Television's 'Today' appear to be
growing in popularity, not least because of the emphasis they give to
local interests and events. The regional radio units have a similar appeal.
Clearly, local newspapers, television and radio can structure their
material so that their audiences' local affiliation make them more responsive to it. Hence it may be that the media's influence will be enhanced with these developments and especially with the spread of local
radio stations (commercial or otherwise). In the case of defence and the
armed forces this is potentially of great significance, for the relevant
public relations organisations have traditionally circulated a great deal
of material with an eye to the 'local angle'. Those aspects of defence
policy questions which have implications for local employment opportunities where defence contractors are located may also achieve new
prominence. Secondly, there is impressionistic evidence to suggest that
the continuous coverage of events in Northern Ireland *has* affected
popular perceptions of both the issues at stake there and of the part the
army has been called upon to play. If the inexorable erosion of popular
support in the United States for the conduct of the Vietnam War was,
as has been claimed, attributable in part to constant exposure to the
brutal suffering it occasioned, one cannot rule out the possibility of a
similar steady development of public disenchantment with all that
'Northern Ireland' connotes.

For people do receive and 'process' information and they are not left completely unaffected or unmoved by the experience. Indeed, research has shown that, in this regard, the media are effective – at least to the extent of bringing hitherto unconsidered matters to popular attention. In one study, for instance, television was shown to have produced impressive effects of this kind. The emphasis the Conservatives placed on the issue of Britain's nuclear capability in the 1964 general election sharply increased, it would appear, voters' assessments of their capacity to handle foreign and security affairs.[37]

The media, or at least the more specialised and 'quality' media, have also served another function. This has been to provide a forum in which the political community, specialised publics and interest groups conduct discussion and analysis of contemporary affairs, including defence policy. Yet, while this has been important for the persons and institutions involved, and might have even indirectly influenced government policy, it is unlikely to have had any profound effect on the attitudes of the public at large. Contrary to what their participants might hope, specialised television and radio programmes have little popular appeal. As for the so-called 'quality press', even the involved and attentive publics in the defence field have been less impressed by these newspapers than is often believed. In Britain there has been only limited informed discussion in the newspapers on broader aspects of defence policy. Certainly *The Times*, the *Observer*, the *Sunday Times* and other British 'heavy' papers suffer by comparison with the *New York Times*, *Le Monde* and several other Continental newspapers in this respect.[38] These media have tended to reflect the attitudes and values of their authors, rather than to have shaped those of their audiences.

In sum, there is little evidence to suggest that the mass media of communication have generally intruded upon the underlying dispositions of the public towards defence to any great effect. The media men are less influential than is commonly supposed. Nor do interest groups and specialist publics seem to have exerted the kind of leverage for which they themselves strive and which their critics fear. Those who have deliberately set out to influence attitudes and mould opinion have not been the main attitude-formers and opinion-makers.

Conclusion

The regular polling of public opinion on political issues has been a feature of only the latter half of the three decades which have elapsed since the end of the Second World War. Consequently such evidence of the shifts in public opinion and attitudes as they provide is fragmentary and incomplete. Moreover even in the regular polling of the last ten to fifteen years little attention has been paid to defence. The polls have been concerned to gauge opinion on the great social and economic issues which have become, increasingly, the overriding preoccupations of British society.

But such evidence that it has been possible to include in this chapter illustrates an important point. As the years have unfolded, Britain has been transformed from a major power with a world-wide Empire into a European country acting in partnership with her near neighbours within the European Economic Community, NATO's Eurogroup and so on. This transformation has been no easy matter. The withdrawal from Empire has involved many agonising decisions and controversies, not least in the field of defence policy. At every juncture political and economic crises have appeared to many involved to foreshadow decline rather than renewal — an end rather than change. To these it has often seemed that the people-at-large have not only acquiesced in Britain's decline, but have positively demanded it in order to indulge a selfish pursuit of comfort, leisure and all the accoutrements of the 'affluent society'. Successive governments, it is felt, have been obliged to acquiesce in these demands — to respond to the pressures of sectional, and even subversive, interests — in order to win power and then hold on to it.

But the evidence suggests a somewhat different picture. Public opinion about defence has remained relatively (and remarkably) stable over the years, not in its demands for a larger or smaller defence effort, but in its support for the policies emanating from the political community, and particularly the government of the day, whichever party has been in power.

As the foregoing discussion has shown, questions of defence policy and provision have been of such low saliency in political debate in Britain since 1945 that they have evoked relatively little expression of public opinion. There have been small groups in both major political parties advocating views about defence which the majorities in both parties have believed to be extremist and it is remarkable how *little* changes in governments have affected defence policy, especially defence expenditure. For in the main defence has been a business which society at large has chosen to leave to its government. In turn governments have shown — in managing the economy and in allocating resources — a keen sense of their obligation to stave off threats to jobs and threats to the quality of life as well as countering threats to national security.

Notes

1. See, for example, *Gallup Political Index,* Report No. 188, March 1976 (London, Gallup Poll, 1976).
2. Defence expenditure was overtaken by spending on education in 1969/70 and by health in 1972/3. Moreover, this trend has continued, regardless of which party has been in government. Labour was in power in 1969 and the Conservatives in 1972.
3. H.L. Childs, *Public Opinion: Nature, Formation, and Role* (D. Van Nostrand, 1965), p. 13.
4. R.C. Blinkley, 'The Concept of Public Opinion in the Social Sciences', *Social Forces,* Vol. 6, pp. 389-96.
5. V.O. Key, *Public Opinion and American Democracy* (Alfred A. Knopf, 1961), p. 14.
6. Naturally, this has different characteristics in different societies. A useful discussion of the notion of 'political culture' is included in R.E. Dowse and J.A. Hughes, *Political Sociology* (London, Wiley, 1972), pp. 226-42.
7. R.E. Lane and D.O. Sears, *Public Opinion* (Prentice-Hall, 1964), p. 17. Among the more prominent studies in this area are: D. Easton and R.D. Hess, 'The Child's Political World', *Midwest Journal of Political Science,* Vol. 6, 1962, pp. 236-7; F.I. Greenstein, *Children and Politics* (Yale University Press, 1965) and a leading general work: H. Hyman, *Political Socialization* (Free Press of Glencoe, 1959).
8. See, for example. D. Kavanagh, *Political Culture* (London, Macmillan, 1972).
9. R.E. Dowse and J.A. Hughes, op. cit., p. 228.
10. J. Frankel, 'Defence, Public Opinion and Parliament' (University of Southampton, 1975. Unpublished). See also J. Frankel, *Britain's Foreign Policy 1945-73* (London, Oxford University Press for RIIA, 1975).
11. For a fuller discussion of Parliament's role in foreign affairs see P.G. Richards, *Parliament and Foreign Affairs* (London, Allen and Unwin,1967).
12. In 1960, for example, the Trade Union Congress (TUC) took up a specific position on a defence issue. A large majority of those members of the public who were aware that this had been done regarded the TUC's concern with the issue as 'improper'. This point is elaborated in W.P. Snyder, *The Politics of British Defence Policy, 1946-62* (Ohio State University Press, 1964), pp. 60-1.
13. The sustained coverage of incidents in Northern Ireland over a period now exceeding seven years may be having some effect, however, not so much in changing views firmly held one way or another but in undermining whatever positive attitudes to the questions at issue a citizen in *Great Britain* may once have held. That is to say, instead of filtering 'noise' according to attitude (or prejudice), people outside Northern Ireland may be 'shutting out' most or all of what they hear. Occasional evidence of popular feeling in Great Britain that Westminster should wash its hands of the affair and bring 'home' British troops may owe something to this phenomenon. (See, for example, *Gallup Political Index.* Reports Nos. 138-149, February-September 1972 (London, Gallup Poll 1972).) Be that as it may, for so long as a bipartisan approach continues in the political community, with little open discussion of withdrawal, strong popular pressure for this course is most unlikely to arise.
14. I am indebted to Mr. R. Hepburn, Jnr. a former student of strategic studies at Aberdeen University, for the information I have been able to include in this section about Parliament's attention to defence in the period

1964-68. See R. Hepburn, Jnr., 'Defence Policy and Parliament 1964-68' (University of Aberdeen, M. Litt. thesis,1976).

15. R. Hepburn, Jnr., op. cit.
16. One of the most illuminating discussions of Parliament's handling of defence in the post-World War II period is that in William Snyder's *The Politics of British Defence Policy*. Snyder says quite bluntly that defence policy debates do not create an informed or critical public. W.P. Snyder, op. cit.,p. 54.
17. Between 1964 and 1968, 256 MPs asked at least one question in the House on matters of defence policy, but only 96 asked more than 5 questions during this period.
18. R. Hepburn, Jnr., op. cit. The establishment, in 1971, of the Defence and External Affairs Sub-Committee of the Select Committee on Expenditure was intended to enable MPs to become more effectively involved in consideration of defence policy options. However, the subcommittee has not concerned itself exclusively with questions of policy. Moreover, when it has done so neither the breadth nor the depth of participation in discussion in the House itself have been conspicuously increased. Nor have the committee's reports been more directly influential. For instance, in March 1976 a subcommittee report urged the government to reconsider its plans for the development of the Multi-Role Combat Aircraft (MRCA). The fact that very shortly after the report was published, the government decided to authorise the development of both the strike and air defence versions of the aircraft suggests that it took little account of the subcommittee's observations. (For a detailed assessment of the work and influence of the Defence Sub-Committee see Masood Hyder, 'Parliament and Defence Affairs: The Defence Sub-Committee of the Expenditure Committee', *Public Administration* (forthcoming).)
19. W.R. Vogt, 'The Armed Forces and the General Public in West Germany', *Defence, the Services and Public Opinion in Britain and Germany*, Report of the Universities-Services Study Group (Scotland) (Edinburgh: HMSO for HQ Scotland (Army), 1973), p. 50.
20. W.P. Snyder, op. cit., p. 68. For a fuller discussion of the role of the backbencher see P.G. Richards, op. cit., particularly Chapters V and VII.
21. According to one authoritative source, MPs' interest in the Institute *has* depended upon whether or not their party is in power. Thus when Labour lost the 1959 general election, and the number of Labour MPs fell sharply, the number belonging to the IISS rose – reaching a maximum of 15 on the eve of the 1964 general election. But the number of Labour members of the Institute rose no further despite the considerable increase in the number of Labour MPs which took place in 1964 and 1966. Between 1964 and 1970, however, Conservative membership in the IISS rose somewhat and included three Shadow Ministers, while in 1968 the Conservative Research Department became a corporate member. A. Barker and M. Rush, *The Member of Parliament and His Information* (Allen and Unwin, 1970) pp. 104-7. See also the International Institute for Strategic Studies List of Members, November 1975.
22. Most of the material for this section has been gleaned from the Nuffield General Election Studies, i.e. R.B. McCallum and A. Readman, *The British General Election of 1945* (Oxford University Press, 1947); H.G. Nicholas, *The British General Election of 1950* (London, Macmillan, 1951); D.E. Butler, *The British General Election of 1951* (London, Macmillan, 1952); D.E. Butler, *The British General Election of 1955* (London, Macmillan, 1955); D.E. Butler and R. Rose, *The British General Election of 1959* (London, Macmillan, 1960); D.E. Butler and A. King, *The British General*

Election of 1964 (London, Macmillan, 1965); D.E. Butler and A. King, *The British General Election of 1966* (London, Macmillan, 1966); D.E. Butler and M. Pinto-Duschinsky, *The British General Election of 1970* (London, Macmillan, 1970); D.E. Butler and D. Kavanagh, *The British General Election of February 1974* (London, Macmillan, 1974); D.F. Butler and D. Kavanagh, *The British General Election of October 1974* (London, Macmillan, 1975).

23. D.E. Butler (1955), op. cit., p. 88.
24. D.E. Butler and D. Kavanagh (Feb. 1974), op. cit., p. 63.
25. D.E. Butler and D. Kavanagh (Oct. 1974), op. cit., p. 54.
26. H. Hanning, 'Defence and British Public Opinion', in *Brassey's Annual, 1970*, pp. 108-18.
27. W.P. Snyder, op. cit., p. 65.
28. See, to take one example, the poll data for July 1967 in *Survey on Defence Expenditure* (London, Gallup Poll, 1967).
29. See W.P. Snyder, op. cit., pp. 91-100.
30. W.P. Snyder, op. cit., p. 61. For full accounts of CND see F. Parkin, *Middle Class Radicalism: the Social Bases of the British Campaign for Nuclear Disarmament* (Manchester University Press, 1968); C. Driver, *The Disarmers: a Study in Protest* (London, 1964); and D.V. Edwards, 'The Movement for Unilateral Disarmament in Britain' (unpublished B.A. thesis, Swarthmore College, March 1962, in the IISS Library, London).
31. There are many accounts of this episode, but a useful examination of the whole issue is to be found in W.D. Muller, 'Trade Union Sponsored Members of Parliament in the Defence Dispute of 1960-61', in *Parliamentary Affairs*, Vol. 23, 1969-70, pp. 258-76.
32. See W.D. Muller, op. cit.
33. See Report of the Committee on Boy Entrants and Young Servicemen (Chairman: Lord Donaldson, OBE) (Cmnd. 4509).
34. Statement on the Defence Estimates 1972 (Cmnd. 4891), p. 32.
35. J.G. Blumler and D. McQuail, *Television in Politics* (London, Faber and Faber, 1968), p. 261.
36. See B.M. Barry, *Sociologists, Economists and Democracy* (London, Macmillan, 1970),pp. 115-16.
37. J.G. Blumler and D. McQuail, op. cit., p. 174.
38. See *Defence and the Mass Media*. Report of a Seminar held at the Royal United Service Institution, 13 October 1970, and in particular the remarks of Michael Howard.

BIBLIOGRAPHY

Books and Theses

Armstrong, De Witt,'The Changing Strategy of British Bases' (Ph.D. Princeton, 1960)

Barnett, C.,*Britain and Her Army* (London, Allen Lane, 1970)

Bartlett, C.J., *The Long Retreat* (London Macmillan, 1972)

Baylis, J., Booth, K., Garnett, J.C. and Williams, P., *Contemporary Strategy: Theories and Policies* (London, Croom Helm, 1975)

Blackett, P.M.S.,*Atomic Weapons and East-West Relations* (London. Cambridge University Press, 1956)

——*Studies of War* (London, Oliver and Boyd, 1962)

Blaxland, G., *The Regiments Depart* (London, Kimber, 1971)

Boardman, R. and Groom, A.J.R., *The Management of Britain's External Relations* (London, Macmillan, 1973)

Brown, N., *Arms without Empire* (London, Penguin, 1967)

Buchan, A., *Nato in the Sixties* (London, *Weidenfeld & Nicolson,* 1960)

Crowe,W.J., 'The Policy Roots of the Modern British Royal Navy' (Ph.D. Princeton, 1967)

Darby, P., *British Defence Policy East of Suez 1947-68* (London, Oxford University Press, 1973)

Divine, D., *The Blunted Sword* (London, Hutchinson, 1964)

——*The Broken Wing* (London, Hutchinson, 1966)

Driver, C., *The Disarmers* (London, Hodder & Stoughton, 1964)

Goold-Adams, R.,Buzzard, A. and Healey, D., *On Limiting Atomic War* (London, Royal Institute for International Affairs, 1956)

Gowing, M. *Independence and Deterrence, Vols. I and II* (London, Macmillan, 1974)

Gretton, P., *Maritime Strategy* (London, Cassell, 1965)

Groom, A.J.R., *British Thinking about Nuclear Weapons* (London, Pinter, 1974)

Hampshire, A.C., *The Royal Navy since 1945* (London, Kimber, 1975)

Higham, R., *The Sources of British Military History* (London, Routledge, 1972)

Johnson, F.A., *Defence by Committee* (London, Oxford University Press, 1960)

de Kadt, E.J., *British Defence Policy and Nuclear War* (London, Cass,

283

1964)

Kennedy, G., *The Economics of Defence* (London, Faber & Faber, 1975)

Kingston-McCloughry, Air Vice-Marshall, *Defence* (London, Stevens, 1960)

Martin, L.W., *The Management of Defence* (London, Macmillan, 1976)

Montgomery, Lord, *The Memoirs of Field Marshal Montgomery* (London, Collins, 1958)

Moulton, J.L., *Defence in a Changing World* (London, Eyre and Spottiswoode, 1964)

Mulley, F., *Politics of Western Defence* (London, Thames & Hudson, 1962)

Northedge, F.S., *Descent from Power* (London, Allen & Unwin, 1974)

O'Ballance, E. *Malaya: the Communist insurgent War* (London, Faber, 1966)

Owen, D., *The Politics of Defence* (London, Jonathan Cape, 1972)

Pierre, A., *Nuclear Politics* (London, Oxford University Press, 1972)

Rosecrance, R., *Defense of the Realm* (New York, Columbia University Press, 1968)

Slessor, J., *Strategy for the West* (London, Cassell, 1954)

—— *The Great Deterrent* (New York, Praeger, 1957)

—— *What Price Coexistence?* (New York, Praeger, 1961)

Snyder, W.P., *The Politics of British Defence Policy, 1945-62* (London, Benn, 1964)

Strachey, J., *On the Prevention of War* (London, Macmillan, 1962)

Thompson, R., *Defeating Communist Insurgency* (London, Chatto & Windus, 1966)

Verrier, A., *An Army for the 60's* (London, Secker & Warburg, 1966)

Wallace, W., *The Foreign Policy Process in Britain* (London, Royal Institute for International Affairs, 1976)

Zuckerman, S., *Scientists and War* (London, Hamilton, 1966)

Short Studies

Brown, N., *British Arms and Strategy 1970-80* (Royal United Services Institution, 1976)

Greenwood, D., *Budgeting for Defence* (Royal United Services Institution, 1972)

Howard, M., *The Central Organization for Defence* (Royal United Services Institution, 1972)

Martin, W., *The Long Recessional* (Adelphi Paper No. 61 1969)

de Weerd, H., *British Defence Policy and NATO* (Santa Monica, Rand,

1964)

Articles

Baylis, J., 'Defence Policy Analysis: the study of changes in post-war British defence policy', *International Relations,* November 1973

Buzzard, A., 'Massive retaliation and graduated deterrence',*World Politics,* January 1956

—— 'Crux of defence Policy', *International Relations,* April 1956

Buzzard, A., Slessor, J. and Lowenthal, R., 'The H-Bomb, massive retaliation, and graduated deterrence', *International Affairs,* April 1956

Carlton, D., 'Great Britain and Nuclear Weapons: The academic inquest', *British Journal of International Studies,* Vol. 2, July 1976

Goldberg, A., 'The atomic origins of the British nuclear deterrent', *International Affairs,* July 1964

—— 'The military origins of the British nuclear deterrent', *International Affairs,* October 1965

Gott, R., 'Evolution of the British Independent Deterrent', *International Affairs,* April 1963

Greenwood, D., 'Why fewer resources for Defence? Economics, Priorities and Threats', *Royal Air Force Quarterly,* Winder 1974

—— 'Constraints and Choices in the transformation of Britain's defence effort since 1945', *British Journal of International Studies,* April 1976

Howard, M., 'Britain's strategic problem East of Suez', *International Affairs,* April 1966

—— 'British defence/commitments and capabilities', *Foreign Affairs,* Vol. 39, 1960-1

—— 'Civil-Military Relations in Great Britain and the United States 1945-58', *Political Science Quarterly,* March 1960

Jacob, I., 'Principles of British Military Thought', *Foreign Affairs,*Vol. 29, 1950-51

Martin, L.W., 'The Market for strategic ideas in Britain: the Sandys Era', *American Political Science Review,* March 1962

Montgomery, Lord, 'The panorama of warfare in a nuclear age', *Royal United Services Institution Journal,* November 1956

Sherfield, Lord, 'Britain's Nuclear Story, 1945-52: Politics and Technology', *The Round Table,* April 1975

Wallace, W., 'World Status without tears' in *Politics in the 50's: the age of affluence,* R. Skidelsky and V. Bogdanor, eds (London, Macmillan, 1968)

INDEX

Aberdeen Studies in Defence
Economics (ASIDES) 19
Acheson, Dean 36, 72, 183-4
Admiralty, British 236; decision-
making role 56, 58
Air barrier, Middle East 56, 167
Air Ministry, British 236
Aircraft, Argosy 175; B29 superfort-
resses 71; Canberra 103; F.111K
200; Hawker Harrier 87; MRCA
149, 281n; TSR 2 268; V-Bomber
78, 94n, 103, 105, 125, 127, 130,
132-4, 140-2, 144, 166, 187, 196
Alexander, A.V. 247
Algeria 238
Allen, H.C. 67
Allied Forces Central Europe
(AFCENT) 204
American civil war (1861-5) 67
Anderson, Sir John 123
Anglo-American relations 66-94; see
also Britain, and United States;
United States, and Britain
Anglo-French Treaty (1947) 96
Anglo-Japanese Alliance (1902) 30
Anglo-Maltese Defence Agreement
(1964) 112
Angola 62
Anti-submarine warfare (ASW) 148-9,
151, 175; Soviet capabilities and
148
Arab-Israeli war, see Six-Day War;
Yom Kippur War
Argentina 36
Armstrong, de Witt 162
Army, British 25, 41, 103, 153, 178,
190, 238, 240-5, 247, 252n,
262-3, 269; Army Department
220; civil authority and 231-2;
manpower and 242; organisation
of 204, 248; public attitudes
towards, 239-41; regimental
system of 235, 248; size and
deployment of, 199; see also
BAOR; Military operations
Association of Jewish Ex-Servicemen
272
Atlantic Alliance see NATO

Atlantic Charter (1973) 115
Atlantic Nuclear Force (ANF) 92n,
140-1
Attlee, Clement 32-3, 118n, 247,
251n, 263; Anglo-Iranian oil crisis
and 38; attitude to defence
planning 32-4; British rearmament
and 36, 74; European cooperation
and 97; United States and 68, 71;
Attlee government, defeat of 126;
military establishment and 234;
Soviet Union and 123
Australia 33, 83
Axis powers 30

Baghdad Pact (1955) 38, 76, 195
Barber, Anthony 203
Barnett, Corelli 61
Barry, Prof. Brian 276-7
Bartlett, C.J. 18, 20, 87, 243
Belgium, British deterrent and 123
Bell, Prof. Coral 62, 83, 86, 92n
Benelux states 34
Berlin 106, 197; Four Power Agree-
ment on 106
Berlin Blockade (1948-9) 35, 71,
73-4, 98-9
Berlin crisis (1958) 79-80
Berlin crisis (1961) 41, 46, 105-6,
197
Bermuda meeting (1957) 77
Bevan, Aneurin 185, 267-8
Bevin, Ernest 34-5, 182, 205; Brussels
Treaty and 34; defence cuts and
35; European cooperation and
197; EDC and 101; European
security and 96, 98; Middle East
and 37, 50n; NATO and 98; Soviet
Union and 96; United States and
35-6, 70, 72-3, 96, 124
Blackett, Prof. P.M.S. 16, 156-8, 161,
164, 170
Blair House meeting (1948) 73
Blatchford, R. 242
Boer War 245
Bomber Command 78
Brandt, W. 111
Bredin, Maj-Gen. H.E.N. 248

For Product Safety Concerns and Information please contact our EU
representative GPSR@taylorandfrancis.com
Taylor & Francis Verlag GmbH, Kaufingerstraße 24, 80331 München, Germany

www.ingramcontent.com/pod-product-compliance
Lightning Source LLC
Chambersburg PA
CBHW061003280326
41935CB00009B/814

*9 7 8 1 0 3 2 4 5 1 9 8 5 *